The American Elections of 1982

The American Elections of 1982

Edited by Thomas E. Mann
and Norman J. Ornstein

American Enterprise Institute for Public Policy Research
Washington and London

Library of Congress Cataloging in Publication Data
Main entry under title:

The American elections of 1982.

(AEI studies ; 389)
Contents: National politics and the 1982 campaign/
Albert R. Hunt—Reapportionment and redistricting/
Alan Ehrenhalt—Parties, PACs, and independent
groups/Larry Sabato—[etc.]
1. United States. Congress—Elections, 1982—Ad-
dresses, essays, lectures. 2. Elections—United States—
Addresses, essays, lectures. 3. United States—Politics
and government—1981–   —Addresses, essays, lectures.
I. Mann, Thomas E. II. Ornstein, Norman J. III. Ameri-
can Enterprise Institute for Public Policy Research.
IV. Series.
JK1968 1982   324.973'0927   83-11843
ISBN 0-8447-3532-9
ISBN 0-8447-3531-0 (pbk.)

AEI studies 389

Printed in the United States of America

Contents

Preface

The American Enterprise Institute's series of studies of American elections was initiated with *The American Elections of 1980*, edited by Austin Ranney. This book follows the lead of the initial volume in striving to provide readers with basic facts as well as analyses of the most recently completed election cycle.

We begin with Albert Hunt's narrative of the twenty-two-month period between Ronald Reagan's inauguration as president of the United States and the midterm elections on November 2, 1982. Hunt, who covered national politics and the congressional and gubernatorial campaigns for the *Wall Street Journal*, traces how developments in Washington both shaped and were shaped by the approaching elections.

Next comes a chapter on reapportionment and redistricting by Alan Ehrenhalt, who directed *Congressional Quarterly*'s election coverage. Ehrenhalt examines the inherently political process of redrawing district lines that follows each decennial census and assesses the consequences of the 1981–1982 congressional redistricting for the 1982 elections and for the shape of politics to come.

In chapter 3 Larry Sabato analyzes the role played by the national political parties and political action committees, including the special breed that relies on independent expenditures rather than on contributions to candidates. Sabato argues that developments in the realm of the political parties may be of greater long-term significance than the more highly publicized PACs.

John Bibby documents in chapter 4 the results of the gubernatorial and state legislative races and explores the extent to which state elections may be more responsive than congressional elections to national politics.

In chapter 5 we look more closely at the House and Senate results and put them into a broader context by examining the ways in which those elections are interpreted by the press, by the public, and by the politicians themselves. The appendixes that follow are not all-inclusive; rather, they present selected data on House, Senate, and state elections in 1982, relating to comparable past elections and including shifts in seats and campaign finance information.

THOMAS E. MANN
NORMAN J. ORNSTEIN
May 1983

The American Elections of 1982

1

National Politics and the 1982 Campaign

Albert R. Hunt

The political mood in the White House Rose Garden was brighter than the sunshine on October 14, 1981. Representative Eugene Atkinson, a Pennsylvania Democrat, was switching parties. The fifty-four-year-old lifelong Democrat was greeted warmly by another famous convert: "I believe that Gene Atkinson's decision will send a loud and clear message to America that our party, the Republican party, stands for the working men and women of this country," declared Ronald Reagan. It was, the president of the United States said, a "historic occasion" symbolizing "the beginning of a new coalition and a new era in American politics."*

Some Democrats worried that the president just might be right. Atkinson was not a typical conservative Democrat who was merely squaring his party affiliation with long-held philosophical beliefs. He was a prototype of the vital blue-collar part of the Democrats' coalition. Beaver County, the heart of his western Pennsylvania district, is full of grimy steel mills and thousands of voters whose fathers and sons spend their working lives in those mills.

To make such a dramatic switch, Atkinson, no doubt, had his political finger in the air. In 1979 freshman Representative Atkinson had an approval rating of 75 from the AFL-CIO. More remarkable, in 1980 he was an active leader in Ted Kennedy's presidential effort in Pennsylvania. (His conversion from a Kennedy Democrat to a Reagan Republican prompted one of his colleagues to call him "the Renee Richards of American politics.")

The year 1981 was a vintage one for Ronald Reagan and the Republicans, and this seemed a fitting finale. In 1980, the Republicans

---

* This was a public appearance. When quotations are not attributed, they either are public statements or are taken from interviews given to the author during the 1982 campaign.

1

not only took the White House but captured control of the Senate for the first time in twenty-six years. The Grand Old Party (GOP) was adjusting well to its governing role. The most significant budget cutbacks in modern times swept through Congress, as did the most massive tax cut in memory.

In the Senate, the Republicans were fortunate to have some of their most able politicians in key slots. Howard Baker, the Tennessee moderate, was as brilliant as he was low key in providing the glue to hold disparate Republicans together on major issues. Chairman Robert Dole of the Finance Committee and Chairman Pete Domenici of the Budget Committee displayed an astuteness and political resourcefulness rivaling that of any Democratic legislator of recent years. In the House, GOP leaders—including Minority Leader Robert Michel of Illinois, Barber Conable of New York, Richard Cheney of Wyoming, and Trent Lott of Mississippi—managed to persuade party skeptics while attracting several dozen conservative Democrats on the big economic issues. The coalition ran roughshod over Speaker Thomas P. ("Tip") O'Neill and the Democratic leadership.

Ronald Reagan

The main focus most of that first year was Ronald Wilson Reagan, the seventy-year-old outsider who took the presidency away from Jimmy Carter in a landslide. Reagan has always been underestimated by the Washington political establishment, so his powers of persuasion and political prowess exceeded all expectations. He dominated the capital to a degree not seen since Lyndon Johnson's pre-Vietnam salad days.

Many factors went into the remarkable Reagan first year, and these are some of the more prominent ones:

• Reagan gave top priority to economic issues. Everything else—foreign policy, social issues, other political matters—was placed on Reagan's back burner in 1981. Budget and tax cuts occupied a great deal of the president's time and energy. The ability to set and keep priorities without being distracted eluded many of Reagan's predecessors, most notably Carter. The Georgia Democrat always seemed to have a dozen balls in the air, never sure which one he would play with on a given day. Reagan rarely juggled more than two balls: budget and taxes.

• Reagan assembled a top staff. Again, this was in stark contrast to his predecessor. Carter turned to his campaign manager, Hamilton Jordan, a Georgian who had contempt for many of the political figures and ways of Washington. Reagan turned to Jim Baker, who

2

was campaign chief for Reagan's chief Republican opponents in 1976 and 1980 (Gerald Ford and George Bush). More important, the talented Baker was a fifty-year-old Texan with a distinct familiarity with Washington. Likewise, for congressional relations, Carter called on Frank Moore, a Georgia crony. Reagan selected Max Friedersdorf, a man he barely knew, but a veteran of the corridors of Congress.

• Reagan was able to articulate his agenda better than any president since John F. Kennedy. Reagan quickly became known as the "Great Communicator," a term that some pundits dismissed as symbolizing the triumph of style over substance. But the ability to communicate effectively is an important ingredient of leadership. It was a hallmark of Winston Churchill, Franklin D. Roosevelt, and most other effective political leaders of this century. Reagan is proficient in making his case in the most attractive and understandable terms.

• Reagan rode the waves of public opinion. In 1981 the majority of Americans clearly favored lower taxes, less government spending in general, fewer federal regulations, and a much tougher foreign policy. Specificity here often created political trouble, but in general, most voters sided with Reagan.

Events, of course, played a role, too. On March 30, 1981, Reagan was shot by John Hinckley, Jr., a deranged young man who hoped to impress a movie actress with this awful act. Press Secretary James Brady was seriously wounded, and two others were also shot. Reagan's life was not in jeopardy, but anytime a seventy-year-old man is shot, it is serious. The president displayed extraordinary presence and humor during the situation; as he was going into the operating room, he asked the surgeon whether he was a Republican. Before this, Reagan's popularity had started to slip in the public opinion polls, but this ordeal reversed that. Weeks later, the president's first major speech after the shooting was to a joint session of Congress where he pushed for spending cutbacks; a few days later, in a test vote, the Democratic-controlled House overwhelmingly backed the president.

Then in June the House voted 217 to 211 for the most sweeping budget cutbacks in decades, with more than two dozen southern Democrats, or "Boll Weevils," in support. The cuts affected a wide array of domestic programs: health, education, urban aid, welfare, food stamps, and jobs programs. A month later, the House, in a 238 to 195 vote, enacted the other part of the Reagan economic package, the massive tax cuts for individuals and corporations.

In their final forms, the budget cutbacks totaled more than $130 billion over four years, starting with $35 billion in fiscal 1982. (There were some actual reductions, but mainly these were cuts from what

3

would have been spending levels with no legislative action.) The tax reductions totaled 25 percent over thirty-three months for individuals, only slightly less than the 30 percent, three-year cuts sought by the administration. The breaks for corporations were even more generous than those the White House had requested. In all, taxes would be cut by almost half a trillion dollars over the next four years.

The president's wooing of the Boll Weevils attracted much attention and provided the winning cushion in the House. More significant, however, was the remarkable Republican unity, the most impressive display of party government in many years. In the House and the Senate, only one Republican dissented on both the budget and the tax cuts. Liberals like Senator John Chafee and Representative James Leach were voting side by side with conservatives such as Senator Jesse Helms and Representative John Rousselot. This cohesion did not carry over to many noneconomic issues, but stuck on budgetary matters, even including the huge defense buildup, which moderate Republicans rhetorically criticized. In the Senate, for instance, a move to reduce funds for the MX mobile missile and B-1 bomber by $115 million failed 47 to 46; Republicans voted 45 to 3 against cuts in these military programs.

It was a euphoric Ronald Reagan who invited the press corps to his secluded mountaintop ranch near Santa Barbara on August 13, 1981, to witness the signing of the budget and tax bills. Not even the heavily overcast day dampened the president's buoyant spirits. These measures signaled "a turnaround of almost a half-century of a course this country has been on," exclaimed the denim-clad president. "They mark an end to the excessive growth in the government bureaucracy and government spending and government taxing." Although this was "only the beginning," President Reagan and his allies confidently predicted Reaganomics would produce a vibrant economy with more growth and jobs and lower inflation and interest rates. Indeed, as some of the more zealous supply-siders argued, the mere passage of a huge tax cut would be such a psychological shot in the arm that the benefits would flow immediately.

Other Republicans were not so sure. They recalled the memorable answer John Anderson gave in the GOP presidential debate during the January 1980 Iowa caucuses when he was asked how the government could cut taxes, increase defense spending, and balance the budget. Very simply, replied Anderson, "with mirrors."

In the summer, Howard Baker, on CBS television's "Face the Nation," acknowledged that the Republicans realized this experimental economics was "a riverboat gamble." But the Senate GOP leader quickly added he had little doubt it would work: "I expect that after we pass this program, the country will pitch in and do what it must do," he declared. "Industry will accelerate the business of new jobs and new investment. Men and women will work more diligently, efficiently, effectively. Churches and philanthropic organizations will begin picking up the slack on social concerns and responsibilities. And you're going to see an esprit de corps in this country."[1]

Realignment?

Many Republicans believed the time was ripe for a periodic political realignment—a possibility a decade earlier that was killed by Richard Nixon and Watergate. But it now seemed an opportune time to usher in a period of conservative Republican domination of American politics. Ronald Reagan might do for his party and philosophy what his former idol, Franklin D. Roosevelt, had done for liberals and Democrats a half-century earlier.

The productivity and popularity of the work of the Ninety-seventh Congress, culminating in the 1982 elections, might determine whether this would be a reality or a political pipedream. "Massive party realignments do not take place in a single election," political scientist Austin Ranney wrote at the beginning of the Reagan administration. "They take place over several elections. The 1932 election, for example, was a massive repudiation of Herbert Hoover and the Republicans because of their failure to cope with the Great Depression. Still, it took the activism of Franklin D. Roosevelt and his New Deal to make the Democrats into the majority party, and it was only after the Democrats' unprecedented gains in the 1934 congressional elections and Roosevelt's landslide reelection in 1936 that the Democrats had clearly replaced the Republicans as the majority party."[2]

Ranney saw a parallel in 1981–1982: "There is little doubt that the 1980 elections gave the Republicans a great opportunity to become again the nation's majority party. Whether or not they take advantage of that opportunity depends upon what the Reagan administration and the Republican Senate do with their power and upon how their uses of it are perceived by the voters. Hence what happens in the 1982 and 1984 elections will tell us a good deal more about whether 1980 was another 1932 or another 1952."[3]

Later in 1981 the president ran into some trouble with additional budget cutbacks. But he bounced back on another issue, snatching victory from the jaws of defeat by persuading the Senate—in a 52-to-48 vote—to agree to the controversial sale of sophisticated radar planes (airborne warning and control system aircraft, known as

AWACS) to Saudi Arabia, despite the opposition of Israel and its powerful allies in this country.

Thus, the GOP viewed the 1982 midterm elections as an opportunity to build on their governing coalition. They thought they passed Ranney's test, having used their power effectively and popularly.

The Democrats had spent most of 1981 on the defensive. In the Senate, where they were unused to minority status, they frequently tried to fashion alternative budget and tax policies but with little success. On defense matters, they tried to sound both tough and critical of Reagan's huge increases in Pentagon outlays. In the House, the Democratic leadership tried to tilt the Reagan budget a little more favorably toward domestic programs and a little less so toward defense. On taxes, they proposed a small cutback on the big individual reductions and tried to outbid the White House in wooing special-interest groups. They were defeated each time. Overall, the Democrats could not decide whether they wanted to oppose the Republican initiatives outright, embrace some and reject others, or try to outdo Reagan on still some others. Some Democrats tried all these approaches in 1981.

Both parties knew that historically midterm elections offer American voters a chance to send a message to politicians. Occasionally, the message is to "stay the course," the theme the GOP adopted for 1982. At other times, it is to reverse the course; but most often, it is to alter the course. These contests traditionally are more about direction than about any broad philosophical mandate.

The elections between presidential contests are for one-third of the Senate, almost three-fourths of the governors, and all of the U.S. House of Representatives. Thus, House races are the most closely watched barometer for national trends. In the dozen midterm elections over the past half-century, the party holding the White House has lost an average of thirty-one seats. But the big losses occur in the second term of a president: the Democrats lost seventy-one seats in 1938 and forty-seven seats in 1966, while the GOP lost forty-eight seats in 1958 and in 1974.

The first midterm contest following a new president's election—the situation facing Reagan and the Republicans in 1982—is different. In this case, the new president is usually still enjoying some of his political honeymoon, and the average losses over the past fifty years have been less than a dozen seats. In 1934, Franklin Roosevelt's Democrats actually picked up nine House seats and ten Senate seats; in 1954, under President Eisenhower, the Republicans lost only eighteen House seats; in 1962, under President Kennedy, the Democrats were barely touched, losing four House seats; in 1970, Richard

Nixon's Republicans lost a dozen seats in the House; and in 1978, even as Jimmy Carter was experiencing more political problems than usual, the Democrats lost only fifteen House seats.

Looking toward the 1982 midterm elections there were 241 Democrats and 192 Republicans in the House of Representatives. In their most upbeat moments, GOP leaders actually talked of taking control of the House in 1982. They counted on picking up about twenty seats and then on persuading a half-dozen conservative Democrats to switch parties; Republicans needed a net gain of twenty-six seats to win control.

Although this seemed overoptimistic, the Republicans enjoyed several advantages. For one, their campaign coffers were overflowing with cash, so they would have more political resources. Second, some analysts thought they might have better candidates than the Democrats were offering. Candidates usually decide to run at least a year before the election, and in late 1981 the political climate was more appealing to an attractive Republican hopeful than to his or her Democratic counterpart. Further, the Republicans thought that redistricting would be a definite plus for them. The areas gaining seats, the West and the Sunbelt regions, were more Republican than the industrial Midwest and Northeast, which were losing congressional districts. The party that controlled redistricting (this varied with different states) would have a big advantage, and generally the Republicans planned to use sophisticated computers and modern technology to overwhelm the Democrats. Finally, the Republicans felt that public opinion was still more on their side; even if not pleased with all the results, the public supported the direction in which Reagan and the Republicans were taking the country. If the economy started to pick up, the GOP thought it could defeat a few prominent Democrats, as when they upset House Democratic Whip John Brademas of Indiana in his bid for reelection in 1980. In 1981 the Republicans never even thought about losing any of their own leaders.

Coyne versus Kostmayer

All the 435 congressional districts have unique political characteristics, so it is very difficult to focus on one race as being illustrative of the entire struggle. Nevertheless, one of the battles certain to attract attention, from the press and from politicians, was the contest in the Eighth Congressional District in Pennsylvania. The center of the district was Bucks County, rich in history and the home of prominent artists, such as author James Michener, and of political diversity.

On the outskirts of Philadelphia, Bucks County is like numerous other affluent suburban districts in the nation. But it also is the home of the original Levittown, a bastion of blue-collar voters. Within a few miles of the city, one can see quaint old farmhouses in the rolling countryside as well as the bellowing blast furnaces at U.S. Steel's huge Fairless plant. Politically, Bucks County is less Republican than a decade ago. Although Ronald Reagan won 56 percent of the vote in the county in 1980, this is a swing district in congressional contests.

The two contestants underscored this. The incumbent, freshman Republican James Coyne, a thirty-five-year-old Harvard Business School graduate, was exceptionally smart and ambitious. He ran as an economic conservative, a champion of supply-side Reaganomics, and as a moderate on most social issues. Independently wealthy, he spent $425,000 in 1980 to defeat a Democratic opponent who spent only half as much. But that opponent, Peter Kostmayer, was coming back in 1982. Kostmayer, a thirty-six-year-old moderate Democrat, was also exceptionally smart and ambitious. Representative Kostmayer had served four years in the House, where he was more involved in procedural matters than in policy; a maverick gadfly, he often criticized his senior colleagues for what he saw as ethical insensitivities. More popular back home than in Washington, Kostmayer was caught by national trends in 1980 and lost to Coyne by less than 4,000 votes: 103,585 to 99,593. The votes had hardly been counted when Kostmayer started running for 1982 and even tried to continue some of the constituent services he had performed while in Congress. These two similar young men—sandy-haired, white Anglo-Saxon Protestants—grew to dislike each other intensely, and their rematch would be interesting to watch.

Only 33 of the 100 Senate seats were up for election in 1982. The Republicans held a 54-to-46 edge, and luck was with them this time. Of the 33 seats contested, 20 were held by Democrats, and only 13 by Republicans.

Moreover, the Republicans were fielding some of their best vote getters in 1982. When a candidate wins 55 percent or more of the vote, it is usually considered a decisive victory. Of the eleven Republican senators seeking reelection, only three had received under 55 percent of the vote in their previous election. A majority of this GOP class were moderates who typically win easily in general elections even though they are from basically Democratic states. Included in this category were John Chafee of Rhode Island, John Danforth of Missouri, and David Durenberger of Minnesota.

Republican strategists thought that in the year ahead there would be only two serious trouble spots. One was California, where Republicans would successfully pressure seventy-five-year-old incumbent Senator S. I. Hayakawa to retire; and although the Democratic candidate, Governor Jerry Brown, was unpopular, none of the GOP aspirants was very impressive. The other trouble spot was Connecticut, where maverick Lowell Weicker faced a tough and divisive primary challenge from Prescott Bush, brother of Vice President George Bush. The Bushes and the Weickers, despite their similar upper-class, prep-school backgrounds, were strongly opposed to each other, and the vice president's brother hoped to capitalize on conservative animosity toward the incumbent. Terry Dolan, head of the independent National Conservative Political Action Committee, promised he could "safely predict" that Lowell Weicker would not return to the Senate after 1982.

On the other side, some of the twenty Democrats up for reelection had won only narrowly in the previous election and were considered vulnerable. Few analysts could forget the 1980 political massacre of liberal senators—McGovern, Culver, Church, Bayh, and Nelson. This time, conservative activists bragged, the same treatment would be given to Donald Riegle of Michigan, Howard Metzenbaum of Ohio, Paul Sarbanes of Maryland, George Mitchell of Maine, and perhaps even Daniel P. Moynihan of New York. They were not as closely identified as liberals as the group in 1980, but Republicans would attack them as big spenders in the way of the Reagan revolution.

Also, some Democratic moderates looked as though they could be beaten, including Tennessee's James Sasser, North Dakota's Quentin Burdick, and Nevada's Howard Cannon, who faced a tough primary. The Republicans even dreamed of toppling some untouchables: eighty-year-old John Stennis of Mississippi, facing his first serious challenge in over three decades, and Minority Leader Robert Byrd of West Virginia, who would be painted as being out of touch with his home state mountaineers. Although some of the GOP targets were overoptimistic, it seemed reasonable to count on toppling a half-dozen incumbent Democratic senators. Of the twenty Democratic seats up for election in 1982, Republicans rated only four as not winnable: the seats held by Henry Jackson of Washington, Edward Kennedy of Massachusetts, Spark Matsunaga of Hawaii, and the redoubtable William Proxmire of Wisconsin.

New Mexico Senate

One contest that both parties focused on was the race in New Mexico. This was not because the candidates were exciting: The incumbent

Republican, Harrison (Jack) Schmitt, lacked charisma, as did the two Democratic hopefuls, former Governor Jerry Apodaca and Attorney General Jeffrey Bingaman. But this was the kind of seat that both parties believed they had an excellent chance of winning: a seat held by a run-of-the-mill Republican incumbent in a Democratic state that was becoming more and more Republican.

New Mexico is a diverse state. About one-third of the voters are Hispanic; they are predominantly Democratic, though less so than in past years. The Little Texas area is full of energy and military complexes, ranchers and small businesses, and either Republicans or very conservative Democrats. With the hard-hit mining industry, some northern New Mexico counties had 30 percent or higher unemployment. New Mexico has been a good political bellwether; only once, in 1976, did New Mexico not vote for the victorious presidential candidate.

Senator Schmitt's chief claim to fame was that, as an astronaut, he once walked on the moon. A geologist with a Ph.D. from Harvard, he is a rigid conservative, much more so than his New Mexican GOP colleague, Pete Domenici, though their voting records are similar. Schmitt lacks Domenici's political warmth and political acumen. Schmitt won 57 percent of the vote in 1976, but that was against an unpopular Democratic incumbent. Still, he ran excellent constituency services; he would be well financed and hard to beat in a state where fewer than 400,000 people would vote. Of the two Democrats, Governor Apodaca was very popular in the Hispanic communities, but carried much political baggage, including a vicious feud with the Albuquerque newspaper. Republicans and Democrats alike thought the tougher Democratic candidate would be Jeff Bingaman, thirty-five years old, clean-cut, and politically in the middle. But he was not very well known or very exciting.

The Governors' Races

Overall, with the numbers favoring the Republicans in 1982, Senate Majority Leader Howard Baker and others thought it important that the GOP gain seats this time. In 1984, nineteen of the thirty-three contested seats would be GOP-held, and in 1986, twenty-two of the thirty-four seats would be Republican-held. So Baker wanted the Republicans to pick up between two and five seats to avoid trouble later.

The effect of national policies on the governors' races was more dubious. To be sure, there was a definite effect, particularly in economically depressed states, which also faced a squeeze on social services due to federal budget cutbacks. These considerations helped Democrats. But local factors dominate most governors' races, which are rarely harbingers of national politics. In 1962, for example, the big news story was the election of industrial state GOP moderates: Michigan's George Romney, Pennsylvania's William Scranton, and Ohio's James Rhodes. Two years later these new governors were ignored as the Republicans nominated Barry Goldwater and suffered a landslide defeat. In 1970, the press focused on the net Democratic gain of eleven state houses and especially on the "new breed" of moderate Democratic southerners: Dale Bumpers of Arkansas, Reubin Askew of Florida, and Jimmy Carter of Georgia. Two years later the Democrats nominated liberal George McGovern and were overwhelmed.

Still, governors' races are the most important elections for many state residents and always involve some politically interesting personalities. In 1982, there were thirty-six governors' races, and the Democrats held twenty of those governorships. (In all, the Democrats had a 27-to-23 edge over the Republicans in the number of governors.) As always, the two largest states, California and New York, were closely watched. Republican hopes for an easy win in New York vanished when unpopular incumbent Hugh Carey decided not to run for a third term. In California, outgoing Governor Jerry Brown was roundly disliked, but this seemed to have little effect on the likely Democratic nominee, Los Angeles Mayor Tom Bradley, who wanted to be the first black governor since Reconstruction. One of the few gubernatorial contests with national implications was that in Texas, featuring Bill Clements, the first GOP governor in more than a century. Clements was an instrumental force in Reagan's big win in Texas in 1980, and national Republicans felt it important to hold this state house for the 1984 presidential race. The major test for the Republicans, however, would be the midwestern heartland; they controlled governorships in Michigan, Ohio, Minnesota, Wisconsin, and Iowa, but none of these incumbents were standing for reelection. This gave the Democrats a golden chance for big gains. (Overall, of the ten largest states, nine had a governor's race in 1982, the exception being New Jersey. On the eve of the election, Republicans held five of the nine seats.)

GOP Problems

As 1982 began, the political picture started to shift, darkening GOP hopes a little. In mid-January, a front-page headline in the *Los Angeles Times* read: "GOP's Grand Hopes for Resurgence Fading." A *Times*—

11

Cable News Network national survey found that 51 percent of likely voters preferred a Democratic congressional candidate, whereas only 35 percent backed a Republican candidate. The same poll found that only 20 percent of the Democrats who voted for Ronald Reagan in 1980 would support a GOP congressional candidate in 1982.[4]

There were several reasons for the changing political climate, among them:

• The economy had failed to respond to the supply-side prescription. The president and his allies had oversold their economic medicine. Instead of immediate improvement and economic vibrancy, the economy stumbled after the Reagan legislative successes. The first month after the budget and tax cuts were passed, not only was economic buoyancy not evident, but the stock market actually declined by almost seventy-nine points. Interest rates remained high, unemployment began to soar, and personal bankruptcies and business failures escalated. Inflation slowed significantly, but that good news was always overshadowed by gloomier events.

• The Republican unity of 1982 had dissolved. Supply-siders claimed that Reagan was not adhering to Reaganomics; some suggested the answer really was a return to the gold standard, an argument rarely heard six months earlier when large tax cuts were supposed to be the panacea. More traditional Republicans complained about the huge budget deficits. Moderates carped that too much was being taken from areas like education. On foreign policy, Reagan began to appear inconsistent. He was tough on the Russians, but lifted the grain embargo. He talked tough about communism, but took no action when the Polish government suppressed the trade union movement there. He alternated between overreacting to and ignoring events in Central America. Relations with the European allies were approaching the low point of the Carter days, in part because the administration had no credible arms control policy. With the abrasive Secretary of State Alexander Haig always in the middle, the Reagan foreign policy team was constantly embroiled in policy and personality struggles.

Thus, moderates began to look for a way to put some distance between themselves and the president on these and other matters. "I fear the Administration thinks it can build a majority party out of white Anglo-Saxon males over 40," charged Senator Bob Packwood, the Oregon Republican who headed the GOP Senate Campaign Committee. "You cannot do it."[5]

Conservatives, though, were not any happier. The White House is "really controlled by the country club set who don't have any appreciation of the average voter," charged Paul Weyrich, a leading New Right activist. In February 1982, the Young Americans for Freedom, a conservative organization and a bastion of Reagan support for years, graded their hero: they gave him a C minus for abandoning the balanced budget, a D plus for deciding against declaring Poland in default on its overdue U.S. bank notes, and a D for his choice of appointments to top jobs. Those in between were thinking of survival. "More and more of us are starting to think it's every man for himself," worried one Republican House member.[6]

• The Democrats were beginning to get their act together. They generally agreed that the Reagan tax cuts were excessive and tilted to the rich; reductions in domestic programs were inequitable and Reagan's promise of a "safety net" to protect the poor was a sham; pressure should be brought on the Federal Reserve to lower interest rates; defense priorities were out of line, with too much being spent on exotic strategic weapons and not enough on conventional forces; and the Reagan foreign policy lacked direction and coherence. This was accepted by Democrats as diverse as Ted Kennedy on the left and Oklahoma Senator David Boren on the right. No doubt, it was much easier to agree on what they did not like than to set a positive agenda. But that is the luxury the party out of power enjoys in midterm elections, and it provided the Democrats with a message for voters in 1982.

• Ronald Reagan's popularity began a predictable drop in the polls. According to the Gallup poll, his overall approval rating dropped to 47 percent in early February from 56 percent four months earlier.[7] There was growing criticism of particular policies and of his general stewardship. His earlier asset of setting one or two priorities now seemed almost a negative—namely, it was felt that he was unable to focus on more than one or two issues or so at a time, a luxury modern presidents do not have as time moves on. In all, Reagan would not provide the big boost in the 1982 elections that the Republicans had anticipated earlier.

By mid-April, a very influential political newsletter, the *Baron Report*, written by Alan Baron, carried the headline: "The Senate: Could Republicans Lose Control?" "As deficit projections, unemployment rates and Presidential disapproval in the polls have increased," Baron wrote, more Republicans feared defections and especially "Republican stay homes on election day." Baron noted that experts in both parties thought it very unlikely that control of the Senate would shift, but mere mention of the possibility signaled a sharp change from six months before.[8]

13

Almost as soon as he sent it to Capitol Hill, Republicans as well as Democrats rejected the president's fiscal 1983 budget. Not only was the economy not responding, but the budget cutbacks were also starting to pinch; people who favored cutting spending found out they did not like cutting programs that affected them. By the spring, top congressional Republicans and Democrats began a series of private sessions with the administration to fashion a compromise budget. Nobody was particularly sanguine about the prospects, but nobody wanted to reject compromise. There were seventeen official members, and the group became known as the "gang of 17." Actually, they made some genuine progress, but political suspicions never disappeared. Finally, with his masterful sense of symbolic moves, Ronald Reagan journeyed to Capitol Hill to meet Tip O'Neill and the gang of 17. Basically, there were to be more domestic cutbacks than the Democrats wanted, a chipping away at Reagan's huge defense increases, some revenue-raising measures that did not affect the basics of the 1981 tax cut, and a lower deficit. Instead of working to hammer out the final specifics, the president and the Speaker spent more time scoring political points against each other. The two political veterans were worlds apart philosophically, politically, and personally. They went through the motions of friendship after working hours but without an abundance of mutual respect. At the final session of the gang of 17, both were posturing for the 1982 election, with O'Neill trying to pin an anti–social security label on the president, and Reagan trying to stick the label of big spender on O'Neill and the Democrats.

When the session broke up in failure, the White House moved to score the initial public relations points. "We had hoped for give-and-take there, and what we found mostly from the other side was mostly take and very little give," complained White House Chief of Staff James Baker. The president, as usual, gave an effective television speech defending his position. But the substantive problems remained. Senate Republicans began gearing up for a tax hike of their own, a rarity in an election year, but it was an acknowledgment that ballooning budget deficits were threatening to send the economy into even more of a tailspin.

On the foreign front, the situation was not much brighter. All the earlier problems remained. Little progress had been made in the volatile Middle East; indeed, many experts felt that Reagan's inaction actually set back Jimmy Carter's achievements there. Relations with one of America's newest friends, China, were souring over the administration's continuing support for Taiwan. Even friendship with right-wing Latin American countries faltered when the United States supported Great Britain following the Argentine invasion of the

British-owned Falkland Islands. William Clark, a friend of Reagan's from California, took over the National Security Council earlier in the year. Although some considered Clark abysmally ignorant on many matters of policy, he provided some direction to foreign policy decision making.

The major shot in the arm occurred in late June when Secretary of State Haig was finally coaxed into resigning. George Shultz, former cabinet member in the Nixon administration, was chosen to take his place. Shultz is enormously respected by politicians of different persuasions, and to many of them his appointment was the best news on the foreign policy front in the eighteen months of the Reagan administration.

The Economy in the Forefront

Still, it was the economic issue that dominated politics in 1982. As unemployment climbed over 9 percent, with no signs of slackening, even lower inflation did not seem to be enough to help the Republicans. Strangely, though, the Democrats remained nervous about the economy. In May, political analyst Kevin Phillips noted that the "ambiguity" of the economic issue made Democrats "leery" of predicting major gains. There still was a tendency to trace economic problems back to the Carter administration, Phillips wrote, and Democrats feared that any short-term recovery in the fall would blur the economic issue.[9]

This ambivalence was present in the Coyne-Kostmayer race mentioned previously. Public opinion surveys showed that the two candidates were almost even and that the economic issue was dominant. Interviews with voters in the sprawling Oxford Valley Shopping Mall in the spring underscored these findings. "We've got to give Reaganomics more time," a factory manager insisted. "We keep hearing things will get better, but they don't," said a female clerk. Some voters urged Representative Coyne, who was campaigning there one day, to stick with the president; others urged him to show more independence.[10]

Representative Kostmayer was concentrating on the issues of rising unemployment, high interest rates, and what he insisted were GOP intentions to cut social security benefits. He charged that a year earlier Coyne had bowed to White House pressure and voted to eliminate the minimum social security benefits; this year (1982), he said, Coyne was supporting slashes in Medicare spending. He called Coyne one of "Reagan's robots" in the House.

Coyne was firm—for the most part. "We've got to be patient and give the president's program some time," he constantly told constituents. Supply-side economics only needed time to deliver as promised, the freshman lawmaker insisted. Thus, he vowed to oppose any tax hike, even a Reagan-supported one.

Yet Coyne did not want to become too closely associated with Reagan and his policies. He insisted that the president's more than $100 billion budget deficit had to be cut to at least $60 billion in the next fiscal year. He proposed to slice the Reagan defense budget by $15 billion but was vague on where other cuts could be made. He signed a letter with two dozen fellow House Republicans insisting that some funds for education spending needed to be restored. He also voted for an expensive mortgage subsidy measure strongly opposed by the White House. In 1981, the *Boston Globe* reported, he voted with Reagan on 69 percent of the key votes but "now is backing away from the President as he [Coyne] tries to stay in office."[11]

No issue concerned Coyne more than social security. "My opponent already is alleging that I want to cut social security benefits. That's a very raw nerve." At the Bensalem Senior Citizens Center in Bucks County, he encountered senior citizens like Scottie Moore who adamantly opposed any cuts in benefits for the elderly; Coyne said he agreed with them.

The young Republican remained confident of victory. "I'll blow him [Kostmayer] out of the water," he insisted. This was based on the hope of improving economic conditions. Coyne had his own political/economic index: if the prime lending rate (running about 16 percent in the spring) dropped below 10 percent, the Republicans would "pick up a lot of seats." If the rate dropped to 12 percent, they would hold their own; but if it was still above 14 percent, they would "suffer some serious retrenchments."[12]

Some 2,000 miles away in New Mexico the situation was not much different. Jeff Bingaman, the Democrats' strongest candidate, easily won the June primary, coming out of the contest with the party relatively unified. He, too, was focusing almost entirely on the economy, assailing the Schmitt-backed 1981 tax cuts as excessive and complaining about some cuts in domestic spending and too much spending for the military.

Jack Schmitt continued to look like an appetizing target. A state Associated Press survey on the most influential New Mexicans placed Senator Schmitt in only ninth place, even running behind the two GOP representatives. He suffered in comparisons made with the more popular Pete Domenici, who was first on that list. "Schmitt isn't thought of as one of our own, like Domenici," said Zora Hesse, the state's Democratic national committeewoman.[13]

An inconsistent voting record also plagued Schmitt. When a GOP-sponsored tax increase first came to the floor as part of the budget resolution, the New Mexico senator supported it. When the bill later came up for a vote, within a matter of minutes Schmitt switched from voting against it to voting for it. When the final version came back from a House-Senate conference committee, he voted against it.

Bingaman had problems too. He had a pedantic style, although he sounded like actor Jimmy Stewart. He had little instinct for going for the political jugular; he refused to make an issue of Schmitt's voting for a gymnasium in the new Senate office building, privately telling aides it was a petty issue. He said that the Schmitt-backed constitutional amendment for a balanced budget was "unworkable," but not wanting to be painted as a liberal he said that he, too, backed a balanced-budget amendment. Yet he could not say how this would be workable.

Schmitt had some decided advantages—constituent services and money, with plans to outspend Bingaman by at least 3 to 2. The help the Democrats received from labor and environmental groups was offset by business political action committees that overwhelmingly backed the incumbent.

On the issues, Schmitt continued to side with Ronald Reagan and his conservative beliefs. He believed antigovernment, antiregulation, and tough defense postures were still popular with the Sunbelt voters. He disagreed with some particulars of the Reagan program but was with the president on the broad questions. Further, he wasted few opportunities to contrast the Reagan philosophy with the discredited Carter administration and Democrats of the past.

New Mexico had been hard hit by the recession, with an unemployment rate of 10 percent, but Schmitt's own polls suggested that the economy would not necessarily be a disadvantage for him. "Our surveys show a real fear factor among voters of returning to what we had several years ago," said Diana Welch, the Schmitt campaign manager.[14]

Pollsters

Two experts who are well qualified to analyze surveys are Robert Teeter, president of Market Opinion Research Company, and Peter Hart, president of Hart Research Associates. Teeter polls for the

o

Republicans—in 1982 he conducted surveys for eighteen Senate candidates, fifteen gubernatorial hopefuls, and dozens of House aspirants. Hart does the same for the Democrats—in 1982 he conducted surveys for ten Senate candidates, eight gubernatorial candidates, and ten House candidates. Though of different parties, these pollsters share common characteristics: both are in their early forties, very bright, insightful, candid about public opinion, and fond of politics and politicians.

As the summer of 1982 approached, these two professionals viewed the unfolding elections similarly. The economic issue, they were confident, would dominate the dialogue through November 2. The president was more popular than his policies. Unanswerable at this point was how the voters would express these views at the polls.

Teeter believed the determining factor would be "whether there's a general sense that economically the country is going in the right direction." A clear majority, he found, thought that Ronald Reagan was more confident in economic matters than his predecessor, Jimmy Carter. If the Republicans could successfully present the argument as a choice between staying with the Reagan program and going back to the unsettled times of preceding years, then the condition of the economy could even help the GOP, Teeter told his clients.

Yet the GOP poll taker saw an Achilles' heel—the fairness issue, coupled with fears about social security. "There is a rather widespread notion that much of the Reagan economic program is slanted to fat cats," Teeter said. There were strong fears of social security cutbacks, he warned; already 28 percent of the public mistakenly believed Reagan had cut general social security benefits. The Republicans had handled this concern clumsily, Teeter said, and it could be potentially devastating.

In early June, Hart and several other political professionals briefed the House Democratic leadership on the election outlook. The main election issue, the Democratic pollster said, should be presented as a "midcourse correction," not as a repudiation of Reagan. The situation, he explained, "is analogous to a trip into the wilderness and finding out your tour guide is drunk. You can't completely admit you failed because then you can't get back to civilization. But you must do something. We have to offer the voters a constructive way to get back to economic civilization."

There were four basic issues, he believed: the economy, the direction of national defense, social security, and the role of government. "But if there is such a thing as a single-issue election, 1982 will come very close to being one as voters focus on the state of the economy," he noted.

Like Teeter, Hart knew that how the issue was cast was critical. If the choice were between the current and the past, that would mean trouble. "The more this election revolves around the past, the stronger the Republicans will be," he wrote. But if the contest were to revolve around the present and the future, Hart maintained, "it clearly will work to our [the Democrats'] advantage." Hart continually advised the Democratic congressional leadership to avoid obstructionism at all costs. "The budget is clearly theirs and I'm delighted," he said several months before the election.

It really was not difficult to convince Tip O'Neill on this matter. The Massachusetts Democrat is fiercely partisan, but he is even more patriotic. Thus, he would not countenance the notion that Reagan, after winning a landslide in 1980, would then be denied votes on his agenda. Tip O'Neill would fight the program every step of the way. But, to the consternation of some younger Democrats and staunch liberals, he made sure that Reagan could never campaign against Democrats as unfair obstructionists.

Both public opinion experts were leery of making outright predictions months ahead of the election. Teeter did say that for the Republicans to make a "decent showing," interest rates had to drop two or three points. He defined "decent" as losing ten to twelve House seats, gaining one or two Senate seats, and losing a couple of governorships. Hart saw a Democratic gain of about twenty House seats, perhaps an even split in the Senate or the loss of two seats, and a gain of about a half-dozen governorships.

Other Factors in the Elections

The economy was the central issue, but there were other important factors that would affect the electoral races, particularly close or marginal contests. Redistricting, to the Republicans' chagrin, had worked slightly to the Democrats' advantage; the Democrats outsmarted the GOP and gained the upper hand in a few major states, principally California, and probably would have a net gain of several seats with the different districts. The Republicans, however, still had a big financial edge in the pivotal contests. White House political aide Lee Atwater dismissed the contention that any election can be bought but admitted that "big bucks" can buy marginal races. Columnist Mark Shields, calling this the GOP's "2% solution," noted that in 1980 twenty-two GOP House seats were won by 2 percent of the vote or less, including the election of nineteen freshmen.[15] Clearly, money could make the difference between a decent showing and a disastrous one if the 1982 elections were to follow a similar pattern.

Some other considerations that emerged in the 1982 election concerned the gender gap, the nuclear freeze issue, and social issues.

The Gender Gap. Traditionally, men and women vote alike. On occasion, they split the vote according to sex. President Eisenhower, for instance, was a little more popular with women voters than with men voters. But this split was much more pronounced in 1980, with men voting heavily for Ronald Reagan and women much less so.

The gender gap continued, with Reagan consistently doing better in the polls with men. At the end of 1981, *Public Opinion* magazine asked: "Does Reagan have a problem with women?" The answer was that "Reagan gets a lower rating among women than men—consistently and systematically. The magnitude of the differences by sex is greater than that of previous presidents, at least back to Eisenhower." But the differences, about eight or ten points, though "not insignificant," the writer cautioned, were "not massive either."[16]

There were several explanations for the gender gap, most of which focused on women. Reagan's opposition to the Equal Rights Amendment and a woman's right to an abortion offended some women voters, as did the absence of any women in the Reagan high command. Certainly, the war/peace issue was a factor, too. Women generally are more dovish than men on the use of force or the control of nuclear weapons. President Reagan's macho image here did not appeal to women as much as to men. In the spring of 1982, the *Wall Street Journal* and pollster Peter Hart met with a dozen women in Richmond, Virginia, for a focus group session. The purpose was to discuss the group's attitudes about politics and the president. Although the group was not large enough to form a representative sample, it did explore, in some depth, the women's feelings. It appeared that they were more leery of Reagan than most men were. Patti Jeffries, a twenty-eight-year-old graphic artist, said unadmiringly, "Ronald Reagan is a man's man."[17]

This session and others suggested that the basic cause of the gender gap was economics. Women generally were more sensitive about Reagan's economic priorities—more for the military and less for domestic social programs—and were more affected by hard times. Almost 35 percent of the families in poverty were headed by a woman, or about double the percentage of all families headed by women. Women continued to make only 59 percent as much as men on the average. (As joblessness soared, women disproportionately were the last hired and the first fired. Many of the most severe budget cutbacks were programs particularly sensitive for women: child care centers and some health and nutritional programs. Senator Nancy Kassebaum, a very prominent GOP woman officeholder, thought this was a "real and serious problem" for her party: "Women feel the economic cutbacks more personally."[18]

There was little doubt that this problem was affecting other Republicans. When asked what would be the Republicans' best strategy for the 1982 election, one GOP strategist replied: "Repeal the Nineteenth Amendment." Leading GOP political consultant John Deardourff warned, "It would be a terrible mistake for Republicans to believe that this is simply some kind of radical feminists' revolution against Republicans. . . . It goes much deeper than that."[19]

Both parties were addressing the issue, though the Republicans did so largely from a defensive vantage point. The White House was trying to focus the spotlight on more visible women in the administration, but the targets were not plentiful. The Democrats were making a capital move out of the issue. California gubernatorial candidate Tom Bradley directed a mailing to everyone in California listed as "Ms." Democratic media consultant Bob Squier aimed much of his political marketing at the women's vote: "I think our party now is the national women's party," he told NBC.[20]

Nuclear Freeze. The movement for a joint U.S.-Soviet freeze on the development and deployment of nuclear weapons was not new. Its major political launching occurred on March 10, 1982, when Senator Edward Kennedy (Democrat, Massachusetts) and Senator Mark Hatfield (Republican, Oregon), along with dozens of other politicians, former diplomats, and church and community leaders, held a press conference to endorse the freeze. The setting was American University in Washington, D.C., where President John F. Kennedy first proposed negotiations that led to the nuclear test ban treaty in the early 1960s. It was a forceful display. Representative Edward Markey (Democrat, Massachusetts) warned: "We are on the verge of blowing ourselves off the face of the earth."

Most Democratic candidates embraced the freeze as a way to attack Reagan's bellicose defense policies. In June, the *New York Times* noted that some Democrats saw the freeze issue, which was "swelling at the local level, as an important political opportunity, one [from] which Democrats, in particular, stand to profit."[21] In the same article, it was reported that Richard Bond, deputy chairman of the Republican National Committee, took issue with this assessment: "Not a single race will be a loser for us" because of the freeze, he predicted. Privately, other Republicans were not sure. Teeter, for instance, said: "The potential is there for the nuclear issue to be a really big one. But it's not there yet." Most, but not all, Republicans opposed the freeze.

Two events during the next couple of months encouraged freeze advocates. In early August, the freeze resolution came to the House floor, with the Reagan administration strongly opposed. The measure was sidetracked in a 204-to-202 vote but only after several GOP sponsors of the resolution switched, succumbing to pressure from Republican leaders. One of these lawmakers was Jim Coyne of Pennsylvania. Freeze supporters were ecstatic despite the legislative loss. They contended that they could make a political point against a dozen or more opponents of the freeze. Then, on September 14, the day of the Wisconsin primary, Badger State citizens voted 3 to 1 for a nuclear freeze resolution.

In the general election, the freeze initiative—advisory, of course, and having no legal effect on national policy—was on the ballots of nine states (Massachusetts, Arizona, California, Montana, Rhode Island, Michigan, Oregon, New Jersey, and North Dakota) and the District of Columbia. It was also on the ballot in nearly thirty localities. Generally, these resolutions supported a joint U.S.-Soviet freeze on the development and deployment of nuclear weapons as long as there could be verification. More than 25 percent of the American people would have a chance to vote on this nonbinding proposition.

Opponents, led by the Reagan administration, belatedly attacked these initiatives, arguing that if a nuclear freeze were put into place, the result would be to lock the United States into a position of nuclear inferiority. Less than a week before the election, Defense Secretary Caspar Weinberger charged that the freeze "would weaken the deterrent forces we rely on to prevent war." Right-wingers charged that the Communists were behind the freeze movement. Sponsors never believed the freeze issue would equal the economic issue, but they hoped it would energize activists and political volunteers and generally make a difference in close contests, usually to the advantage of Democrats.

Social Issues. In the past couple of elections, conservatives argued that Republicans' successes were aided, in large part, by the so-called social issues—abortion, the ban on school prayer, school busing for purposes of racial integration, affirmative action programs for women and blacks, gun control, and crime. Conservatives were against all these. In the 1980 Senate races, in particular, the New Right activists claimed credit for a number of Democratic scalps. Independent groups, particularly the National Conservative Political Action Committee (NCPAC) and North Carolina Republican Senator Jesse Helms's Congressional Club, would spend millions of dollars concentrating on most of these issues again in 1982.

In some ways, these issues were a mirror image of the freeze. Conservative activists also knew that the social issues would not supersede the issue of the economy. But they hoped the other issues would play a role in bringing out otherwise passive voters and supply the critical margin in close contests. Sometimes, the two might cancel each other out. In California, for example, GOP politician Stuart Spencer had predicted for months that any Democratic gains in the voter turnout on the freeze initiative would be offset by conservative gains from a handgun initiative that was also on the ballot.

In August, Democratic political consultant David Garth conducted a poll on the effect of these social issues. On some issues, the conservatives had little public support; by large margins the public opposed strict prohibitions on abortion and did not agree with the Moral Majority and other right-wing groups. On issues like school prayer, though, the conservatives held a lopsided majority. But Garth concluded that the "public is more liberal on social issues than is currently believed" and dismissed the New Right as a potent political force. In a survey of 1,000 voters he found that only 21 percent rated social issues as their primary concern (about half of these were liberals), whereas 72 percent considered the economy their primary concern.[22] One prominent Republican politician ventured: "With double-digit unemployment, high interest rates, and record bankruptcies, people no longer have the luxury to focus on social issues."

Whatever appeal these measures enjoyed was further diminished in September. A handful of conservatives, led by Jesse Helms and sometimes by Orrin Hatch of Utah, tied up the Senate for almost the entire month trying to push antiabortion and school prayer measures. The spectacle of devoting the final month of the session to these matters when the economy was in sorry shape angered even conservative stalwarts such as Barry Goldwater.

Events in the Fall of 1982

September marked the end of most of the primaries. The results clearly suggested a tilt to the center, perhaps even to the left.

Republican moderates like Pete Wilson in California and Millicent Fenwick in New Jersey defeated conservative rivals in Senate primaries. Also, most, though not all, of the GOP gubernatorial winners were centrists. Democrats also moved a little to the left, defeating conservative Governor Edward King in Massachusetts and Ohio Representative Ron Mottl, one of the few northerners who had voted for key parts of Reagan's economic package. William Safire's *New York Times* column on the primaries carried the headline "The Libs Are Coming!" and the conservative pundit suggested that the primaries provided "the first straw of a Great Liberal Comeback or at least a sharp lurch amid a longer term conservative trend."[23]

Meanwhile, in Washington, the issue of the economy kept coming up. Over the summer, Ronald Reagan, the great tax cutter, had shocked some of his followers by favoring a tax increase. Only months earlier the president had flatly rejected any tax hikes. But Capitol Hill Republicans, led by Senate Finance Committee Chairman Bob Dole, kept pushing, and the president finally relented in hopes of reducing the burgeoning deficit. Actually, the Reagan-backed measure would impose levies, or user fees, mainly on upper-income individuals or corporations and would undo some of the excesses of the 1981 tax legislation. Reagan got a lot in return: assurances that the major parts of his 1981 tax cuts would not be affected. But the legislation produced a bitter fight, mainly within the Republican party. Representative Jack Kemp (Republican, New York), the chief supply-side politician in Congress, opposed his old mentor, Ronald Reagan. The bill eventually passed the House 226 to 207, with the Republicans 103 to 89, and the Democrats 123 to 118, in favor. The measure went back to the Senate, where it cleared 52 to 47, with nine Democrats—including Ted Kennedy—providing Reagan with the winning margin. Opponents argued that the $98.3 billion, three-year tax hike would hurt the president politically, both because of particular features of the bill and because of the appearance of inconsistency. Supporters like Bob Dole argued that it was more popular to reduce the deficit by taxing affluent special interests.

Reagan, however, was eager to placate his conservative critics. The opportunity soon arrived in the form of a $14 billion supplemental appropriations bill that Congress passed before heading home for the August recess. In fact, the legislation was almost $1.3 million less than the president sought, but Congress had altered the budget priorities, taking from defense and giving to domestic programs. The president, eager to regain the anti–big government ground, vetoed the bill with a blistering warning against big spenders.

The House, as expected, easily overrode the veto. But needing only about three-fifths of the Republicans in the GOP-controlled Senate, the White House fully expected victory there. Yet, it was not to be—the Senate voted 60 to 30 to override the veto, exactly the two-thirds vote necessary. Dole had warned that an override "might bust the president," but many lawmakers were furious because Reagan seemed to be playing political games with them and had such little knowledge of the substance of the bill. (The White House complained about a provision in the bill giving $211 million for community service jobs for the elderly, but when asked about this, Reagan supported the program, pleading: "This one slipped by me.") It was not the liberal big spenders who defeated the president on this one. Voting to override the veto were Chairman Pete Domenici of the Budget Committee and such stalwart conservatives as Charles Grassley of Iowa. Some loyal Reaganites, such as John Tower of Texas, did not even bother to stay in town to vote. It was not a good day for the president.

Having a veto overridden is not novel, however, and Reagan still had a splendid legislative record in the Ninety-seventh Congress. But the September 10 vote, less than eight weeks before the midterm election, dramatized both the evaporation of Reagan's once magical hold over Congress and the end of any vestige of GOP unity on tough issues.

Even so, the president showed little remorse. He warned Congress that it had "better practice" veto votes because he would give them plenty of opportunities to use them. The lawmakers viewed the politics differently—of the twenty-six senators who were present for the veto vote and were standing for reelection, twenty-four voted to override the president, including seven of the nine Republicans. The Democrats thought this fight focused on budget priorities, not on big spending, and with unemployment climbing toward double-digit levels, they viewed it as a winning issue.

Several days later, the House Democrats passed a $1 billion "jobs" bill, underscoring new-found confidence in their old bread-and-butter issues. The measure, which passed the House 223 to 169, was more artifice than anything else. For one, it was obvious that Senate action was not possible, so this really was a political gesture. Also, most of the jobs were temporary and makeshift, so that even if the program worked as promised, it would not make much difference. More than 11 million Americans were unemployed, and this legislation aimed to employ 200,000. In Michigan, for example, 636,000 citizens were officially unemployed, and according to the most optimistic analysis the bill would provide 12,000 temporary jobs there. But it gave the Democrats political talking points for the election.

Indeed, the Democrats were escaping their disarray and divisiveness. Reaganomics, or more appropriately anti-Reaganomics, was a powerful bond bringing together disparate Democrats. Over the summer, as the Democrats held a midterm convention in Philadelphia, fears of feuding gave way to unity and harmony. James Perry, in the *Wall Street Journal*, observed: "The ordinarily fractious Democrats came to Philadelphia for three days and held a national party convention that turned out to be as placid as Sunday's supper at the Union League Club."[24] (All of the presidential hopefuls were there, as were most other Democratic notables. An exception was former President Jimmy Carter, who was fishing in Canada; few Democrats lamented his absence.)

Times were tougher for Ronald Reagan and the Republicans. The economy was getting worse, not better, and the Republicans were trying to run away from it. In early October, Adam Clymer, chief political correspondent of the *New York Times*, reported that GOP House candidates were eschewing national issues and trying, out of necessity, to focus on local matters.[25] Reagan's performance was under growing attack. Serious people questioned whether he was able to grasp the complex issues facing him. Few politicians were eager to criticize the president personally, but it was open season on his policies.

The most knowledgeable Reagan analyst is probably Lou Cannon, White House correspondent for the *Washington Post* and a Reagan watcher for more than a decade and a half. In September 1982, Cannon's book *Reagan* was published. It is remarkably even-handed and may be the finest biography ever written about a president in office. "Reagan's idea of a President," Cannon writes, "was of a leader who could rally the country to a cause with the power of his voice and use public opinion as a catalyst for change."[26] After all, Franklin Roosevelt was Reagan's first political idol and his model stylistically. Reagan held up this side of his presidency with enormous talent. But the other side—amounting almost to disengagement from important matters of state—is detailed in Cannon's description of the administration's decision making in the MX mobile missile controversy. Reagan was removed from the process, had little knowledge of or interest in this key matter, and demonstrated that "he knew practically nothing" about the decisions being reached.

By the fall, Reagan was starting to alienate some important constituency groups. Many blue-collar voters whom he had wooed away from the Democrats in 1980 were increasingly disgusted with the economy. Women, who were skeptical of his policies to begin with, now were more anti-Reagan (and anti-Republican) than two years earlier.

But most antagonistic toward the administration were blacks. Reagan never had much black support—in 1980 over 90 percent of the black vote went to Jimmy Carter. By the fall of 1982, however, Peter Hart ventured that "blacks despised Reagan."[27] The president certainly is no racist, but he often seems insensitive to the concerns of blacks. He had to be dragged—by Republicans like Bob Dole—into supporting an extension of the Voting Rights Act even though it had overwhelming support in Congress. Even when he tried to address some black concerns, it often backfired. On September 17, the president spoke to the National Black Republican Council. His message was an all-out assault on the Great Society programs of the mid-1960s. This speech, the *New York Times* noted, "provided fresh ammunition for critics who say he is trying to reverse the racial progress of the last 20 years."[28]

The fear was not that Republicans would lose black votes; except for some moderates in a few industrial states, the GOP was not getting many black votes anyway. But the political concern was that black animosity toward Reagan would produce a much bigger than usual outpouring of black voters on election day. That had already happened in 1981, in a special congressional election in Mississippi and in the Virginia gubernatorial election. On both occasions, blacks provided Democrats with their margins of victory. Nowhere was black resentment of the Republican party more dramatic than in Alabama, where blacks were wholeheartedly supporting the Democratic nominee for governor: George Corley Wallace.

A Balanced Budget

In general, the economic issue was helping Democrats even more than a few months earlier. The September New York Times–CBS poll found that 61 percent of registered voters said they would trust Congress more than President Reagan on the economy.[29]

Yet there was one bright spot for Republicans in most of these surveys: voters still identified the Democrats as the party of big government and thought the Republicans were more likely to cut spending. No issue, Republican strategists felt, was more tailor-made to exploit this advantage, as well as to distract attention from skyrocketing unemployment, than the proposed constitutional amendment to require a balanced budget. Although it appeared ludicrous that an administration producing record deficits now climbing to $200 billion a year could, with a straight face, talk about a balanced-budget amendment, this was precisely what Reagan was bracing to do, with great gusto, in the closing weeks of the campaign.

For two years the House Democratic leadership had bottled up this amendment in the hostile Judiciary Committee. There is another way to get a measure to the full House—the rarely used discharge petition, when at least 218 members, or over half the body, sign a petition directing a measure to the floor. Although backers of the amendment had nearly 200 signatures, it was doubtful they could get those tough final signatures before the election; even if they did, House Speaker O'Neill could use procedural tactics to prevent a vote before November 2.

The White House and House GOP leaders hatched a plan. First, in mid-September, the president insisted Congress return for a post-election lame-duck session. Prominent Republican lawmakers tried to persuade him that this was a bad idea, but Reagan wanted Congress to come back to pass the military spending measure; he also wanted the vehicle of a pending session to hammer away at the balanced-budget amendment. The White House hoped that this issue would alter the economic agenda into a debate over government rather than one over the economy. In late September, only days before scheduled adjournment, heavy Republican pressure produced the final signatures for the discharge petition, and Reagan and company prepared their assault on Tip O'Neill's obstructionism.

The plot did not unfold, however, as planned. Not only did the Speaker not bottle up the amendment, but he brought it to the floor for a vote—immediately. On October 1, as Congress was about to adjourn for the elections, the amendment, which had earlier cleared the Senate 68 to 32, reached the House floor. Substantively, even some of the amendment's sponsors thought this was a bad idea. Either it would not work—it was full of loopholes—and would be another case of politicians promising something and not delivering, or it would work and produce economic chaos. Many economists thought, for example, that balancing the budget at the time would have turned a recession into a depression. Conservative experts were almost as critical as liberals, but the amendment continued to appeal to average voters frustrated over what they perceived as an out-of-control government. The House voted 236 to 187 for the measure, but this was 46 votes short of the two-thirds required to pass a constitutional amendment.

Reagan was off balance politically. The White House tried to turn the vote to its advantage. The president came before the television cameras that afternoon and, while ducking most questions, blasted the House vote and called on voters to "count heads and take names" in the November elections. He neglected to point out that some of the names included those of prominent Republicans who voted against the amendment, such as former House Minority Leader John Rhodes and ardent supply-sider Jack Kemp. A White House aide boasted that "the issue is a winner for us no matter how you slice it. It gives us a platform on which to tell the country that we need a Republican Congress to get the Amendment through in the future."[30]

Tip O'Neill, with strong support from lieutenants such as House Democratic Whip Thomas Foley of Washington, had followed his instincts here and robbed the Republicans of an issue. The Massachusetts Democrat, beaten so soundly throughout 1981 and even part of 1982, had outsmarted his rivals this time.

Both Teeter and Hart could see movement toward the Democrats though its size and scope were unclear. Another pollster, Patrick Caddell, believed a Democratic landslide was in the offing: the Democrats might pick up forty or more House seats and possibly capture control of the Senate. Recent elections, Jimmy Carter's pollster maintained, demonstrated "a pattern of stunning voter swings in the final weeks, and even days, and predominately against the party in power."[31]

Teeter and Hart were less certain. "We're beginning to see a little movement away from the Republicans, but it's too early to know whether it's a tidal wave," Teeter declared a month before the election. Voter turnout, everyone agreed, was critical. The conventional wisdom was that high turnouts helped Democrats and low turnouts aided Republicans, but the more relevant issue was who voted. It seemed that Democrats were more bouyant in 1982 and Republicans more dismayed—the opposite of 1978 and 1980—and thus the surveys might be underestimating Democratic voters and overestimating Republican voters. "This is one of those things that is almost beyond the art of polling," Teeter declared. "We can only measure it in the last couple of weeks and maybe not even then." The GOP poll taker saw a positive sign in that the election year tax increase "fizzled almost right away as an issue in this election."

Maybe the most pertinent question, Bob Teeter thought, was why the Republicans were even competitive, given the state of the economy. He answered his own question, pointing out several GOP arguments that were credible with voters, such as: it took a while to get into this mess and it will take a long time to get out of it; we do not want to go back to the *status quo ante*; inflation and interest rates are down, and there is some light at the end of the tunnel; if we adhere to these policies, the economy will be much better a year from now. The Republican theme urging voters to "stay the course" was not without appeal, Teeter thought.

Hart agreed that there were crosscurrents. "People express four strong beliefs on the economy," he noted. "First, Reaganomics is not working. And the economy is lousy. But also they don't want to give up on Reagan, and, finally, they don't want to go back to the old ways."

Still, Hart argued that some perspective was necessary. "When

29

people ask why we aren't picking up forty seats," the Democrat said, "I remind them that only a year ago there was talk of the Republicans taking over the House." Moreover, he was pleased with recent developments. "The Republicans—Helms and company—looked like crazies on the abortion–social issues stuff. And we won on the veto override. The Democrats were pictured as standing for jobs. When the issue is jobs, the battle is being fought on our turf."

The stock market was starting to surge, but that did not worry Hart much. In September he advised his clients to

> take an offensive position against the Republicans on the basis that they feel the solution to the economy resides on Wall Street rather than Main Street. We would make the focus on the economic issue the small businessman . . . we should urge voters to ask their supermarket manager, their pharmacist, their hardware store manager, their local lunch counter proprietor, etc., how many people they have hired recently and if they feel the economy is picking up.

The Last Unemployment Report before the Elections

Hart also wanted his clients to take full advantage of the September unemployment report, which would be issued October 8 and would be the final jobless data before the election. Most analysts expected the rate to rise to double-digit levels. Hart understandably wanted the Democrats to take advantage of this and attack Reaganomics but warned that the public "wants more than scapegoats . . . the voters need help that goes beyond a simple rejection of Ronald Reagan. . . . We urge your campaign to talk about two or three proposals you have formulated to improve the economy, especially in the private sector and with regard to small business."

The September unemployment report was issued Friday morning. The rise to 10.1 percent was not unexpected, but it still sent political shock waves across the country. The media attention was extraordinary: "10.1% Jobless 42 Year High" blared the *Pittsburgh Post Gazette*.[32] CBS ran a special program Friday night, and part of it focused on hearings before the congressional Joint Economic Committee. One blue-collar worker, while explaining his inability to find a job for months, broke down in tears; it was devastating as well as dramatic.[33]

Reagan met that day with new Mexican President Miguel de la Madrid on the Mexican-U.S. border and, earlier, in an elaborate ceremony in San Diego, signed an export trade bill, which the president claimed would create "hundreds of thousands of new jobs." Try as he might, the president could not divert attention from unemployment. Democrats and labor leaders all over America expressed outrage at the latest unemployment figures and placed the blame squarely on the Reagan administration. Things did not get any better for the White House when five days later it was revealed that another worker had filed for unemployment benefits: Ron Reagan, the president's son, who had been temporarily laid off by the Joffrey Ballet.

The Nonpolitical Speech

The next week Reagan went on television to talk about the economy. The speech was billed as "nonpolitical" so the networks would carry it. Two of the three networks—CBS and NBC—accepted that description.

The Great Communicator's speech, however, was as polished as it was political. Economic problems all were placed at someone else's doorstep—that of the Democrats, previous administrations, Congress, everyone it seemed but the president. He cited "years, even decades of past mistakes" and claimed "it's easy to lose touch with reality when it is other people's money that you are spending." The Democratic response, by Michigan Senator Donald Riegle, predictably drew a much smaller audience and also predictably blasted Reagan and the "millionaires" in his government. The Michigan Democrat suggested that the rich were prospering while the poor suffered under Reaganomics. Both speeches were aimed at the middle class.

The president ended his so-called nonpolitical speech with a plea to "stay the course," the GOP campaign slogan in 1982. But one of the few critics of this entire performance was Robert Kaiser, who, writing in the *Washington Post*, was worried that television executives had decided "whether a Presidential address on the economy five days after an announcement of 10.1 percent unemployment and 20 days before a national election is news instead of politicking." This type of television "soap opera," orchestrated by Reagan, always goes "unnoted" or unreported by television news, Kaiser noted.[34]

Media Coverage of the Elections

In general, media coverage of the elections was erratic. When Jerry Brown and Pete Wilson held an important foreign policy debate in their Senate contest, none of the Los Angeles television stations broadcast it. Political columnist David Broder noted that the three main Los Angeles stations "are owned and operated" by ABC, CBS, and NBC and that their considerable profits are aided by election year

31

advertising: "Television swallows those dollars and, then, often on its news shows and commentaries, joins the denunciation of the distorted and negative messages of the 30 second ad it runs." But, Broder added, the networks' stations then refuse to run a half-hour-long debate. The dean of Washington political reporters then did some research on what network executives had offered southern California voters instead that evening: NBC watchers saw "Real People," featuring a cat that predicts the weather; CBS audiences watched an episode of "Seven Brides for Seven Brothers"; and those tuned in to ABC saw the Rock Hudson film *Ice Station Zebra*.[35] It was not only the big television concerns, however, that abdicated journalistic responsibility. When the two Texas gubernatorial candidates had a debate in Amarillo, neither of the Houston newspapers even bothered to cover it, although Houston is Texas's largest city.

There were other crazy-quilt sidelights to the campaign, not the least of which were the wild gyrations in the polls. The best example may be Connecticut. In mid-October, a *New York Times* poll said Democrat Toby Moffett was five points ahead of Republican incumbent Lowell Weicker. The same day, a *Hartford Courant* poll said its survey showed Weicker up by sixteen points. Both reexamined their data—the *Times* decided Weicker might be ahead after all, while the *Courant* concluded that the momentum had shifted to Moffett.

There was also plenty of nasty and negative campaigning in 1982; hitting-below-the-belt tactics had worked in 1980, and political strategists, like generals, are always using what worked in the last war. Some of it was simply petty. Republicans, for example, painted West Virginia Senator Robert Byrd as being aloof from his home state when Byrd actually made numerous phone calls to West Virginians practically every day and went to the state almost every weekend.

Some of the campaign tactics were more serious. Jerry Brown ran a pro–nuclear freeze ad, which clearly suggested that a vote for Pete Wilson might be a vote to blow up the world. In Tennessee, Republican Robin Beard's campaign accused Democrat Jim Sasser of "murder" for supporting an abortion measure and in another ad featured a likeness of Fidel Castro lighting a cigar and thanking "Señor Sasser" for supporting foreign aid.

The new rule of political consultants, David Broder wrote, "is to get a good shot at your opponent before he or she gets in one on you." The problem, he concluded, is that such negative campaigns lead to "gutless government where the art of survival means avoiding any controversial stands that an opponent could use in a future 'attack' ad."[36] Some independent groups, particularly NCPAC, reveled in these tactics. This negativism, the *Los Angeles Times* reported, "was fostered by widespread voter disenchantment and cynicism," but the result was to produce still more cynical citizens.[37]

Yet, some of this campaign strategy backfired. Brown and Beard were decisively defeated, and their negative commercials hurt them. This surely does not mark the end of negative campaigns, but it may cause future campaign strategists to be a little more careful or selective. (Some negative ads are quite legitimate. In Virginia, Democrat Dick Davis ran a verbatim tape that showed his foe, Republican Paul Trible, stammering and stumbling when asked about his greatest achievement.)

Social Security Again

Much political hoopla flowed from the social security issue, too. The Reagan administration had tried to chip away at some peripheral social security benefits and had created political problems in the process. The elderly usually vote more Republican than Democratic, but this time the GOP was genuinely worried about these voters, as the Democrats repeatedly insisted the Republicans wanted to take benefits away from old folks.

In reality, the social security trust fund faced some potentially severe short-term problems over the next decade. The next Congress had to either raise taxes or cut back benefits, and most Democrats knew this in 1982. But it was too good a political issue for them to ignore.

Then the Republicans gave the Democrats an election year bonus. In early September, the House Republican Campaign Committee sent out a fund-raising mailing that addressed the social security issue. It asked which remedy the individuals on the mailing list favored. One of the options was to make social security voluntary—which to most recipients meant destroying the system. Democrats got hold of the letter almost immediately but shrewdly held it until a week before the election, when they leaked it. The Republicans were horrified, and the Democrats ecstatic. Tip O'Neill called on Reagan to "repudiate immediately" any suggestion that social security be made voluntary. Yet, another Democrat privately admitted: "Social security is to us what the balanced budget is to the Republicans—we both know we're demagoguing, but it's too good to pass up."

The Home Stretch

As the election entered the final two weeks, the Democrats—buoyed by the social security and unemployment issues—were gaining confidence. In the House, they started to talk confidently of major gains in the Midwest and perhaps even in the Sunbelt, too. They talked seriously about defeating House GOP leader Bob Michel, who had won his Peoria district in the past two elections with 66 percent and 62 percent of the vote. Michel's nervousness was underscored when he told a visiting *Boston Globe* reporter: "I don't intend to put any distance between our President and myself."[38] Only days later, however, he broke with the president on the issue of trade sanctions against the Soviet pipeline. The largest employer in his district was Caterpillar Tractor Company, whose payroll had dropped by almost one-third over the past three years. Caterpillar was one of the U.S. companies most adversely affected by the pipeline sanctions.

Pennsylvania's Eighth Congressional District mirrored these national trends. Democrat Kostmayer emphasized unemployment and social security repeatedly. He accused Coyne of voting to reduce social security benefits. Coyne actually taped a radio spot saying he had "voted against every bill that would cut social security benefits," indicating that he was countering the Democrats' charges.

The nuclear freeze was topical here, especially since Coyne had provided the deciding vote against it in the House. Even worse, the incumbent waffled in trying to explain his action, offering different explanations to different groups. Kostmayer was not going to let Bucks County voters forget that Coyne had succumbed to party pressure. One Kostmayer campaign ad was entitled "The Story of How the Cookie Crumbles."

Coyne continued to insist that the country's economic woes were caused by policies of the past and consistently called Kostmayer a "left-wing liberal." But he also began to pull back from the Reagan administration. The president "deserves something better than an average grade but certainly not an A," Coyne told the *Yardley News*.[39] "I've opposed him about a third of the time and, of course, most strongly on things like Jim Watt. I was the first Republican member of Congress to call for Watt's resignation."

Kostmayer waffled too on issues like the balanced-budget amendment and on the sort of specific jobs programs he proposed. If elected, he promised to assemble a jobs task force and to appoint an aide to bring employment to Bucks County. These weren't satisfactory answers, but Kostmayer had an important advantage: people thought the economy was in bad shape, and, as in 1980, critics were not held as accountable as incumbents.

Terry Weldon, the Kostmayer campaign manager (who, curiously, performed the same task for Coyne in the 1980 race), noted that while the freeze vote was helpful, "the unemployment situation is the overwhelming issue." There were the parochial matters that affect all congressional contests, and the prime rate had come down to the acceptable 12 percent level Coyne wanted, but joblessness was dominant anyway. In a typical Kostmayer television commercial, the Democrat stood before an empty factory and asked: "How much longer are we going to permit jobs to be lost overseas or to the Sunbelt?" while decrying the 10.1 percent unemployment rate. "The immensity of unemployment as the cutting issue" in this district, columnists Evans and Novak discovered, was underscored in a small survey in which even Republicans said that the Democrats would do a better job of reducing unemployment.[40]

The Battle for the Senate

In the final week of the elections, much of the attention was on the Senate races. On October 27, David Broder wrote in the *Washington Post* that the Democrats were "in striking range" of taking control of the Senate. This respected political reporter found a "surge of support for Democrats from California to New Jersey."[41]

Ironically, the national economy often seemed to affect the governors' races as much as, if not more than, the Senate and House contests. Few of the Republican governors had ever been enthusiastic about Reaganomics, which would clearly cut back on federal largess to their states. But most of the GOP governors stayed with Reagan throughout most of 1981.

As 1982 progressed, though, the state candidates increasingly sought to create some distance between themselves and the president. Even conservatives such as Lewis Lehrman in New York criticized Reagan's and the Republicans' campaign theme of "stay the course," arguing that the course was not working very well. Some articulate and bright Republicans, like Clarence Brown in Ohio, simply were overwhelmed by economic conditions. Even in Texas, which GOP Governor Bill Clements had boasted was resistant to the national recession, the economic issue dominated the closing weeks when unemployment jumped 25 percent to 8.4 percent.

Naturally, some state house races were dominated by local considerations. In Illinois, for example, GOP Governor James Thompson was expected to trounce Democrat Adlai Stevenson, not because of national trends or even because Thompson was such a great governor, but because Stevenson once complained that Thompson had called him a "wimp"—a charge the governor did not deny, and the public apparently accepted. Still, most Republicans even searched for ways to break with the Reagan administration. In Oregon, for instance, conservative incumbent GOP Governor Victor Atiyeh sent a well-

35

publicized missive to Budget Director David Stockman complaining: "Don't tell me how tough it is. Don't tell me what you inherited. . . . Don't tell me how something can't be done." He then demanded action in lowering budget deficits and interest rates.[42]

Many of the Republican gubernatorial candidates relied on blue-collar voters for support: Reagan was alienating them, and there was fear that this would spill over. As early as late summer, GOP Senate campaign committee strategist Vince Breglio was lamenting that "the blues are going home" to their political nest, the Democratic party.

As David Broder acknowledged, however, the chance of any Democratic takeover of the Senate remained very slim. But some Republicans thought to be shoo-ins a few months earlier were now fighting for their lives. In Missouri, millionaire John Danforth, despite having an edge in campaign funds, was running even with State Senator Harriet Woods. In Minnesota, popular incumbent Senator David Durenberger was confronted by Mark Dayton, a young multimillionaire who was spending more than $6 million of his own money on the race. In New Jersey, Representative Millicent Fenwick, an overwhelming favorite over the summer, was running a second-rate campaign and in danger of being overtaken by businessman Frank Lautenberg. GOP moderates like Rhode Island's John Chafee and Vermont's Robert Stafford were battling for their political lives. Ironically, Republican prospects in California and Connecticut— initially, the GOP's two most worrisome contests—were much brighter. Out West, Republicans now rated Utah's Orrin Hatch as safe and felt that they had a chance to unseat incumbent Democrats Howard Cannon of Nevada and John Melcher of Montana.

No race was more of a tossup, though, than the one in New Mexico. Both Schmitt and Bingaman were cautiously optimistic. Most surveys showed Schmitt with a slight and declining lead. On October 26, the ZIA Research poll in New Mexico showed the incumbent Republican ahead 47 percent to 40 percent. (Bingaman led among women, 44 percent to 43 percent, whereas Schmitt was well ahead among men, 52 percent to 35 percent.) That was not welcome news, however, for Schmitt; anytime an incumbent is ahead by only seven points and has less than 50 percent of the vote in a two-way race, he is in trouble since most undecided voters probably do not like him much.

Was Bingaman tough enough to win? In mid-October, the *Baltimore Sun* predicted that a "Democratic breakthrough seems less likely" than earlier, as Bingaman's "hesitant style . . . may not be quite the formula for unseating Schmitt."[43] Only a week later, however, the *New York Times* reported that Schmitt's reelection drive "seems to be in trouble."[44]

Bingaman was gaining more confidence as election day neared, and Schmitt was showing signs of panic. In late summer, the Democrats decided they needed a stronger message to solidify the party's base. Polls, for example, showed Bingaman winning only a little more than half the Hispanic vote. So new commercials were aimed at unemployment, social security, education, and the need to control defense spending. Schmitt was chastised for being antienvironment and anti–social security and was blamed—with no explanation—for the fact that 60,000 New Mexicans were out of work. The ex-astronaut also was portrayed as a do-nothing legislator: "What on earth has Jack Schmitt done for you?" (This ingenuous phrase actually was coined by Ted Kennedy, when he campaigned for Jeff Bingaman.)

Sensing that things were not going well, Schmitt, in mid-October, launched two decidedly negative commercials. One charged that the state's attorney general had failed to prosecute prisoners responsible for the 1980 New Mexico state prison riot in which thirty-three inmates had died. The other accused Bingaman of trying to get the governor to pardon a hardened criminal who was on the most-wanted list of the Federal Bureau of Investigation.

The commercials were misleading, as it turned out. On the issue of the pardon, all Bingaman had done was provide a legal opinion to the governor that it was legally permissible to comply with a U.S. Justice Department request that the felon be given a conditional release. As far as the prison riots were concerned, both a citizens' advisory committee on the subject and the president of the New Mexico Association of District Attorneys pointed out that it was the local district attorney, not the state attorney general, who had responsibility for the prosecution.

Bingaman's response, featuring aggressive personal appearances, a short commercial, and surrogate attacks on Schmitt's tactics, was masterful. "For eight or nine days the newspapers and television news shows contained stories about the controversy, the nature of the ads and our response," noted Les Francis, a Washington political consultant advising Bingaman. "Too, Schmitt mishandled the situation terribly; first he said the ads would be pulled; then he kept them on."

A week before the election, the Democrats' final poll showed Bingaman pulling five points ahead of his opponent. Also, the public believed, by 51 percent to 13 percent, the Bingaman version and not the Schmitt version of the controversy. No wonder the *Washington Post*'s knowledgeable southwestern correspondent Dan Balz concluded that the Schmitt commercials had boomeranged.[45]

Four days before the election President Reagan came to Roswell, New Mexico, to campaign for Jack Schmitt. But even the Republican forces found this a mixed blessing; Reagan, they feared, would stir the Democrats to vote against their man as much as he would inspire the GOP faithful.

Teeter and Hart

The two pollsters adjusted their election outlook very little at the end. "This is an election of money issues; unemployment is the focal point," lamented Teeter. Only a few days before, Hart had advised clients to keep stressing joblessness, painting the GOP as being oblivious to the real pain of unemployment: "The bottom line is that Democrats mean jobs."

Two nonissues, both agreed, were the stock market surge—Main Street did not care much about Wall Street—and the balanced-budget amendment. "To my surprise the Republicans didn't get anywhere with the balanced-budget issue," said Hart. Although unemployment plainly was helping the Democrats, both pollsters agreed that many voters were reluctant not to give Reaganomics a chance. Thus, it was hard to determine whether Reagan was a plus or a minus for many of the GOP candidates.

The more Hart analyzed his data, the more he became convinced that the successful overriding of the presidential veto of the appropriations bill in September was a seminal political event, as half the congressional Republicans deserted the president on this one. "The Republican line was to accuse the Democrats of being the party of tax and tax, spend and spend," the Democratic pollster ventured. "But this vote said the Republicans decided instead each of us has to save ourselves. This cut the ground out from under their national message."

Both Teeter and Hart were predicting about two dozen House gains for the Democrats, an even give or take of one or two seats on either side in the Senate, and about a half-dozen Democratic gubernatorial victories. If either side enjoyed a last-minute boost, they agreed it would more likely be the Democrats in the form of a protest vote. Both used the term "midcourse correction" to describe the probable message coming out of these midterm elections.

Reagan's Campaign Efforts

Reagan tried to garner votes for Republicans in the last two weeks of the elections, but the results were mixed. He stirred some Republican passions wherever he went. But he also lambasted Senator Don Riegle as "the demagogue from Michigan." The nuclear freeze movement was inspired, he said, "by some who want the weakening of America." He said House Majority Leader Jim Wright was engaged in "hypocrisy," and in noting that the Pac-man video game has been described as a "round thing that gobbles up money," he told a group of conservative Texans: "I thought that was Tip O'Neill."

The president had an embarrassing problem in the final days of the elections. Many Republican candidates, ranging from candidates in most of the northern and midwestern states to conservatives such as Senate aspirant Paul Trible in Virginia, did not want the president to campaign at the end. One day in the last week he spent a whole day in North Carolina campaigning for House candidates, particularly for a heavily favored conservative running against an incumbent Democrat who was recently picked up for drunk driving. This looked like a case, the *New York Times* noted, of the White House seizing "an opportunity for the President to take credit for a probable victory."[46]

Where he was welcomed, the president left a message that was sometimes confusing. In Peoria, in an appearance for Bob Michel, he delivered "two directly conflicting political messages," Lou Cannon reported.[47] One warned of the dangers of dealing with the Soviet Union; the other boasted of his administration's efforts to increase grain sales to the Russians. In the closing days of the elections the Reagan theme was to be "hope" (Republicans) versus "fear" (Democrats). But as the president went out West, to Montana, he felt compelled instead to respond to Democratic attacks on social security. This, reports indicated, "overshadowed the 'hope versus fear' line and was fighting the battle on the Democrats' turf."[48] (The White House was also eager to take credit for any victory where the president campaigned and insisted that Nevada GOP senatorial candidate Chic Hecht rose in the polls after Reagan campaigned for him. But Peter Hart, who was polling for the Democratic gubernatorial candidate in Nevada, a week before Reagan set foot in the state, found Hecht pulling even with incumbent Senator Howard Cannon.)

On the eve of the election, Reagan made a national speech for the Republicans; former senator and secretary of state Edmund Muskie spoke for the Democrats. Neither speech was memorable.

The Election Results

As the results poured in election night, it was obviously quite a good Democratic year. The Democrats picked up twenty-six House seats, not a landslide, but enough to cause a sharp shift in the balance of power in the Ninety-eighth Congress. To prevail in the House in 1983, Reagan would have to make major concessions.

In Pennsylvania, Peter Kostmayer defeated Republican Jim Coyne by a little more than 2,000 votes. This time, unlike the previous election, the two candidates each spent about the same amount, about $500,000. The race was settled in industrial lower Bucks County, where Kostmayer won by more than 17,000 votes, or about 6,000 more votes than in the previous election. In Peoria, GOP leader Bob Michel trailed for a while but hung on to squeeze out a narrow victory.

The Republicans' 54-to-46 edge in the Senate was unchanged, as few seats changed. The Democrats won seats in New Mexico and New Jersey, while the Republicans took over the Virginia and Nevada seats (every other incumbent won). Pete Wilson beat Jerry Brown in California. In New Mexico, Jeff Bingaman won with almost 54 percent of the vote, doing especially well in Hispanic communities.

Senate Majority Leader Baker and other GOP functionaries insisted that overall the elections were a vote of confidence for the Republican-run Senate. Actually, the outcome reflected only the electoral arithmetic of 1982. Of all the votes for the Senate, 55 percent went to the Democrats, but more Democratic incumbents had been up for election, so net gains were difficult to assess. That situation will be reversed in 1984 and 1986.

In the governors' races, the Democrats made their biggest gains, increasing their margin by seven to a 34-to-16 advantage. The only major disappointment was in California, where Tom Bradley barely lost a chance at becoming this century's first black governor. Republican Jim Thompson held on in Illinois but only by about 5,000 votes over former Senator Adlai Stevenson. The Democrats recaptured Texas, with Mark White winning. Lieutenant Governor Mario Cuomo won in New York, and George Wallace, with a large black vote, easily returned to the Alabama state house. The Democrats now controlled six of the ten largest states; they also picked up a net gain of 177 state legislators.

The election clearly had to be a disappointment to Reagan. The GOP hopes of solidifying the 1980 gains and building a new governing coalition were dealt a severe setback. But, with double-digit unemployment, some White House aides insisted it could have been much worse. Howard Baker obviously was pleased at keeping the same majority margin in the Senate. Yet the six Republican senators who won with only 51 percent of the vote did not send out any encouraging signals about lock-step loyalty in 1983 and 1984.

The one clear winner election night was Thomas P. O'Neill. He had suffered more than any other political leader in the past two years. But his strategy of giving the Republicans their chance, or some political rope, paid off on election night. With a 269-to-166 Democratic margin in the House, Tip O'Neill will be expected to put together serious Democratic alternatives in the Ninety-eighth Congress, a task that could prove impossible. But on election night it was hard for him to think of problems. Eugene Atkinson, who left the party O'Neill revered, was trounced. So was John LeBoutillier, the abrasive young New York conservative Republican who loved to insult O'Neill. Just about all the Speaker's friends were winning easily. Watching the election returns come in that night, the Speaker waved his cigar, smiled, and declared: "It's a great night for the Irish."[49]

Notes

1. CBS, "Face the Nation," August 2, 1981.

2. Austin Ranney, "The Carter Administration," in Ranney, ed., *The American Elections of 1980* (Washington, D.C.: American Enterprise Institute, 1981), p. 2.

3. Ibid., pp. 2–3.

4. George Skelton, "GOP's Grand Hopes for Resurgence Fading," *Los Angeles Times*, January 16, 1982.

5. Albert R. Hunt, "GOP Unity Dissolves As Reagan Policies Irk Both Wings of Party," *Wall Street Journal*, February 17, 1982.

6. Ibid.

7. Gallup poll, February 1982.

8. Alan Baron, *Baron Report*, April 12, 1982.

9. Kevin Phillips, *American Political Report*, May 7, 1982.

10. Dennis Farney and Albert Hunt, "Any Budget Plan Faces Hard Time in Congress despite Public Unease," *Wall Street Journal*, April 10, 1982.

11. David Nyhan, "Running against Reaganomics," *Boston Globe*, May 23, 1982.

12. Farney and Hunt, "Any Budget Plan Faces Hard Time in Congress."

13. Albert R. Hunt, "Can the Republicans Hold On to New Mexico?" *Wall Street Journal*, September 14, 1982.

14. Ibid.

15. Mark Shields, "The GOP's 2% Solution," *Washington Post*, June 11, 1982.

16. "Does Reagan Have a Problem with Women?" *Public Opinion* (December/January 1982), p. 48.

17. Albert R. Hunt, "Wider Gulf Indicated between the President and Women Voters," *Wall Street Journal*, May 6, 1982.

18. Ibid.

19. NBC Nightly News, October 27, 1982.

20. Ibid.

21. Judith Miller, "Democrats Seize Weapons Freeze as Issue for Fall," *New York Times*, June 20, 1982.

22. David Garth, "Social Issues in 1982: Rhetoric versus Reality," *The Garth Analysis*, August 1982.

23. William Safire, "The Libs Are Coming!" *New York Times*, October 1, 1982.

24. James M. Perry, "Democrats Parade Leading '84 Hopefuls, Some New Ideas at Philadelphia Meeting," *Wall Street Journal*, June 28, 1982.

25. Adam Clymer, "Republican Candidates for House Focus Campaigns on Local Issues," *New York Times*, October 4, 1982.

26. Lou Cannon, *Reagan* (New York: G. P. Putnam's Sons, 1982), p. 371.

27. Jack Nelson, "Democratic Pollster Sees Heavy Black Turnout," *Los Angeles Times*, October 5, 1982.

28. Howell Raines, "Reagan and Blacks," *New York Times*, September 17, 1982.

29. New York Times–CBS poll, September 1982.

30. Steven R. Weisman, "House Vote: Who Won?" *New York Times*, October 2, 1982.

31. Patrick Caddell, "Why the Democrats May Win Big," *Washington Post*, October 17, 1982.

32. *Pittsburgh Post Gazette*, October 9, 1982.

33. CBS Special, October 8, 1982.

34. Robert G. Kaiser, "Blowing Smoke and Calling It Reality," *Washington Post*, October 17, 1982.

35. David S. Broder, "The Networks Blank Out a Debate," *Washington Post*, October 10, 1982.

36. David S. Broder, "When Campaigns Get Mean," *Washington Post*, October 31, 1982.

37. Robert Shogan, "Activists Unleash Tide of Political Negativism," *Los Angeles Times*, October 25, 1982.

38. David Rogers, "Back Home in Peoria, Rep. Michel Runs Hard against a Newcomer," *Boston Globe*, September 24, 1982.

39. "The Race for Congress," *Yardley News*, October 21, 1982.

40. Rowland Evans and Robert Novak, "A Sword Hanging over the GOP," *Washington Post*, October 29, 1982.

41. David S. Broder, "Democrats in 'Striking Range' of Senate Majority," *Washington Post*, October 27, 1982.

42. Robert W. Merry, ". . . and Atiyeh vs. Kulongoski atop Oregon Card," *Wall Street Journal*, September 23, 1982.

43. Fred Barnes, "Schmitt Leads Hesitant Bingaman in N.M. Senate Race," *Baltimore Sun*, October 13, 1982.

44. Steven V. Roberts, "Schmitt, Astronaut Now in Senate, Struggles to Hold New Mexico Seat," *New York Times*, October 21, 1982.

45. Dan Balz, "Negative Ads Have Backfired on Schmitt's Slipping Campaign," *Washington Post*, October 26, 1982.

46. Howell Raines, "President Alters Campaign Strategy," *New York Times*, October 26, 1982.

47. Lou Cannon, "President's 2 Message Conflict," *Washington Post*, October 21, 1982.

48. Rich Jaroslovsky, "Reagan in West to Conclude GOP Campaign," *Wall Street Journal*, October 29, 1982.

49. Mary McGrory, "A Good Night As Projected, for the Democrats— and the Irish," *Washington Post*, November 4, 1982.

2

Reapportionment and Redistricting

Alan Ehrenhalt

Students of congressional redistricting sometimes forget, at least for a while, the fiendish unpredictability of American politics. The massive presence of population data, demographic analysis, and precinct voting history can foster the illusion that carving up a state's congressional districts is a species of exact science. Only when the election returns come in is it clear how much like the rest of politics redistricting is.

In the spring of 1981, when legislatures throughout the country began redrawing district lines to reflect population data in the previous year's census, a few political results seemed all but certain. The movement of population and House seats to southern and western states seemed to dictate a strengthened Sunbelt conservatism in the Ninety-eighth Congress. The enormous Republican advantage in preparation for the process seemed to guarantee not only a conservative trend but also a partisan windfall of a dozen seats or more. Much of this change was likely to come at the expense of minorities, whose representation was concentrated in underpopulated inner-city districts ripe for elimination.

These events did not take place, for a number of reasons that this essay will try to trace. Of the predictions commonly heard when the process began, only one consistently came true—that it would be a messy and unpleasant affair whose closest observers would complain that there must be a better way to deal with a problem certain to recur every ten years.

The Commands of the Census

Rarely has a census revealed such sharp regional shifts of population and political power in the United States as the 1980 census did. The 1970s provoked endless debate about the move from Frostbelt to Sunbelt, but the census figures left little room for argument about what was happening.

The numbers dictated that seventeen House seats would have to move from one state to another, and every one of those was to move in the same direction. No state in the Northeast or Midwest gained a seat; no state in the Southwest lost one. New York learned that it would be giving up five of the thirty-nine districts it had during the previous decade, the largest such reapportionment loss any state has suffered in this century. Florida learned that it would be gaining four seats, punctuating one of the swiftest accessions to major-state status in American history. When John F. Kennedy was elected president in 1960, there were only eight House members from Florida. In the Ninety-eighth Congress, there are nineteen.

In no other recent census had the regional gains and losses been so clear-cut. True, California and Florida had been the big gainers after the 1970 census, but not all the South and West had shared their good fortune: Alabama and Tennessee had each lost a seat. Although much of the Frostbelt had lost representation in 1960 to give California its reapportionment bonanza of eight new seats, there had been pockets of Frostbelt growth. Michigan and New Jersey, still reaping the last benefits of postwar suburban expansion, each gained a seat at that time.

Within each state, the population changes recorded by the 1980 census were nearly as striking. In every region of the country, people not only were leaving the inner cities, as they had been doing for a generation, but also were moving beyond the first ring of suburbs to newly built communities that stood on land used for farming a decade earlier.

Virtually all inner-city districts, north and south, were major population losers in the 1970s. The five most massive declines were in districts in New York City (the Bronx and Brooklyn), Detroit, St. Louis, and Cleveland; all those districts had black or Hispanic representation.[1] More surprising was the decline in districts that included the older suburbs—elite bedroom communities built before World War II and the first tract home suburbs constructed after the war.

Illinois shows the pattern clearly. The district with the heaviest population losses in Illinois over the decade was the First District, an overwhelmingly black constituency on Chicago's Near South Side that has had a black representative since 1929. The district lost 20 percent of its population during the 1970s as housing opened up elsewhere in the city and blacks were able to leave the tenement-style South Side neighborhoods to which earlier segregation had confined them.

As blacks continued to spread out within the city, ethnic working-class whites left the outlying bungalow neighborhoods of the South and West sides. The Southwest Side Fifth District, traditional home of policemen, steelworkers, and packinghouse workers of Irish and Polish descent, lost 15 percent of its population.

Yet these ethnic migrants did not settle in the more established Chicago suburbs. The inner-suburban Tenth District, whose bedroom communities such as Evanston and Winnetka have sent wealthy commuters into downtown Chicago for most of the century, actually suffered its own 6 percent population loss in the 1970s. The district was not declining economically—it remained near the top in all national economic rankings at the time of the census. But children were growing up and moving away, and there were few new families coming in to replace them, in part because housing in these older suburbs was so expensive.

Chicago's younger families were bypassing the familiar Evanston and Winnetka for subdivisions in towns such as Schaumburg, Elk Grove Village, and Hoffman Estates, some of them built on land that was growing corn in 1970. In Illinois, as in most of the country, the "growth districts" were the ones concentrated 30 to 50 miles from the city limits. Nearly all these constituencies were securely in Republican control. The Illinois Twelfth District, northwest of Chicago's inner suburban ring, grew 32.6 percent in the 1970s, a period in which it was represented by conservative Republican Philip M. Crane. The Fourteenth District, an equivalent distance west of the city, grew 34.8 percent. It was the preserve of veteran Republican John N. Erlenborn, labor's chief antagonist on the House Education and Labor Committee.

The twin migrations of the 1970s—from Frostbelt to Sunbelt and from the cities to the metropolitan fringe—seemed to dictate only one political result for the 1980s. Resourceful Democratic candidates might find a way to win some of the new districts in the Sunbelt and the suburbs, but they would do it only by assuming the local political coloration. The ultimate shift, it was argued convincingly, would have to be toward conservatism. "If you move a seat from a big city ghetto out to the suburbs," said Richard M. Scammon, political demographer and former director of the Census Bureau, "it doesn't make any difference if you elect another Democrat. It's the kind of Democrat you're going to elect. . . . This is going to cut back on the representation of people who have been for liberal issues."[2]

Predictions such as these led to some early militance on the part of inner-city Democrats in the House, an ironic reversal of what happened in 1920 when rural legislators were outraged by census figures showing an urban majority in the nation for the first time. Those rural militants, dealing from a position of unquestioned strength in Congress, knew exactly what to do. They simply canceled reapportionment for the entire decade of the 1920s, leaving districts as they had been before World War I.

Their urban counterparts of 1981 had no such hopes. But they suggested a variety of solutions to their problem. Representative Robert Garcia (Democrat, New York), chairman of the House Census Subcommittee and representative of the single most underpopulated district in the country (his Bronx Twenty-first District had lost half its people in the 1970s), urged that the Census Bureau adjust its urban figures to account for blacks and Hispanics missed in the regular head count. Representative Mary Rose Oakar, a Cleveland Democrat whose constituency lost 19 percent of its residents in the decade, proposed enlarging the size of the House. "There's nothing sacrosanct about the number 435," she insisted.

The Perils of Partisanship

Congressional redistricting is one of those games that is more fun to watch than to play. For the reporter, the academic, and the armchair politician, it offers just about everything: backroom intrigue, personal rivalry, mounds of statistics, and the certainty that national government will be affected for years to come, one way or the other.

For the typical state legislator drawing the lines, it offers comparatively little. Unless he is planning to run for Congress himself, the process is not crucial to his own political future. It is more than likely to make him an enemy of at least one member of the state's congressional delegation (no new congressional district map pleases everybody); it often involves tedious late-night bargaining for weeks on end; and it is nearly always irrelevant to his state legislative constituents. Most of the legislators who chair redistricting committees emerge vowing never to do it again.

It was clear from the outset that the post-1980 redistricting would be even more burdensome than those in the past. Federal courts had made it clear that districts had to be virtually identical in population (a 3 percent variance had been declared unconstitutional by the U.S. Supreme Court in 1969), and computerization for the first time permitted mapmakers to generate, on a moment's notice, detailed voting histories down to the precinct level. Statistically, at least, there was far more to argue over than there had been in 1970.

Whatever the local burden, though, there was a good deal for national Republicans to be cheerful about in early 1981. Besides the shift of political power to the suburbs and the Sunbelt, they could count on a clear advantage in the computer technology that seemed crucial to winning a modern redistricting war. The Republican National Committee had spent several years helping the party's state legislators prepare for the task. Republican consulting firms such as the Rose Institute in California and Market Opinion Research in Michigan had been feeding precinct data to GOP mapmakers all over the country. "Gerrymanders do work, given computers," said Alan Heslop, director of the Rose Institute. "There is a prospect that a party which has control in 1980 can so abuse its power that it will still be in control in 1990."[3]

Democrats in most states had no help from the party's national organization and no access to the kinds of information Republicans were using. Some of them foresaw disaster. "We may be operating in the 19th Century and they may be operating in the 21st Century," said a legislator in Washington State. "They've done their homework on this and they'll shoot it to us."[4] A consultant to the Texas AFL-CIO reported shortly after that state's process had begun that "the Republicans had expertise and computer capability and the Democrats were all grins and no leadership."[5]

In May 1981, as the first few states were completing their congressional maps, it appeared that Republicans were headed for the triumph that demographics and computers seemed to promise them— a gain of a dozen or more House seats in 1982 based on redistricting alone. On April 30, the last day of Indiana's legislative session, the Republicans had unveiled and passed a new map that both sides conceded was a remarkably skillful gerrymander.

Indiana had to lose a seat in reapportionment, but the state GOP, taking advantage of more than $250,000 worth of demographic information supplied by Market Opinion Research, did more than one seat's worth of damage to the Democrats. The new map, signed immediately by Republican Governor Robert Orr, dismembered two Democratic districts rather than one and created a brand new Republican seat in the Indianapolis suburbs. "The Democrats are going to have to face the political reality that we are going to do everything we can to hurt them within the restraints of the court rulings," said one author of the plan.[6]

Few in the national GOP could have suspected that Indiana would be perhaps the last triumph they would savor in the entire yearlong process. From the end of April on, virtually everything that could possibly go wrong for them did go wrong. The remainder of the season brought a remarkable string of Republican defeats, missed opportunities, and, at best, political standoffs.

At the end of the summer, Democrats in California did to the opposition what had been done to *them* in Indiana, but on a much larger scale. The Democratic party controlled both legislative chambers and the governorship in California, and the legislators entrusted the entire task of redistricting to U.S. Representative Phillip Burton, who said nothing about it in public until September 15, the day his plan passed. Most of the state legislators had not seen a copy of the Burton map at the time it was approved overwhelmingly in both the Senate and the House. Nor had his Democratic congressional colleagues seen it. "You're in your mother's arms," he reassured them.

Burton's objective was to take the existing California map, on which Democrats had a 22–21 majority, and create a new forty-five-seat map that would increase the party majority to 27–18. Two brand new Democratic districts were created, both with political allies of Burton in mind. Three GOP-held districts were carved up beyond recognition. Two pairs of Republican incumbents, both in southern California, were obliged to run against each other or accept difficult reelection odds elsewhere.

Republicans had expected bad news in California, but they had not counted on anything quite so blatant. Republican U.S. Representative William M. Thomas, who was supposed to be the redistricting liaison for the GOP House delegation but whom Burton never consulted, accused Burton of "personally placing his thumb print on the state of California." Republicans managed to get the Burton map on a referendum for decision at the 1982 primary, on June 8, but the state supreme court, on a 4–3 vote, made that move essentially irrelevant by ruling that the Burton districts would remain in effect for 1982 even if they were disapproved in the referendum (as they ultimately were).[7]

All by itself, the Burton map virtually eliminated any practical possibility of a twelve-seat national Republican windfall in redistricting. To make up for even a four-seat loss in California, the GOP would have had to redraw more than fifteen districts for partisan reversal in states where they had the political advantage. As the 1982 election year grew closer, it became clear that California, not Indiana, would approximate the national situation.

In New Jersey, where a Republican governor was elected in November 1981 to replace an outgoing Democrat, Democrats in the legislature moved a "midnight redistricting bill" that did the same partisan work as Burton's had in California, albeit less elegantly. Governor Brendan T. Byrne signed the new plan into law the day before he left office in January 1982.

Jutting across county lines and township lines and breaking up political communities that had been left intact for generations, the redrawn New Jersey map eliminated one Republican district, paired two GOP incumbents in another, and rearranged the lines in Bergen

County to make reelection difficult for the Republican who had been representing much of it.

Republicans challenged the map and won a fleeting success when a federal court declared the map's population variances too great to meet constitutional standards. But the U.S. Supreme Court followed the California precedent and allowed the map to stand for 1982, pending a later review.

While these reverses were taking place, Republicans were encountering trouble in states that they had assumed were under their control. In Washington state, where all the branches of government were in Republican hands, a problem emerged within the majority party. The legislature moved quickly in 1981, with the help of a $175,000 Rose Institute computer system, to pass a map weakening at least one of the state's five incumbent House Democrats. But the plan drew resistance from a moderate Republican, Representative Joel Pritchard, who felt it would have made his safe district in the Seattle suburbs uncomfortably close.

Pritchard's complaint convinced his ally John Spellman, the state's Republican governor, and Spellman vetoed the expensive document. When the legislature finally managed to agree on a map that pleased Spellman, in February 1982, it turned out to be one that protected all five of the Democrats, rewarding the GOP majority only with a secure hold on the newly created Eighth District near Seattle, a seat that virtually any Republican could have taken regardless of the way the lines were drawn.

Far worse, from a Republican point of view, was the situation in Texas. The GOP was not even close to a legislative majority there, but it had a strong and aggressive governor in William Clements and state-of-the-art technical sophistication.

Clements managed to strike a bargain with the legislature's most influential conservative Democrat, House Speaker Billy Clayton, and their chosen victim was Democratic U.S. Representative Jim Mattox, a hot-tempered populist who had tangled with the leadership of both parties during his years in Austin. Mattox's congressional district was made so heavily Republican that he abandoned it to run for state attorney general. Just to the west, a new "mid-cities" constituency between Dallas and Forth Worth, one of three in the state added by reapportionment, was given a Republican coloration despite the heavy Democratic advantage in the legislature.

The Clements-Clayton map, however, did not make it to the primary. First the Justice Department ruled it invalid under the Voting Rights Act, arguing that the balance of Hispanic voters in two south Texas districts was not equal enough. That made little partisan difference, but it rendered the entire state map temporarily unusable, and a three-judge federal panel took advantage of that opportunity to redraw most of the lines in the Dallas–Fort Worth area, restoring a Democratic majority in the Mattox district. Mattox himself decided to continue his campaign for attorney general, but a Democrat of similar populist inclination, state Representative John Bryant, was the eventual nominee and easy winner. In November, the last sliver of Republican good fortune in Texas disappeared when the mid-cities district was won by conservative Democrat Tom Vandergriff, the former mayor of Arlington. Of the three new Texas seats created by population growth, the GOP thus did not get any, even though much of the growth was in Republican-leaning areas.

Texas held its 1982 congressional voting under the lines approved by the federal judges in February, even though the U.S. Supreme Court agreed with Republican contentions that the judges had exceeded their authority in redrawing the Dallas-area districts. The Court said the error did not have to be corrected before the 1982 general election, and no changes were made.

The Wisdom of the Courts

One serious flaw in the early predictions of a national Republican redistricting bonanza was the failure to reckon with unfriendly federal courts. Although all federal judges are nominally nonpartisan, all are sponsored by either Democratic or Republican national administrations, and their decisions in congressional redistricting have a more than random tendency to favor the party that appointed them. The remapping issue is only slightly less partisan in federal court than it is in a state capital, and most of the federal judicial panels that made important redistricting decisions in 1981 and 1982 happened to have Democratic-appointee majorities.

In Missouri, for example, it would be hard to ignore the political backgrounds of the three judges who drew the state's nine new congressional districts. One was a former Democratic state senator, another had been elected a county prosecutor as a Democrat, and the third was a former Republican state chairman.[8] Few were surprised when this tribunal voted 2–1 in favor of a new map that preserved all the underpopulated districts around St. Louis and eliminated a rural Republican seat in the central part of the state. "The city of St. Louis doesn't have enough population for one congressional district, let alone two," complained the Republican-appointed judge, Kenneth Wangelin.[9] But his brethren chose to listen to other arguments.

The Missouri panel acted with unusual dispatch, if not haste. The state legislature had twice failed to agree on a redistricting bill, both in its regular 1981 session and in a special session late in the year, but the 1982 primary was still more than seven months away when the court announced its decision on December 28, 1981. Instead of prodding the legislature to try again, the judges settled the issue in a single stroke, pleasing nearly all the state's Democrats and infuriating the Republicans.

In Missouri, as in several other important states, federal courts were a crucial bargaining chip for Democrats in the legislature. Once Democrats were certain that redistricting in their state would move to a friendly court upon deadlock, they had little incentive to make a legislative compromise with Republicans.

In Kansas, where only minor adjustments were needed to comply with the census, Republicans controlled both chambers of the legislature. But Democratic Governor John Carlin held veto power, and he refused to accept either of two maps the legislature sent him. Carlin argued that the plans split the Wichita area unnecessarily between two districts.

Republicans might be forgiven for thinking Carlin had other reasons in mind. When the governor and the legislature could not agree, the issue went to a federal panel with two Democratic appointees. They quickly imposed a new map weakening the state's one shaky Republican incumbent, Jim Jeffries, by adding to his district the University of Kansas community in Lawrence. Jeffries decided to retire, and the district went Democratic in November.

Minnesota faced the opposite political situation—a Democratic legislature and a Republican governor, Albert H. Quie. When the legislature failed to offer a map that Quie would accept, a three-judge panel—two Democratic appointees and one Republican appointee—took over. In March 1982, the panel produced a 2–1 party-line vote in favor of a map produced by Democrats in the Minnesota senate.

It was a map almost any Democrat could love. Although Minnesota neither gained nor lost a seat in reapportionment, the judges redrew district lines throughout the state, eliminating a seat in rural southern Minnesota and adding a new one with a Democratic majority in blue-collar Twin Cities suburbs. The court said the resulting "four-four" split (four rural and four metropolitan districts) most nearly matched the state population.

In any case, it forced upon Republicans a game of musical chairs that left GOP Representative Arlen Erdahl, who had been representing the state's southeastern farm counties, without a place to seek reelection. Erdahl eventually moved to the newly created suburban district ringing St. Paul and Minneapolis, but the Democratic registration advantage and the poor Republican year proved to be too much for him.

Still another court friendly to Democrats was the three-judge federal panel in Michigan, with the familiar 2–1 lineup of Democratic appointees. This panel bestowed on the state the same map that had cleared both chambers of the Democratic legislature but had been vetoed by GOP Governor William G. Milliken on the ground that it would give Democrats more House seats than statewide party strength justified.

This map, unlike some of the others, did not ultimately prove to be a disaster for Republicans. The one seat that had to be sacrificed to reapportionment was a Democratic seat in the Detroit suburbs, a relatively painless choice because the incumbent, James J. Blanchard, was running for governor. The map did produce one Republican casualty, however, in first-term Representative Jim Dunn, whose Sixth District was given the heavily Democratic city of Pontiac. The vote in Pontiac turned Dunn out of office in November.

In Illinois, where the legislature was politically divided and unable to reach agreement, Republicans had no reason to oppose court intervention. The redistricting issue went to a three-judge panel with two Republican appointees. A decade earlier, in a similar situation, two Republican appointees had chosen a map eliminating a district in Chicago that Democratic legislators very much wanted to save.

In a move that embittered much of the Illinois GOP House delegation, however, one of the Republican appointees chose to vote with the one Carter-appointed judge, accepting intact a map drawn by Democratic legislators for the purpose of protecting as many Democrats as possible. All the underpopulated districts in Chicago were retained, chiefly by extending them into just enough suburban territory to make up their population deficits. Two Republican districts were eliminated in the suburbs, where growth had been brisk.

The court's map had its partisan effect before the fall campaign ever started. Twenty-year veteran Robert McClory retired rather than face a primary contest with fellow Republican John Edward Porter, and twenty-four-year veteran Edward J. Derwinski, forced to contest his GOP primary in territory largely unfamiliar to him, lost to Republican colleague George M. O'Brien.

Among the largest states, only New York, Ohio, and Pennsylvania gave Republicans much semblance of satisfaction. New York's staggering sacrifice of five seats had to be negotiated among a Republican senate and a Democratic assembly, and they surprised many observers by reaching agreement, prodded by a relatively patient federal panel that constantly threatened to step in but never actually assumed control. Two Democratic districts and two Republican districts were eliminated, and one "fair fight" was set up in New York City's northern suburbs between Democrat Peter J. Peyser and Republican Benjamin Gilman in a nominally marginal district. Gilman's victory in November, along with Republican Representative Guy J. Molinari's victory over Brooklyn Democratic Representative Leo Zeferetti, whose old seat was one of those eliminated, allowed the GOP to claim modest success statewide.

Ohio's legislature, also split between the parties, managed to pass a new congressional map on March 24, 1982, the day before a federal court had said it would take over. Ohio had to give up two House seats, and each party sacrificed one—a Democratic district in Cleveland and a rural GOP district in central Ohio. Republicans were given an extra gift when the Democratic Speaker of the state house, Vernal Riffe, agreed to alter the district of first-term Democratic Representative Bob Shamansky of Columbus, complicating Shamansky's reelection. Shamansky had angered the Speaker by making a gubernatorial endorsement earlier in the year, when Riffe was considering a gubernatorial campaign himself. Shamansky lost in November with the new district lines.

Pennsylvania was the only one of the ten largest states in which Republicans had complete political control, and they used it to effective partisan purpose. To bring the state down to the required twenty-three districts, the legislature eliminated two Democratic seats, one in Philadelphia and one in the western part of the state. Both choices forced pairs of Democratic incumbents to run against each other in primaries, ending the House careers of Representative Joseph F. Smith in Philadelphia and Representative Don Bailey in the west. Besides forcing Democrats to bear the entire burden of the two-seat reapportionment sacrifice, the mapmakers did their best to strengthen Representative Eugene Atkinson, who had abandoned his lifelong ties and become a Republican in October 1981, partly at the prodding of the Reagan administration.

The new map helped save the Pennsylvania GOP from disaster in what turned out to be a Democratic year at the polls. Democrats unseated four of the state's Republican incumbents (including Atkinson, who lost badly despite the mapmaking help), but because the Smith and Bailey districts were the ones chosen for dismantling, the GOP entered the Ninety-eighth Congress with ten seats remaining. Had Democrats controlled redistricting in Pennsylvania, the Republican contingent might have been reduced to eight or fewer.

While partisanship was complicating the process virtually everywhere, one state was struggling through a redistricting that seemed more difficult because partisanship was officially absent—it had been made illegal. In a burst of "good government" altruism, Iowa's Republican legislature voted in 1980 to turn its redistricting over to a computer operated by the state's nonpartisan Legislative Service Bureau and programmed to ignore partisan concerns and the wishes of incumbents. The only relevant concerns were to be compactness, population equality, and respect for traditional community boundaries.

The computer did what it was told. It also happened to draw a map placing two of the state's three Republican House members—Jim Leach and Tom Tauke—in the same district. That caused a highly partisan uproar among GOP officials, who saw no reason why Iowa's majority party should suffer disproportionately in the interests of good government. The legislature refused to accept the map, as it was legally permitted to do, and asked the computer experts to try again. "It looks like a Democratic computer wrote it," complained an aide to GOP Governor Robert Ray.[10]

On its second attempt, the computer still appeared not to have heard the message. It gave Leach and Tauke separate districts, but placed so many new Democrats in Tauke's district that reelection would have been difficult for him.

The computer's third map looked little better to Republicans than the others. It seemed to weaken the state's third GOP incumbent, Cooper Evans, as badly as the second would have weakened Tauke. But by this time, some of the legislators who had backed the nonpartisan approach were beginning to wonder whether they were giving the concept a bad name. Over Evans's objections, the third map cleared the legislature and was signed by Ray.

This was one redistricting saga that had a happy ending for Republicans. All three incumbents were reelected, and Evans, who seemed an almost certain loser early in the campaign, emerged with a plurality of more than 20,000 votes over his surprised Democratic challenger.

But the Iowa case points up the difficulty in trying to take politics out of the redistricting process. It may be possible in any state, given good faith on both sides, to draw a congressional map both parties can accept. But it is impossible to pretend that there are no political consequences or to make the majority party accept a product that causes it to feel like the minority.

The Obsession with Numbers

While the two political parties were scrambling for advantage in the legislatures and the courts, they were learning to manipulate the rigid standards of population equality that the U.S. Supreme Court had gradually imposed on them over the past two decades. This was a process in which the rules sometimes seemed to come out of the pages of *Alice in Wonderland.* States that drew districts varying in population by less than 1 percent were told to redraw them more closely, even though the census itself could not claim accuracy with that degree of precision.

It was all the legacy of *Wesberry* v. *Sanders,* the 1964 decision in which the U.S. Supreme Court first said congressional districts had to be "substantially equal" in population. *Wesberry* simply extended to the congressional level a principle the court had declared for state legislatures two years earlier. Before those decisions, several states permitted gross disparities in congressional districts—in Georgia, where Wesberry filed his suit, one rural district had 272,164 people, and one urban district 823,860. The Court said that such large differences denied voters in the overcrowded constituency their right to equal representation. There was no hint at the time that "substantially equal" would ever be interpreted to mandate absolute equality.

By the end of the 1960s, however, the Court had decided that "substantial" was not good enough and insisted on the exact (or seemingly exact) head counting that has been required ever since. In *Kirkpatrick* v. *Preisler,* in 1969, the justices ruled that a population difference of 3.1 percent among ten Missouri districts was unacceptable. Justice William Brennan, speaking for a 6–3 court majority, said that any variance of population, "no matter how small," can be justified only by a "good faith" effort toward precise equality.[11]

Thus Missouri, and New York, whose 6.6 percent maximum variances were declared invalid by a similar decision the same year, had to return to work and draw new districts of virtually identical size—according to 1960 census figures then nearly a decade old. Some of the New York districts redrawn to "equality" after the 1969 decisions were shown to vary by as much as 80 percent when the 1970 census was taken only a few months later.

It is fair to say that the logic of *Kirkpatrick* has escaped most legislators who have considered it in the years since it was handed down. Nevertheless, it became the law of the land, and it was the governing principle for the congressional redistricting that followed the census in 1980.

In June 1983 the Supreme Court advanced its rigid population standard to the brink of absurdity. It issued a 5–4 decision in *Karcher* vs. *Daggett* that struck down New Jersey's congressional districts because they varied in population by a maximum of 0.69 percent. Justice William Brennan's majority opinion held that the legislature could have come closer if it had tried, rejecting the argument of four dissenting justices that 0.69 was within the census margin of error and thus amounted to "the functional equivalent of zero."

The Court sidestepped the real issue that motivated the Republican plaintiffs in the New Jersey case, the fact that the map was a blatant Democratic gerrymander. One justice, John Paul Stevens, said he was more concerned about the gerrymander than about absolute equality. But he chose to side with Brennan, providing the vote that seems certain to lock rigid population standards into place for years to come.

The Court did provide a small loophole. It held that a legislature could justify a deviation from equality by showing that it was necessary to accomplish one of several other desired ends, including compactness, community integrity, and, somewhat bizarrely, avoidance of contests between incumbents. But the court left no clue to how legislatures might prove the deviation was necessary. It seems safe to conclude that absolute equality will remain the one solid principle of redistricting, regardless of the political effect.

Through the years, of course, many values besides equal population have been urged on those drawing congressional maps. Citizens are more likely to participate in the election process, for example, if a state's districts are compact and easy to comprehend. It is conducive to political stability for a map to be the product of both political parties, working together, rather than of one party straining for political advantage. Some scholars have suggested that communities of interest, whether geographical, ethnic, or otherwise, ought to be concentrated within individual districts to give them a stronger voice in Washington. Others argue that communities of interest ought to be divided between districts, making elections more competitive and forcing legislators to respond to a variety of points of view.

Those values may not all be consistent, but rigid population standards are the enemy of each of them. The rule in 1981 was "no exceptions"—for compactness, bipartisanship, community of interest, competition, or any other political reasons. The result in 1982 was a set of districts throughout the nation that slice in and out of cities, counties, and townships in a pattern that confuses voters and candidates alike but maintains scrupulous attention to population equality.

When Phillip Burton was accused of drawing an outrageous partisan gerrymander in California, one meant to cost Republicans as many as five seats in the state's House delegation, he could say with pride that his map was loyal to the Court's edict: the average variance in population between the districts was sixty-seven people.[12]

Since the late 1960s, it has been taken for granted that congressional maps will cross city and county lines. In any state with more than a handful of districts, it is impossible to make them equal in population without crossing such lines. Once a mapmaker knows he can split even the smallest subdivision with impunity, there is little to restrain his partisan instincts.

It is sometimes assumed that before *Wesberry*, states routinely gerrymandered congressional districts for partisan purposes. In fact, this was a limited practice. What most states did, unless gains or losses from reapportionment forced them to redraw their lines, was simply to leave the districts as they were, regardless of population changes. This was a gerrymander in itself, since it guaranteed over-representation of the rural areas that were losing population. But it was the only form of mischief most states bothered to practice.

After the 1960 census, for example, twenty-five states were left with the same size House delegation they had had during the previous decade. Some eighteen of those twenty-five did not redistrict at all. Of the nine states that redrew all their district boundaries, eight were forced to because they either gained or lost representation.[13]

In the states that gained new districts, moreover, there was no serious effort in the old days to place the new seats in rural areas that were losing population. The usual approach was to place a new district in a growing metropolitan area while making sure the existing rural constituencies were preserved.

In theory, a state legislature could have done untold mischief in the years before *Wesberry*. A million Democrats could have been crowded into one district so that 200,000 Republicans would have a district to themselves next door. But these gross disparities were almost never created by design. They were the result of decades of demographic change.

In those years, there was a powerful natural brake on partisan gerrymandering. Counties, cities, and smaller communities represented a pressure group asking legislators not to tamper with district lines. Cities did not want to be in three congressional districts if they could be in one. Counties did not want to switch representation in Washington every ten years to serve partisan purposes. State legislators ignored that pressure at their own political risk. In some states, the pressure was written into law in the form of language in the state constitution prohibiting the breaking of county lines in drawing districts.

Most counties in most states remained within the same congressional district for decades. In Indiana, for example, the legislature in 1932 created a Seventh District in the southwest part of the state and included in it Monroe County, where Bloomington was the county seat. For forty years, the county remained part of the same constituency. The map grew to be unfair because the Seventh District was underpopulated, but it was never given a purely partisan over-haul, even though the Republicans had sufficient control of the state government to perform one.

In the years since *Wesberry*, things have been different. In 1971, Monroe County was split—Bloomington stayed in the Seventh District while other townships went to the neighboring Eighth District to equalize population. In 1981, the Republican legislature used the precedent to partisan advantage. It drew a line down Third Street in Bloomington, giving part of the city to shaky Republican incumbent Joel Deckard, but not the part most likely to vote against him. Deckard's Eighth District was redrawn to share Bloomington with Democrat Lee H. Hamilton of the Ninth District, who habitually wins by such large margins that Democratic votes added to his total would be essentially wasted.

It is possible to say that the Bloomington ploy failed or that it almost worked. Less than a month before the 1982 election, Deckard drove his car into a tree and was charged with driving while intoxi-cated. He came within 7,000 votes of reelection, an indirect testimony to the skill of the Republican mapmakers. In the old Eighth District, Deckard would almost certainly have been beaten by a substantial margin.

The Indiana redistricting proved, among other things, that a congressional map can be partisan and compact at the same time. The state's ten new districts are of similar geographical size and nicely squared off—more appealing to look at, in fact, than the less blatantly partisan set of districts they replaced. There are few of the tell-tale squiggles that have been associated with gerrymandering since Elbridge Gerry.

Yet not every state legislature had as much concern for the aesthetics of its partisanship. New Jersey's Democrats, slipping their congressional map into law only a few hours before the arrival of the Republican governor who would have vetoed it, produced what can only be described as a monstrosity. Virtually every district in the northern part of the state juts and squiggles and curves back on itself so many times that the overall effect is that of a maze, rather than a collection of political entities. These districts are almost impossible to define demographically, let alone to understand politi-cally. They are slices of counties and townships, equal in population but otherwise meaningless. GOP Representative Marge Roukema, in order to travel southwest through her Fifth District from Bergen County at one end to the Trenton suburbs at the other, must pass through three other districts before returning to her own.

Districts like these raise the question of whether the democratic process can work effectively if political units are so confusing as to discourage participation. Earlier in the nation's history, from 1901 to 1911, Congress required by law that districts be composed of compact territory. But there has been no attempt to legislate compactness since then, and no court has pronounced itself willing to speak on the issue.

The Question of Minorities

Whatever redistricting might have done for the two political parties, it carried the potential of disaster for minorities. Eight of the ten most underpopulated constituencies in the country had elected a black or Hispanic representative in 1980. All eight were in states that had to give up at least one House seat, and if those states simply followed population movement, the minority seats would be the first to go. Congress would reconvene in 1983 with far fewer than the eighteen blacks and six Hispanics who had served as members the year before.[14]

In the end, nothing like that happened. Every black House member who sought reelection won it, and four new blacks were chosen to join them, bringing the total to twenty-one, an all-time record. The number of Hispanics in the House went from six to nine. Those who had predicted a decline in minority membership had ignored the power of the federal judiciary, the importance of the Voting Rights Act, and the leverage that blacks and Hispanics can have in state politics.

For most black congressional incumbents, that leverage never really had to be spelled out. In Ohio, for example, it turned out to be surprisingly easy for veteran Democrat Louis Stokes to survive local population changes and keep his House seat on Cleveland's mostly black East Side.

Stokes's district had lost nearly a quarter of its people in the 1970s and needed more than 150,000 new constituents to reach the number that each of the state's districts would need under the one man, one vote, requirement. Ohio had to drop two districts for the 1980s, and one was bound to be in the Cleveland area. Stokes's district could have been carved away and used to make up the smaller population deficits of the three other Cleveland districts, all represented by white Democrats.

Yet if this was good mathematics, state legislators were nearly unanimous in considering it bad politics. There was never any enthusiasm in Columbus for alienating Stokes, his constituency, or his political organization, the Twenty-first District Congressional Caucus. In Ohio and in every other state facing a similar situation, there was always another way to spread the political sacrifices, and the other way was always chosen.

The other three Cleveland Democrats all had constituencies that were more nearly full size. But none had a core of political followers who would see the dismantling of their districts as a continuation of historic bias. Rather than spread Stokes's 351,000 remaining constituents among three other districts, the legislature carved up the nearby Nineteenth District, belonging to first-term Democrat Dennis E. Eckart, and used the population of this district to give Stokes a full-sized district.[15]

Stokes was given a redrawn constituency expanded just far enough into Cleveland's suburbs to solve the population problem, but not far enough to threaten his political security. The new Twenty-first District is only 62 percent black (compared with 79 percent on the old map), but it reelected Stokes in 1982 with 86 percent of the vote.

One senior black House member, however, seemed an inevitable casualty of redistricting. William Clay of Missouri represented a district that had seen a massive population decline in the 1970s, and the only way to meet population requirements was to bring in nearly 200,000 whites in ethnic south St. Louis and suburban St. Louis County. Over seven House terms, Clay had never built a broad biracial constituency. "I don't represent all people," he said in 1981.[16]

Still, Clay's allies in the Missouri legislature vowed to do everything possible to give him a district in which he would have a chance to survive a Democratic primary against a white opponent. "I have vowed to shut down the Capitol if necessary," said a state senator close to the representative.[17]

In the end, the Missouri map had to be drawn in court, and though the 2–1 Democratic majority among the judges was crucial, the militance of Clay's backers had its effect as well. The judges drew him a district with nearly all his old constituents remaining and managed to make it 52 percent black. Republicans called it a blatant racial gerrymander, insisting that Clay's underpopulated district was the obvious one to eliminate at a time when Missouri had to give up one seat. "The area that lost the most population in the state is metropolitan St. Louis," said the state GOP chairman. "What the judges did was preserve a black congressman's district simply because he is black."[18]

Clay still had to deal with a credible white primary challenger who chose busing as the major issue for the campaign, but over three months the incumbent clearly outdid him in organizing and campaigning, and the carefully drawn district lines allowed him to win renomination.

Missouri was one of several states where the judicial preference for a Democratic map automatically benefited minorities. In some cases, however, minority rights were cited as an explicit reason for the choice. A prime example was Illinois, where there were two seats to be sacrificed and three black incumbents to protect.

The court, which in this case had a majority of Republican appointees, argued that the Democratic redistricting plan was fairer to blacks. It left three Chicago districts with 70 percent black majorities, where a Republican map would have reduced one of them—represented by first-term Democrat Gus Savage—below 60 percent. Elected in an upset in 1980, Savage was on shaky political ground anyway. The Republican map would have left him open to a serious white primary challenge. In the version of the map that finally became law, he narrowly overcame a black primary opponent.

The Illinois case points up the subtle influence of the 1965 Voting Rights Act in situations where it has no legal force. Illinois is not covered by the act, and besides, the law does not require courts to submit their maps for the Justice Department's approval. Only legislatures have to do that.

During its seventeen years of life, the Voting Rights Act has acquired a moral and political significance beyond its legal boundaries. Faced with a choice of whom to disappoint in redistricting, federal courts made it a clear practice not to disappoint minorities. Clay acknowledged that fact at the height of his own remapping controversy. "I think my chances in the court are far better," he said, "than they would have been in the Missouri Senate or House."[19]

In the South, blacks were playing a different game with different rules. On the positive side, they could take advantage not only of the spirit of the Voting Rights Act but of its literal wording. As written in 1965 and later extended, the act forbade legislatures in the covered states from drawing any new district that diluted minority voting strength. In these states, which include all of the Deep South, the dilution did not have to be intentional to render the new district lines invalid. All congressional maps drawn by legislatures in these states had to clear the Justice Department before they could take effect.

Still, the psychology of southern redistricting was a problem for blacks. The initial breakthroughs had not yet come for them in most of the Deep South states, so success could not be defined as protecting House seats already won. As the 1980s began, only Texas and

Tennessee had a black member in their House delegations. The only way to claim conspicuous progress through redistricting was to elect a black candidate in states such as Mississippi, South Carolina, and Alabama, which had large black populations but whose House delegations had been all white throughout this century.

As the process began, it was not clear how much help the Justice Department would be to the minority cause. Blacks were no significant part of the Reagan constituency in 1980; the administration might have been expected to give conservative legislatures the benefit of the doubt in drawing new district lines. The Nixon Justice Department had essentially done that a decade earlier.

As it turned out, the Justice Department interpreted the Voting Rights Act with surprising strictness in dealing with some of the southern states. In December 1981, it threw out North Carolina's map, arguing that the legislature had created a "strangely irregular" district for veteran Democratic Representative L. H. Fountain just so Fountain would not have to represent Durham, with its large and politically active black community. The legislature then drew a new district with Durham in it, and Fountain promptly announced his retirement.

A few months later, the Justice Department acted against Mississippi. It refused to accept a map virtually identical to the state's old one, on the grounds that the old one had itself been discriminatory, even though it had cleared the Nixon Justice Department in 1972.

When blacks began to vote in significant numbers in Mississippi in the mid-1960s, the state had changed its congressional map to eliminate the traditional "Delta district" along the Louisiana border. The Delta region had a clear black majority. What the Justice Department said in 1982—reversing its stand of a decade earlier—was that the absence of a Delta district was a dilution of black voting strength. The legislature went back, redrew the map, and moved the existing Second District farther into the Delta, giving the district a 53 percent black majority. The Justice Department accepted that revision.

Civil rights activists in Mississippi viewed this with mixed emotions. They saw the importance of creating a black-majority district in the Delta, but they worried that 53 percent was too small a majority to elect a black candidate. State Senator Henry Kirksey, a black Democrat and a professional cartographer who had offered his own alternative map to the legislature, insisted that a 65 percent black population would be needed to send Mississippi's first black representative of the century to Washington. "We're not satisfied," echoed Owen Cooper, director of the Delta Ministry and a leader of the minority cause.[20]

Cooper and Kirksey turned out to be right in their pessimism, but just barely. In November, black Democrat Robert Clark, a colleague of Kirksey in the Mississippi senate, fell fewer than 3,000 votes short against a conservative white Republican, Webb Franklin. Clark needed about 15 percent of the white vote, and the indications were he did not get it.

The end result in North Carolina was similar. By redrawing Fountain's district and bringing about his retirement, the legislature opened the way for a candidacy by a black Durham lawyer, H. M. "Mickey" Michaux. The front-runner in his district's Democratic primary, Michaux lost in a runoff to a conservative white opponent, I. T. Valentine, who had been an ally of Fountain. This was a defeat within the Democratic party—unlike the one in Mississippi—but it represented much the same thing. Blacks won a victory through federal intervention but were unable to sustain it at the polls.

Mississippi and North Carolina did not typify the entire southern story. In Alabama, black legislators complained that the newly drawn congressional map carefully spread the state's black population so equally that none of the constituencies would have enough black voters to inconvenience the white incumbents. Although the state is more than one-fourth black, no district was drawn to have a black electorate of more than 34 percent. The Justice Department rejected those complaints. Similarly, in Louisiana, the National Association for the Advancement of Colored People protested that the legislature had split the city of New Orleans between two districts to avoid giving the city a black-majority district. This complaint was also rejected by the Justice Department. There clearly was a point, hard to define but easy to notice, beyond which the government was unwilling to apply affirmative action to congressional districting.

In Georgia and Texas, the remapping process turned into a complicated three-cornered struggle in which Republicans formed an ad hoc alliance with segments of the black community against the local Democratic party.

The Dallas and Atlanta metropolitan areas presented similar political situations. Each contained two districts in which a substantial black vote helped elect moderate white Democrats to Congress. In both cities, it was clearly possible to redraw one of the districts to include a black population so large that a black candidate could win. But that would most likely give the other district to a conservative Republican. This was exactly what state GOP leaders wanted, not only to pick up a House seat but to make a conspicuous gesture, altruistic or not, to the black community.

In Texas, Republican Governor Clements proposed to make

Democrat Martin Frost's Dallas-based Twenty-fourth District 64 percent black, adding black votes from the neighboring Fifth District, and thus making fellow Democrat Jim Mattox's loss to a GOP challenger in the Fifth District a virtual certainty. "The black community of Dallas wants its own representation," Clements insisted, "and they are not better served by two liberal white Democrats."[21]

Some local black officeholders clearly felt the same way. "Congressman Mattox is Anglo, and Congressman Frost is Jewish," said Lucy Patterson, a former member of the Dallas city council. "They cannot fully understand the needs of the black community."[22]

Other Dallas blacks, however, disagreed. "Blacks now have substantial influence on two congressional districts," said local activist Thomas Jones. "I'm not interested in trading two Democratic friends for one congressman who might not even turn out to be minority."[23]

It was a bitter dispute. The Coalition for Minority Representation, which backed Clements's position, repeatedly accused the other side of selling out to the white power structure. During one session of the legislature, the coalition chairman, John Price, had to be restrained after he poked his finger in the face of a legislator who took the opposite view.[24]

In the end, the Clements plan never received a full test, because the federal judges invalidated it, arguing that it improperly packed minority voters into the Twenty-fourth District. As a result, both the Fifth and the Twenty-fourth districts remained firmly Democratic in 1982. Frost, restored to a white-majority district by the federal panel, won easily over Lucy Patterson, who changed parties to challenge him and drew barely a quarter of the vote.

The process was different in Georgia, but the result was similar. The legislature passed up the opportunity, urged upon it by some Atlanta-area blacks, to create a two-thirds black majority district and make the neighboring constituency Republican. The Justice Department, in a ruling that seemed to contradict the federal court action in Texas, ruled that the state's new map diluted the voting strength of Atlanta blacks by *not* packing them into a single district. The legislature returned to work, made Democrat Wyche Fowler's Fifth District 65 percent black, and reduced the black population in Democrat Elliott Levitas's Fourth District to 17 percent. That made both incumbents clearly vulnerable—Fowler to a black primary challenger and Levitas to a Republican.

But Fowler drew no black primary opponent of established reputation, and Levitas overcame a well-financed Republican opponent with surprising ease. The test for them will come in 1984 and later in the decade.

Through years of argument over redistricting, blacks and Hispanics have been allies against what they saw as white discrimination. The post-1980 process, however, produced the first important case in which the federal government intervened in behalf of one group at the other's expense.

This happened in New York City. Under pressure from Hispanic leaders to create a second Hispanic district in the city, the legislature went to unusual cartographic lengths to draw one. It came up with a new Eleventh District that stretched awkwardly from Brooklyn to Manhattan's Lower East Side and all the way north to Harlem.

Districts in New York City, along with a limited number in other places outside the Deep South, are covered by the Voting Rights Act because chronically low voter turnout has kept their voting under the threshold needed for exemption. When the Justice Department looked at the new Eleventh District in the spring of 1982, it decided that the unusual lines "needlessly fragmented" the votes of Brooklyn blacks, cramming them into the adjoining Twelfth District to keep the Eleventh District Hispanic. The legislature redrew the map to meet these objections, and the Eleventh District emerged as a black-majority district. Its new representative, Edolphus Towns, is one of four new blacks in the Ninety-eighth Congress and the only one who can trace his election directly to redistricting.

The New York case marked one of the few clear defeats Hispanics suffered in the redistricting process. Elsewhere, things went well for them. In California, the two new Hispanic House members—Esteban Torres and Matthew (Marty) Martinez—owe their presence largely to Phillip Burton.

Burton's map deliberately created two Los Angeles–area seats that Hispanics had an excellent chance to win. Martinez had to survive a rough general election challenge from Republican Representative John Rousselot, whose old district Burton had eliminated, but the voters ultimately rejected Rousselot's militant conservatism.

New Mexico gained a third congressional district with its brisk population growth during the 1970s, and the seat went to Democrat Bill Richardson, who despite his Anglo name is half-Mexican and grew up in Mexico City. Richardson won in a newly drawn constituency covering the mostly Hispanic and Indian northern part of the state. Conservatives in the legislature wanted to divide the three districts on an east-west axis, which would have made Richardson's chore very difficult, but Hispanic legislators lobbied aggressively and prevailed.

Texas, whose population also grew by more than a quarter during the 1970s, was entitled to carve out three additional districts for the next decade. It was agreed early in the process that one of the three would be in south Texas and would favor Hispanics. Shortly before the 1982 primary, the federal judges eliminated any real doubt that the new Twenty-seventh District, stretching from Corpus Christi down to Brownsville on the Mexican border, would choose a Hispanic representative. They adjusted the boundaries to make the district about 60 percent Hispanic, rather than 50 percent, and the district went on to elect Solomon P. Ortiz, the sheriff in Corpus Christi.

November and Afterward

By the summer of 1982, it was clear there would not be a Republican windfall from redistricting. So the overall result November 2 was not a shock to either party. But it was striking.

Of the seventeen brand-new districts in eleven southern and western states, the Democrats won ten, even though Ronald Reagan had carried all of the states in 1980 and Gerald R. Ford had taken all but three in 1976.[25] Beyond that, the returns refuted the theory that reapportionment would be a boon for conservatives regardless of partisan result.

The group of ten Democrats chosen in newly created districts included only one—Tom Vandergriff of Texas—who seemed a possible candidate for Boll Weevil status in the House. Three others, Ortiz and Mike Andrews of Texas and Jim Cooper of Tennessee, appeared likely to float between national Democratic positions and those normally associated with the South. The remaining six—Richardson of New Mexico, Jim McNulty of Arizona, Richard Lehman and Jim Bates of California, and Larry Smith and Buddy McKay of Florida—are national Democrats by any standard.

The "conservative windfall" theory fell victim to the rapidly changing two-party system in the Sunbelt. Liberal thinking is still in the minority in these states, but as conservative Democrats migrate to the Republican side, liberals *within* the Democratic party are growing stronger—not weaker. A liberal Democrat has a better chance today of winning nomination in a Texas district, for example, than at any other time in recent history. In the fall, if he is lucky enough to be running in a relatively good year for Democrats nationally, he can survive the general election with a little help from conservative Democrats who opposed him in the primary but retain some residual loyalty to their party at the congressional level.

For every new district created in the Sunbelt, one was eliminated in the East or Midwest. It is not always easy to "find" these dropped constituencies, since some states take advantage of the reapportionment situation to redesign their maps entirely. Only one district had to go in Indiana, but the Republican legislature dismembered two, both Democratic, in order to create a new GOP seat.

The best estimate is that reapportionment caused the disappearance of nine Democratic seats and seven Republican ones, with South Dakota having to combine its two districts, one belonging to each party. Democrats thus did pay a price for the population decline in urban Democratic areas, but considering the extent of that decline, it was a modest one. Had Republicans not managed to force Pennsylvania's two-seat sacrifice entirely onto the Democrats, the net national result would have been more GOP seats eliminated than Democratic ones.

Moreover, not all the Democrats who saw their districts erased ended up leaving Congress. The Massachusetts legislature placed Democrat Barney Frank in a merged district where 70 percent of the constituency belonged to moderate Republican Margaret M. Heckler, but Frank successfully turned the election into a referendum on Reaganomics and dispatched Heckler easily. First-term Democrat Dennis E. Eckart of Ohio saw his Cleveland-area district carved off the map, but he took advantage of Republican Representative J. William Stanton's retirement to move into Stanton's nearby constituency, win a second term, and force the GOP to bear the reapportionment loss. In South Dakota, where Democratic Representative Tom Daschle and Republican Representative Clint Roberts both had to run statewide, Daschle was the winner.

If the reapportionment result was roughly a partisan standoff, however, the net result from *redistricting* was unfavorable to Republicans. Several marginal GOP incumbents—notably Paul N. Findley in Illinois, Harold E. Hollenbeck in New Jersey, and Jim Dunn in Michigan—had to run in constituencies that remained essentially intact but were given crucial new pockets of Democratic voting strength.

Findley, Dunn, and Hollenbeck had moderate House voting records, but they had supported the Reagan economic program in 1981, and they encountered Democratic challengers determined to make that the focus of the campaign. This was not the year for them to be taking on new Democratic territory; had the first election within the new district lines taken place in 1980, most likely all three would have survived. But among the many Republican problems of redistricting was its bad timing for the GOP in national politics. Resourceful incumbents such as Findley, Dunn, and Hollenbeck were forced to plead for Democratic votes in unfamiliar territory in a year of economic devastation under a Republican president.

The results of redistricting were clearest in Dunn's case. Elected in 1980 as a resolute conservative, he had carefully built an independent House voting record, working hard at constituent service and promoting legislation to bring jobs to hard-hit central Michigan. He was a solid winner in 1982 in the parts of his district he had been representing. Unfortunately for him, however, redistricting had added the city of Pontiac, a Democratic stronghold with a large black population and an unemployment rate nearing 30 percent. Dunn's only chance was a low voter turnout in Pontiac, but the turnout there was higher than normal, bringing a districtwide margin of about 6,000 votes to Democrat Bob Carr, the man Dunn had unseated two years earlier.

There are several other Republican stories like that. Besides Dunn, Findley, and Hollenbeck, perhaps half a dozen defeated GOP incumbents could argue plausibly that redistricting was their downfall in 1982. But even by the most generous account, redistricting did not produce half of the party's twenty-six incumbent House defeats. In most states, incumbents of either party seriously inconvenienced by redistricting were distinct exceptions.

The coming of a new congressional map always makes many House members nervous and cautious in their roll call voting; they do not know a year in advance exactly which constituents they will have to please. But in the vast majority of cases, redistricting has little effect on whether the incumbent wins or loses. In 1982, as in 1972, the only comparable year of universal redrawing, the reelection rate for incumbents was well over 90 percent. Judging by the victory margins alone, it would be difficult to tell that new lines were even in place.

So members like Jim Dunn are not typical. A more typical case might be that of Elwood H. Hillis, a quiet Indiana Republican who has served in the House since 1970. Hillis saw his district changed beyond recognition for 1982, shifted to the northwest part of the state and given more than 250,000 new voters. But by election day, these voters had been systematically introduced to Hillis through a steady stream of franked mail advertising him as an effective public servant.

This free advertising is perfectly legal. House rules allow members to use the frank to send mail not only to their current constituents but to those in areas in which, because of redistricting, they will be running in the next election.[26]

This privilege, of course, is not offered to challengers. It all but assumes that that the election is over and the incumbent candidate has won. In 1982, several House members declared the "extended frank" unethical and chose not to use it. But they tended to be members who were already politically secure. For the average incumbent facing the uncertainties of a changed constituency, the extended frank, however questionable, is a good insurance policy on reelection. It is an important reason why the reelection rate does not go down simply because incumbents have to run in strange territory. Hillis, who drew 62 percent of the vote in 1980 in the friendly confines of his old district, used the franking privilege and drew 61 percent of the vote in the new district two years later, despite the area's serious economic problems.

Because incumbents of both parties did so well in 1982, the election returns may mask some long-range political changes likely to show up before the end of the decade. Districts that changed dramatically—and still reelected their incumbents by wide margins— may spring a few surprises once those incumbents depart.

The districts to watch during the remainder of the 1980s are traditional Democratic constituencies, long based in big cities but expanded into suburban areas to make up population deficits in 1982. Democratic incumbents such as Sidney R. Yates in Chicago and Robert A. Young in St. Louis had to be given huge new suburban additions in order to keep their districts intact. Neither had any problems in 1982, and both may be able to win reelection routinely as long as they want to seek it. But sooner or later, Republicans will have a chance to contest those districts without an incumbent Democrat on the ballot, and Democrats may not find them easy to hold, especially if this happens in a year that is unfavorable for them nationally.

If the 1970s provide any precedent, the media will treat redistricting as a two-year story: little effort will be made in 1990 to assess the impact of the redrawn district lines over five elections. If such an attempt is made, however, it could provide some belated consolation for Republicans who are currently wondering how the situation could have turned out as badly for them as it did.

Notes

1. *Congressional Quarterly*, January 10, 1981, p. 73.
2. Ibid., p. 70.
3. *Seattle Times*, April 13, 1981.
4. Ibid.
5. *Dallas Times-Herald*, May 18, 1981.
6. Alan Murray, "Governor Gerry's Monuments," *Congressional Quarterly*, May 9, 1981, p. 811.

7. By rejecting the Burton districts on June 8, 1982, California set up a vote that November on a proposal to have the state's districts redrawn by a bipartisan commission. But that plan was also rejected, on November 2. That left it up to the legislature to revise Burton's original map. In January 1983, shortly before Democratic Governor Edmund G. Brown, Jr., was to be replaced by Republican George Deukmejian, the legislature passed and Brown signed into law a new set of forty-five districts that made only modest changes in the Burton map. Republicans announced their intention to challenge that product in court.

8. *St. Louis Globe-Democrat*, December 30, 1981.

9. Ibid.

10. *Des Moines Register*, April 23, 1981.

11. Nelson Polsby, ed., *Reapportionment in the 1970s* (Berkeley, Calif.: University of California Press, 1971), p. 20.

12. Phil Duncan, "A Recipe for Gerrymandering," *Congressional Quarterly*, February 27, 1982, p. 354.

13. Andrew Hacker, *Congressional Districting: The Issue of Equal Representation* (Washington, D.C.: Brookings Institution, 1964), p. 100.

14. Two Hispanics—Ron de Lugo of the Virgin Islands and Baltasar Corrada of Puerto Rico—are nonvoting delegates to the House.

15. Eckart moved and won reelection in the Eleventh District.

16. *New York Times*, August 2, 1982.

17. *Kansas City Times*, June 11, 1981.

18. *St. Louis Post-Dispatch*, December 29, 1981.

19. Ibid., December 20, 1981.

20. *Jackson Clarion-Ledger*, June 10, 1982.

21. *Houston Chronicle*, March 2, 1982.

22. *Dallas Times-Herald*, December 2, 1981.

23. Ibid., May 17, 1981.

24. Ibid., June 2, 1981.

25. Rob Gurwitt, "Redistricting Bitter Disappointment to GOP," *Congressional Quarterly*, November 6, 1982, p. 2787.

26. Alan Ehrenhalt, "Incumbency Insurance: The Extended Frank," *Congressional Quarterly*, June 19, 1982, p. 1499.

3

Parties, PACs, and Independent Groups

Larry Sabato

The new technologies make parties, if not obsolete, certainly obsolescent.

JOSEPH NAPOLITAN, Political Consultant[1]
July 1979

In a circular chase that is dominating congressional politics as never before, the candidates are courting the PACs, and the PAC-men are courting the candidates. . . . [PACs have] proliferated beyond any expectation, pouring far more money into campaigns than ever before. Today the power of PACs threatens to undermine America's system of representative democracy.

Time[2]
October 1982

[The National Conservative Political Action Committee] is on its way out, and I hope its kind of activity will disappear from the political landscape.

U.S. SENATOR ROBERT C. BYRD (Democrat, West Virginia)[3]
November 1982

New political axioms regularly gain acceptance both in the years leading up to each national election and in the election's immediate aftermath, and 1982 is no exception. Three particular self-evident truths about the process of modern American elections and the power

The author wishes to thank Ed Blakely, communications director of the National Republican Congressional Committee; Kent Cooper, assistant director for public disclosure, Federal Election Commission; Robert Hirschfeld, director of radio-TV for the Democratic National Committee; Ann Lewis, political director of the Democratic National Committee; and Michael J. Malbin, resident fellow at the American Enterprise Institute for Public Policy Research, for their review of this article.

of the principal electoral organizations have gained currency in recent times. First, many pundits have declared that political parties are irreversibly atrophying and becoming irrelevant in an age of independent voting behavior when campaigns are masterminded by extra-party political consultants. Second, political action committees have been pronounced the most significant political organizations on the horizon; indeed, to judge by some accounts in the popular press, PACs virtually dominated the conduct and determined the outcome of the 1982 midterm congressional elections. A third axiom, while contradicting the second one somewhat, has been accepted most widely of all following the November 1982 general election: the independent New Right groups, which appeared to be so successful in the 1980 elections, have been rebuked into submission and, quite possibly, into extinction.

To varying degrees, these maxims are fictions, and the midterm election provides evidence that contradicts each one, as this chapter will show. The financial and organizational activities and campaign technology of the national and state parties in 1982 will be examined first, for their development is the most significant structural aspect of the midterm election—one that signifies a healthy change for the better in American political life. Once the parties' midterm vibrancy has been reported, the usurpers of press attention, the PACs, will be analyzed. There are many trends to note in the recent workings of political action committees, but perhaps none is more important than the strengthening of their diversity—a pattern that does not lend itself so easily to broad-stroke, sinister, and monolithic generalization. Finally, a very special kind of PAC will be set aside for review. Independent groups that emphasize opponents' shortcomings have been dominated by right-wing interests for years, but in 1982 for the first time, liberal committees with the same goals and tactics (if different targets) began to appear at the battlefront. Neither ideological cluster of independents was notably successful in the midterm elections, but their failures in one election cycle have hardly signaled their demise.

The Political Parties in the Midterm Elections

In 1982, to a much greater degree than in any previous modern election, the political parties directly assisted their candidates with critically important campaign tasks. The Republican party has been doing so since the mid-1970s, of course, but its efforts were considerably expanded in 1982. Also important, the Democratic party, though still outclassed by the GOP in virtually every area where technology can help a political party, took the first crucial steps toward modernizing its organization, using the Republican national operation as its model. In the 1982 midterm elections, the "atrophied" parties were showing new muscle—and they were anything but irrelevant.

Just as it has been for almost a decade, the Republican party was the pacesetter. The GOP proved anew in 1982 that though the Federal Election Campaign Act of 1971 and subsequent amendments[4] weakened the political parties in numerous ways,[5] the statutes also provided openings that an aggressive party could exploit. For example, FECA limits to $5,000 per election[6] the *direct* campaign contributions a party can make to each of its House candidates, but several provisions in the law permit parties to provide major "in-kind" assistance (such as polling and media production) to House candidates. These services (to be discussed shortly) are rendered and paid for primarily under the FECA provision for "coordinated expenditures,"[7] whereby the national and state parties can spend their funds on behalf of federal candidates up to a certain amount (adjusted for inflation every election year). In 1982 the national party *and* the state party could each contribute as much as $18,440 in coordinated expenditures,[8] *in addition to* the direct contributions of $5,000 per election. All told, party committees could add a maximum of $66,880 to the coffers of each House candidate in 1982.

Much more money could be given to Senate contenders. Although direct contributions are limited to $17,500 per candidate for all national party committees combined, the national and state parties could each spend the greater of $36,880 or two cents per voter in each state. Thus, depending on the size of the state, from $91,260 to almost $1.33 million (in California) could be spent by the party committees for their Senate candidates.[9]

Such massive sums were but a pipedream for the Democrats in 1982, but not for the Republicans. The national GOP committees (the Republican National Committee, National Republican Congressional Committee, and National Republican Senatorial Committee) raised enough money to give nearly the legal limit to more than seven dozen House candidates and most Senate candidates. Moreover, the GOP national committees were so awash in money that, as in 1980, they were able to pick up the contribution tab for many of their state party affiliates as well. (This is permitted as long as the state party agrees to let the national party act as its agent.)[10]

In every one of thirty-nine selected 1982 House races (including all twenty-nine contests in which incumbents were defeated), GOP contributions to party candidates exceeded Democratic donations.[11]

Similarly, in fully twenty-eight of thirty-three Senate races, the Republicans gave more in direct contributions and coordinated expenditures to party candidates than the Democrats did. In most cases the gap between the parties was huge, even in key contests targeted by both parties, such as California's open Senate seat. In that race, GOP committees donated $1,340,068 to Republican Pete Wilson, the eventual winner; Democrat Edmund G. "Jerry" Brown, Jr., received a paltry $149,553 from his party. Long-shot Republican Senate candidates, such as Florida's Van B. Poole, Massachusetts's Raymond Shamie, Michigan's Philip E. Ruppe, and Texas's James M. Collins, also received their full measure. Perhaps more important, they received the money relatively early, for as Gary Jacobson has noted, "early money is seed money for the entire campaign effort [and] is needed to organize, plan, and raise more money."[12] Party money helps to break the "loser cycle" faced by most challengers, who cannot raise much money from PACs and individuals until they demonstrate "winning potential"—which they cannot do until they have money for early media coverage, polling, and organization.

Overall in 1981–1982, the national Republican party committees gave $18.6 million in direct contributions or coordinated expenditures to their congressional candidates, compared with $3.3 million in Democratic expenditures, and the GOP groups spent more than six times as much money as their Democratic party counterparts ($189.8 million to $31.2 million).[13] The Republican lead has been growing in recent years. In 1977–1978 the GOP had a 3-to-1 advantage, and by 1979–1980 a 4-to-1 lead. The electoral effects of such a yawning financial divide are obvious to professionals on both sides. By mid-October 1982, U.S. Representative Tony Coelho (Democrat, California), chairman of the Democratic Congressional Campaign Committee, had funds set aside for less than a half-dozen late-blooming challengers. "For me, it's going to be a matter of hoping I guess the right ones; it's going to be like finding the needles in the haystack," Coelho remarked ruefully. "The Republicans can just cover the whole stack."[14]

Much of the Republican party's progress is due to an increasingly sophisticated direct mail effort.[15] The GOP committees have permanent, regularly "freshened" lists of more than 1.7 million mail donors, compared with Democratic small-contributor lists less than one-seventh as voluminous. As a consequence, a far larger percentage of Democratic net receipts are derived from donors of over $500; the Republicans, in a reversal of their "fat cat" image, take in the bulk of their proceeds from small givers.[16]

Republican Polling and Media

The large amount of GOP financial contributions was only a part of the remarkably advanced effort waged by the Republicans in 1982. Services provided by the party, paid for by coordinated expenditures or nonfederal "soft money,"[17] were showpieces of state-of-the-art campaign technology.

Especially impressive was the Republican polling operation. The national campaign committees carefully monitored public opinion trends in the closing weeks of the campaign in selected states and districts where tight contests were being waged. Daily "tracking polls" in each area were used for this purpose, whereby 150 to 200 new respondents were interviewed each evening and added to the existing polling sample of approximately 500.[18] Simultaneously, the most dated group of 150 to 200 respondents (usually those taken three evenings earlier) was dropped from the sample. In this "moving averages" fashion, a continuously updated trend line was established in every targeted campaign, enabling party strategists to relate the effects of specific campaign events (such as the introduction of a new advertising package or a presidential visit) on the electorate (as indicated by the candidate preferences of respondents).[19]

The National Republican Senatorial Committee, for example, invested more than a half-million dollars in tracking for thirteen close Senate contests. Cumulatively, the results in mid-October alerted GOP strategists to the danger of a disproportionately low voter turnout among Republican party identifiers. Consequently, the committee sent out a $1.3 million direct mail appeal to 7 million Republican households, exhorting voters to go to the polls and preserve President Reagan's Senate majority.

In individual campaigns as well, the tracking polls were often of immense value. Republican U.S. Senator John Danforth of Missouri, for one, may well owe his very narrow reelection to the "intelligence advantage" the polls gave him over his Democratic opponent, State Senator Harriett F. Woods.[20] As Woods gained on Danforth, and then passed him in voter support as measured by both public and private surveys, GOP strategists in Washington were following the developments. Their tracking suggested appropriate adjustments in Danforth's media advertising campaign,[21] and Danforth was able to surge ahead in the final hours. Neither the Woods campaign nor the national Democratic party had any similar polling system; the Woods effort, in fact, was "flying blind" in the crucial closing days when polling information like Danforth's could possibly have enabled Woods to counteract the Republican's new strategy and to win.

Polling data were not the only useful information provided to marginal campaigns by the GOP. The Republican National Committee had direct computer links with more than three dozen House campaigns. Portable video display terminals were located in the district headquarters of the selected campaigns, all linked to the RNC's master computer. The setup ensured instant communication and gave the candidates automatic access to the RNC's centralized data on the voting records of Democratic House incumbents, for example.

The national party provided yet another major boost to its congressional nominees through the media services division. The National Republican Congressional Committee produced about 180 television advertisements and provided other media services to ninety-two GOP House candidates (forty-eight incumbents and forty-four challengers)—a record number, compared with eight candidates in 1978 and fifty in 1980. The commercials were of a high technical quality, were keyed to national Republican themes, and were backed up by extensive research and audience testing. Moreover, the packages were produced at a far lower cost than that charged by independent political consultants, who are usually motivated at least as much by pure profit as by party promotion. The NRCC even purchased media time for many candidates, saving campaigns as much as 90 percent of the normal 15 percent commission fee levied by independent consultants and ad placement agencies.[22]

Perhaps of greater importance were the "institutional" advertising packages prepared and aired by the GOP throughout 1981 and 1982. Designed to support not specific candidates but the generic Republican label and the policies of President Reagan, the 1982 institutional ads followed a developmental pattern established in 1980. During that year's presidential campaign, the GOP aired a $9.5 million series of commercials that attacked the Democratic Congress and lampooned its leaders. Each commercial ended with the tag line, "Vote Republican—for a change."[23] Survey research clearly showed that the ads were effective, and so once in power in 1981, the RNC aired a $2.3 million advertising package designed to capitalize on President Reagan's congressional budget successes, on the theme of "Republicans: leadership that works for a change."

The 1982 midterm election package, on which the Republicans spent almost $15 million, followed naturally from the institutional campaigns. It began in late spring with commercials produced by Korey and Kay advertising agency of New York, including a controversial ad featuring actors who resembled former President Jimmy Carter and House Speaker Thomas P. "Tip" O'Neill looking on as a lawyer read a will: "To Ronald Reagan we leave a recession. . . ."[24]

The theme of "Republicans are beginning to make things better" developed by these ads then gave way in the summer to the slogan "give the guy a chance," designed by San Francisco media consultant Hal Larson for the RNC. In this series, for example, Republicans tried to counter Democratic charges that the Reagan administration was damaging the social security system. In what many consultants regarded as one of the most effective political commercials of the year, a white-haired avuncular mailman was seen delivering social security checks that contained the July 1982 automatic 7.4 percent cost-of-living increase:

> I'm probably one of the most popular people in town. . . . [Reagan] promised that raise and he kept his promise in spite of the sticks-in-the-mud who tried to keep him from doing what we elected him to do. . . . For gosh sake, let's give the guy a chance.

The ad was so successful in convincing senior citizens that Reagan had increased rather than decreased their payments (as measured by White House pollster Richard Wirthlin's surveys)[25] that its first run in July was followed by an encore in August. An autumn update of the commercial also appeared in which the postman reported, "Well, I'm still delivering those social security checks." Not surprisingly, this spot was extensively run in media markets with large concentrations of elderly voters.

The final phase of the GOP's institutional advertising occurred during the traditional autumn campaign. Using a slogan suggested by the Washington consulting firm of Bailey-Deardourff, the GOP issued a clarion call to "stay the course" in the run-up to the general election. All kinds of people filmed in a "man-in-the-street" format urged voters not to "go back" but to stick with the president and his programs and to give his ideas more time to work. President Reagan himself took up the standard, closing his October 13 nationally televised "nonpartisan" speech on the economy with an admonition to "stay the course." Both public and private polls indicated that the catch phrase, and the sophisticated media behind it, probably had the desired effect on many Americans. A mid-October Associated Press/NBC poll, for instance, found that 52 percent of the public believed the president's economic policies had not had enough time to work, compared with only 38 percent who had expressed similar patience in midsummer.[26] (This finding is even more remarkable, given that the poll was taken shortly after the unemployment rate broke the 10 percent barrier for the first time since World War II.)

The president's slogan, in fact, seemed so effective to one endangered Democratic House incumbent, Abraham "Chick" Kazen of Texas, that he adopted "stay the course" as his own reelection directive. (Kazen won another term.)

Not all Republican candidates, however, were as enthusiastic as the Democrats' Kazen in welcoming the institutional package in 1982. The effect of an institutional ad campaign is to nationalize all party candidacies, but in the midterm elections, some Republican nominees were naturally attempting to distance themselves from the Reagan administration in the midst of a recession. The 1982 Republican institutional package, then, was working at cross-purposes with the efforts of some GOP candidates, and though shrewd use of the media can eliminate some of the conflict, it may also be true that institutional ad campaigns are usually better suited to the party out of presidential power.

Whatever the actual effect of the GOP's national advertising, the media and polling services as well as the guarantee of full party financing offered by the Republicans were of immense value in recruiting top-quality candidates. "We locked them in with our resources," admitted Richard Bond of the Republican National Committee.[27] Once "locked in," the candidates became part of a centralized campaign effort run not only from the Republican National Committee but also from the White House, where an "assets and priorities" group was meeting weekly from January 1982 onward.[28] Coordinated by Lee Atwater, the deputy assistant to the president for political affairs, the group continuously scrutinized all House and Senate races, deciding which were of high priority and which were marginal—and thus eligible for extra aid and attention. Of special concern was the allocation of "human resources," particularly the time and travels of the president, vice president, and cabinet officers. President Reagan's political moves were carefully scheduled by the group. The president was filmed separately (the film was to be inserted into district and state television commercials) with most GOP candidates for the House, the Senate, and the governorship. The itinerary for presidential barnstorming was determined by the group with the help of polling data, and Reagan's fund-raising potential was used to the fullest, from direct mail packages bearing the presidential signature to closed-circuit speeches via satellite to a series of party fund-raising affairs. Rarely, if ever, has the White House worked so closely and so well with its party operatives. Never has the new campaign technology been so effectively employed by a presidential administration at midterm.

Republican Campaign Technology and the Election Results

This description of the superb 1982 Republican campaign organiza-tion leads inevitably to one question: If the GOP ran such a fine cam-paign, why did Republicans lose twenty-six House seats? Patrick Caddell, pollster for President Carter and many other Democrats, suggested two reasons several weeks before the election:

> First, a number of recent elections have shown that a can-didate funded at a level adequate for his or her message to get across—or to reach a threshold of public awareness—can prevail. Second, if a candidate is riding a tide of the right issues and themes, that tide can rush over a seawall of money.[29]

Caddell's two conditions for cushioning the impact of Republican money and services did, in fact, exist in 1982. The Democrats made a fair amount of organizational and technological progress in 1982, so their candidates were not at the same level of disadvantage as in 1980. Although Democrats spent significantly less than Republicans in most marginal contests, they were able to raise enough money to be reasonably competitive. Democrats, in other words, were far below the Republican spending ceilings, but they spent enough to keep from falling beneath the threshold of potential victory. Primarily because of their edge in incumbency, Democrats continue to do better than hold their own in raising funds both from individuals and from political action committees.[30] Above all, the issues of the election (predominantly unemployment, the economy, and social security) inevitably favored the Democratic party in the midterm of a Republi-can presidency.

Although Democrats achieved moderate advances in 1982, it can be argued that they should have done much better—and the explana-tion for their relative lack of success is clearly tied to the abundance of Republican money and campaign services. According to traditional models of midterm election behavior, the Republicans ought to have lost up to twice as many House seats as they actually did. Edward R. Tufte, for example, has demonstrated that, in the aggregate, con-gressional election results are referendums that are greatly responsive to the level of presidential popularity and the change in real per capita disposable income before the election.[31] His equation, highly predictive in past years, forecast a Republican loss of about forty-five seats in 1982. Before the election, Tufte himself, recognizing the potency of GOP financing and organization, scaled the likely loss back to forty seats, and in retrospect it is obvious that he did not sufficiently allow for Republican campaign advantages. Also before the election, Gary Jacobson and Samuel Kernell ventured an accurate guess that Democrats would do less well than Tufte's equation indicated because of the GOP's success in using their money and services to recruit outstanding candidates. As they explained it:

> Each specific pair of candidates and campaigns presents a particular choice, and the voting decision depends heavily on the alternatives offered. In contests between incumbents and challengers, the choice is largely determined by the quality and resources of the challenger. Attractive, well-financed challengers can seriously threaten incumbents; most incumbents are reelected easily because they do not face such challengers. . . .
>
> If 1982 is not a Republican disaster, national-level Republican party committees will be the reason. First, they have raised enormous amounts of money to spend on the campaigns. . . .
>
> Equally important, Republicans have figured out what to do with their money. They have used it to recruit and train high-quality candidates as well as to help finance their campaigns (the promise of money, of course, helping to recruit strong candidates). At present, it appears that both parties will be fielding strong challengers in 1982, but for very different reasons. Strong Democratic challengers have been attracted in the usual way: by their belief that serious economic problems and Reagan's declining popularity make it a good year to go after Republican incumbents. Strong Republican challengers have emerged despite unfavorable national conditions through the work and money of national-level party committees. The party has managed to organize a strong countercyclical thrust—strong enough to convince many observers of national politics that 1982 will not be an especially good Democratic year.[32]

Thus, the Republicans were able to buy a hedge against normal midterm losses by attracting strong candidates early, and by using their financial and technological tools for what White House political director Ed Rollins frequently called the "2 percent solution": concentrating resources on marginal races where an additional technology-generated 2 percent of the vote could tip the election. Many successful Republican candidates across the country clearly owed their victories to the 2 percent solution. Nowhere has this been more visible than in the Senate contests. In 1980 and 1982 Republicans have won nineteen Senate seats where their candidates received less than 53 percent of the vote. By contrast, Democrats have won just four such races. It is no accident that the GOP has done better in Senate contests than in House contests, because FECA permits the greatest party activity in Senate elections and the GOP campaign advantages are therefore magnified.

Democratic Progress in 1982

Thomas E. Cronin, an academic-turned-politician who ran unsuccessfully as the 1982 Democratic nominee for Congress against Republican U.S. Representative Ken Kramer of Colorado, described his contact with the national Democratic party this way:

> The Democratic Congressional Campaign Committee said I was an attractive candidate; they encouraged me and said they were delighted I was running, but I didn't get anything. They had trouble raising money and concentrated on [Democratic] incumbents and open seats. Besides, I got in the race late and was considered a low priority as a challenger against an incumbent. In any case, it was annoying to receive a letter from [the] Democratic National Committee . . . saying, "Thank you, it's great having candidates like you." I feel like sending it back and telling [them], "A lot of help you guys were." They provided a lot of talk, what Texans refer to as "all hat and no cattle."[33]

Most Democratic congressional nominees would undoubtedly second Cronin's plaint, and in many respects it is justified. In almost every major category, the national Democratic party committees are pale shadows of their Republican counterparts. For years the Democratic party was lulled into organizational complacency by electoral success and by dependency on the AFL-CIO's Committee on Political Education (COPE) and the personal office staffs of incumbent congressmen. But the sweeping nature of their 1980 defeats, the activism of New Right challengers, and the embarrassing comparison with Republican party operations have begun to move Democrats toward modernization. By no stretch of the imagination can Democratic party efforts in 1982 be called comparable to those of the Republicans, and labor was still the mainstay of the Democratic party's electoral activities. (In fact, in some areas such as voter registration and getting out the vote, labor became even more vital to Democratic success in 1982.) But the midterm congressional campaign is nonetheless significant for the Democrats because it provides the first tangible evidence of revival and renewal for their national party organization. Democrats now know that drastic changes in their operations are in order, and they have started down the path that Republicans first walked almost a decade ago.

Even so, the national Democratic party Senate and House campaign committees more than tripled their fund-raising proceeds in 1981–1982, compared with those in the previous election cycle. The Senatorial Campaign Committee registered large gains, raising a total of $5.6 million, compared with $1.6 million in 1980. Of this, $3.4 million came from the new "Leadership Circle" described below. The Democratic Congressional Campaign Committee collected even more money in 1982, $6.5 million; it had also performed somewhat better than its Senate ally in 1980, having raised $2.0 million then. The Democratic National Committee, saddled with debt approaching $10 million after the 1968 presidential election, finally cleared the books of its obligations in June 1982. In all three cases, accumulations of relatively large contributions (gifts of $500 or more) were responsible for the advances, a result of more aggressive solicitation of PACs, businesses, and traditional party financiers. Special big-donor "clubs," which guarantee access for party officeholders through regularly scheduled dinners and meetings, played a role in increasing top-dollar gifts. As for the Senate, Senator Alan Cranston of California formed a Leadership Circle with an annual admission fee of $15,000 per person or PAC. The Leadership Circle, with 153 members (112 individuals and 41 PACs), raised over $3 million and provided all of the $2.5 million the Democratic Senatorial Campaign Committee disbursed to Senate candidates. The House committee's group is called the Speaker's Club and has an admission charge of $5,000 a year for an individual and $15,000 a year for a PAC. (The DNC and all three Republican campaign committees have similar affiliated groups.)

Yet despite the preponderance of large gifts, the Democratic party also recognized the importance of expanding the small-donor base for the first time. In 1981 the DNC contracted with the direct mail firm of Craver, Mathews, Smith and Company to begin an extensive program of mail solicitation. Using especially the social security issue and drawing on lists of demographically targeted registered Democratic voters in addition to contributors to previous presidential candidates (such as George McGovern and Morris Udall), the firm was able to expand the DNC's sustaining list of contributors from 25,000 in 1981 to more than 220,000 by the end of 1982. Significantly, the Democrats demonstrated the self-discipline necessary to develop a successful direct mail program by reinvesting the proceeds of early "prospecting" mailings in additional solicitations.[34] Although it will take years to reach the GOP's level of sophistication

—and thus the gap in party proceeds will probably continue to grow in the interim—the Democrats' direct mail investment should begin to pay some dividends by 1984, and certainly by 1986.

Democrats copied their opponents not only in direct mail but also in other campaign activities in 1982. For several years the GOP has been sending press releases critical of the votes of incumbent Democratic congressmen to the television, radio, and newspaper outlets in their home districts, and in 1982 the Democrats followed suit, targeting vulnerable GOP incumbents for the negative media treatment. Democrats also began to imitate the successful GOP "Tidewater conferences," whereby party officials regularly gather on retreat in a relaxed, off-the-record atmosphere to discuss political strategy and policy issues. Senate Minority Leader Robert Byrd sponsored such a conference for Democratic senators and their wives in West Virginia in October 1981, and by all accounts it helped Democrats to regroup and act as a more cohesive Senate minority. Because of the pressure of congressional business, plans for a second gathering in 1982 were scrapped, but others may be held in the future.

For several election cycles, too, the Republicans have been stressing campaign organization, get-out-the-vote activity, and staff and candidate training. Beginning with their midterm convention in Philadelphia June 25–27, the Democrats adopted the same techniques. Instead of discussing controversial issues as in the previous midterm convention, this party conclave was devoted in good part to a series of workshops on practical political skills, from fund raising and press relations to proper use of polls and effective response to attacks from the New Right. Throughout 1981 and 1982 the DNC and the party's Congressional Campaign Committee held a series of seminars and "national training academies" in Washington and in other major cities across the country in which candidates and their staffs were schooled in modern campaign techniques. Additionally, the DNC, with the help of political consultant and organizational specialist Matt Reese, worked to strengthen the state parties in eighteen states. The ability to identify, register, and turn out party voters was particularly emphasized, and efforts in a number of states (such as Texas and New Mexico) were cited by nonpartisan observers in the upsets of favored Republican incumbent officials.

Of all their activities, the Democrats secured the most notice for their institutional advertising program. Ten thirty-second radio commercials were created, some featuring national Democratic "stars" such as U.S. Representatives Claude Pepper discussing the social security issue and Morris K. Udall focusing on the environment. Copies of the ads were made available to all fifty state parties and to party candidates. (A handful of state parties and about twenty Democratic candidates actually bought time to air them.) The national Democratic party itself paid $20,000 to air new radio commercials in the final hours of the 1982 campaign as well.

Five thirty-second television spots were also produced, one of them featuring "Dixie," the Republican elephant, blundering through a china shop and smashing ware labeled "social security," "jobs," and so on, as an announcer intoned: "Two years ago, we trusted the Republicans to mind the store in Washington. They promised us they'd bring prosperity and respect to America's heritage of fairness and compassion. . . . The Republicans have made a mess of things."[35] Other commercials closed with the tag line, "It isn't fair. It's Republican."[36] One featured a social security card being clipped away by scissors as the Republicans were accused of repeatedly trying to cut benefits.[37] Another showed a 1982 unemployment line that dissolved into a photo of a Great Depression dole queue. A third ad cleverly demonstrated the Democratic view of "trickle-down" Reaganomics, as the champagne of the tax benefits gushed into the sparkling crystal glasses of the wealthy, while only a few drops of tax relief reached the tin cup of the average person below. Finally came an encore for James A. Willders, an unemployed Baltimore blue-collar worker who was featured in a 1980 GOP institutional commercial roaming through a deserted factory, angrily asking, "If the Democrats are so good for working people, then how come so many people aren't working?"[38] In 1982 Willders returned to the house of his father, and he announced his homecoming in a Democratic ad with a touching climax:

> Remember me? In 1980 the Republicans paid me to go on television because they promised us they would make things better, and I believed them. Well, since they've been in control, unemployment is the highest since the Great Depression and businesses are closing down every day. Millions of Americans are without jobs, and we've got to do something. I'm a Democrat, but I voted Republican once—and it's a mistake I'll never make again. And I didn't get paid to say this.[39]

Except as a courtesy of the evening news broadcasts, many, if not most, Americans never had a chance to see any of these ads, since only about $1 million was raised by the DNC to air them, mainly in secondary markets. (Some state and local parties, however, as well as a few individual candidates, also financed showings of the spots, adding as much as another $1 million in air time for the package.) But at least the usefulness of institutional advertising has now been acknowledged by both parties, and as the Democrats' financial position improves, their offerings will be more widely shown. Their spots may also be produced internally, thanks to a $390,000 loan to the Democrats' Congressional Campaign Committee by former New York Governor and Mrs. Averell Harriman. With the loan, the party purchased a building on Capitol Hill to be used as a media center for Democratic candidates. By 1984 the party may be able to produce television and radio advertisements for its own use and that of its nominees, much as the GOP does (though the Republican media division is far more expansive and technically advanced than anything the Democrats can hope to construct in the near future).

Political Action Committees in 1982: Developing Diversity, Coordination, and Sophistication

Although the innovations of party activity in 1982 may well have more long-term significance for the American political system, it was the political action committees that received the lion's share of attention in the midterm elections. As the focus of press coverage and media publicity that occasionally became unbalanced, the PACs were generally pictured as a sinister and sometimes monolithic force practicing a kind of legal bribery and dominating the political process to an excessive degree.

There is no question that a disturbing correlation sometimes exists between votes cast in Congress and special-interest money contributed during election campaigns. But in the absence of full public financing of congressional campaigns, the hope must be for James Madison's solution: the flourishing of competing interests so that the resources of any single interest will become less significant.[40]

The developments of 1982 give reason to believe that PACs as a group are becoming somewhat more diverse and balanced, as labor and liberal PACs responded to the corporate challenge. PACs of all kinds are clearly becoming better coordinated and are using more sophisticated targeting methods as well. Campaign activities beyond the mere contribution of money are beginning to take center stage in some of the larger PACs.

Basic Facts about PACs

The term "political action committee" is used to describe and define any political committee that has not been directly authorized by a candidate or political party. The term includes two types of PACs: (1) a separate segregated political fund connected to a corporation, trade association, or labor organization; (2) an independent political committee without any connected organization. In 1974, when their permissible activities were more clearly defined,[41] there were 608 PACs, with labor PACs outnumbering corporate committees by 201 to 89. By 1976, 1,146 PACs were in existence, the increase being due mainly to a 1975 ruling by the Federal Election Commission clearly permitting corporations to form PACs. Corporate committees now exceeded labor ones by 433 to 224. The greatest growth since 1976 has continued to be among corporate and the independent "nonconnected" PACs. By the end of 1982, 3,371 political action committees had been formed: 1,570 by corporations,[42] 380 by labor unions, 746 by independent organizations, 628 by trade associations,[43] and 47 by cooperatives.[44] The potpourri of PACs included everything from BeefPAC, EggPAC, and LardPAC to Whataburger, Inc.'s Whata-PAC and the beer distributors' appropriately named SixPAC. There are at least twenty pro-Israel PACs, but the Italians, Romanians, and Armenians, among other American ethnics, are also represented. Past, present, and future presidential contenders have PACs to finance their travels and contribute to potential supporters' campaigns. In 1982 Ronald Reagan's Citizens for the Republic,[45] Edward Kennedy's Fund for a Democratic Majority, Walter Mondale's Committee for the Future of America, and Howard Baker's Republican Majority Fund were the most active.[46] Even Time Inc., whose subsidiary magazine ran a cover story "exposé" on PACs during the 1982 election, has a political committee.

In contributions as well as number, PACs have expanded. PACs gave $11.6 million to congressional candidates in 1974, or about 15.7 percent of the total amount of campaign funds raised that year. By 1980 27.4 percent of congressional candidates' war chests were contributed by PACs ($55.2 million of $201.5 million total), and in 1982 the PAC proportion of the total increased slightly, to 27.6 percent (or $83.1 million of $300.8 million overall).[47] In recent years, including 1982, PACs have accounted for a larger proportion of funds for House candidates than for Senate contenders, partly because of the large role played by the political parties in Senate contests.[48] Although the average PAC spends less than $25,000 in an election cycle, and eight out of ten spend less than $50,000, more than two dozen PACs are multimillion-dollar operations. In 1982 the biggest givers among labor unions included the United Auto Workers, the Machinists, and the National Education Association; among trade associations, the National Association of Realtors, the American Medical Association, the National Association of Homebuilders, and the American Bankers Association; and among corporations, Tenneco, Winn-Dixie Stores, and the Harris Corporation. The largest fund-raisers of all are the independent political committees, such as the National Conservative Political Action Committee and Jesse Helms's National Congressional Club.

The Left Comes Alive in 1982

Despite estimates that corporate and conservative PACs spent well over twice as much as labor and liberal PACs in 1982, both the unions and the left were more active, and politically shrewd, than they have been since the era of PACs dawned. First, much like the Democratic party, they were spurred to greater effort by the severe drubbing they received in 1980. Second, they showed much greater savvy in targeting marginal races and in using the money at their disposal, and they have also begun to offer some of the same auxiliary services that corporate and independent conservative groups offer. In many of the twenty-two cases where Democratic challengers defeated Republican House incumbents in 1982, for example, the challengers were able to compete effectively for PAC money with their opponents, despite the heavy tilt among PACs toward incumbents and despite the GOP advantage of larger corporate and conservative PAC treasuries.[49] Selective targeting by labor committees, women's groups, environmental organizations, and new nuclear freeze PACs was largely responsible for the challengers' fund-raising success. Although right and left are far from equally represented among PACs and some interests are wholly unrepresented—Senator Robert Dole of Kansas has noted that "there aren't any Poor PACs or Food Stamp PACs"—the PAC system seemed to become more diversified and balanced in 1982. One ideology or party or set of interests has no near monopoly on PAC power.

Labor, in particular, was a more important electoral factor in 1982 than in any year since 1976, and the increased tempo of its activity on behalf of Democrats helped to neutralize the effect of vast GOP expenditures.[50] At least 3 million members of union households were reportedly added to the voter rolls by the registration drives coordinated by the AFL-CIO's Committee on Political Education in 1981 and 1982. An estimated 150,000 COPE volunteers and several thousand paid staffers canvassed union neighborhoods and organized get-out-the-vote drives, assisted by COPE's computerized data on almost 15 million union members. Targeted, personalized direct mail appeals were used extensively by labor for the first time, and technological improvements were made in the traditional labor phone bank system. With the hired help of Democratic consultant Peter D.

Hart, COPE developed its own polling operation (which was used, for example, to test membership support for labor-backed candidates). Computer terminals were installed in some state labor headquarters to give instant access to COPE's data banks. A program of regional conferences to train state and local labor activists in campaign skills was expanded. Individual unions, such as the Communications Workers of America, the United Auto Workers, the American Federation of State, County, and Municipal Employees, and the two teachers' unions (the National Education Association and the American Federation of Teachers), also undertook major supplementary activities.

Even more so than in the past, labor cast its lot with the Democrats, giving only token amounts to past Republican friends and concentrating the lion's share on Democratic campaigns. Challengers and open seat contenders, not only incumbents, benefited from labor's 1982 largess. In 1980 Democratic Senate incumbents received 65 percent of labor's contribution, but in 1982 the proportion declined to 55 percent. In House campaigns, the change is even more dramatic: Democratic incumbents secured 67 percent of labor's donations in 1980, but just 51 percent in 1982. Democratic challengers were the main beneficiaries of labor's shift from incumbent financing. Although many forces—not just labor—shaped the election results of the midterm contests, labor could take great solace and satisfaction from its batting average. In labor's best showing since the Watergate year of 1974, COPE-endorsed candidates won twenty of thirty-one Senate contests in which labor had taken a stand (64.5 percent), compared with 34 percent in 1980 and 40 percent in 1978. In House races, 237 of 376 COPE-backed contenders won (63 percent), about the same as in recent elections. Exit polls also indicated that union members voted heavily, casting about 35 percent of all ballots even though they make up only a quarter of the electorate.[51] Union voters returned to the Democratic fold as well, voting more than 2 to 1 for Democratic congressional candidates after a relatively high rate of defection in 1980.

Other liberal groups complemented the work of organized labor in 1982. Angered by the death of the Equal Rights Amendment and by some of Reagan's foreign and domestic policies, women's groups generated considerable money and volunteer support for favored candidates.[52] The National Organization for Women (NOW), the largest of the feminist groups, contributed a half-million dollars to congressional candidates (the overwhelming majority of them Democrats) and donated another $1 million to state candidates. Other women's organizations, such as the National Women's Political Caucus, the Women's Campaign Fund, and the National Abortion

Rights Action League, added well over $1 million to the coffers of sympathetic candidates, mostly Democrats.

What the ERA did for women's activism, Interior Secretary James Watt accomplished for environmentalists.[53] The Sierra Club computerized the 1.1 million names from its 1981 petition drive seeking Watt's ouster, supplying them to candidates endorsed by the club's PAC for direct mail fund raising. (That was no small gift; liberal direct mail consultants report that James Watt's name stimulates as much giving on the left as the mention of Edward Kennedy's name does in mailings to conservatives.) The combined work of the Sierra Club, the League of Conservation Voters, Friends of the Earth, and Environmental Action mobilized thousands of volunteers and contributed more than $900,000 to congressional candidates, again mainly Democrats.

Similarly, Democrats gained from the mushrooming growth of PACs supporting a nuclear weapons freeze,[54] obviously a popular cause in a year when pronuclear referendums won in eight of nine states and twenty-seven of twenty-nine localities (plus the District of Columbia) where the issue was on the ballot. PeacePAC, an affiliate of the Council for a Livable World, gave about $73,000 to fifty-two House candidates supporting a nuclear weapons freeze. The council itself contributed $458,511 to eighteen profreeze Senate contenders. (Of the council and PeacePAC's seventy-one candidates, forty-seven were elected.)[55] Other PACs active on the nuclear freeze front included FreezePAC, SANE, the National Committee for an Effective Congress, the Fund for a Democratic Majority, Friends of the Earth, and Democrats for the 80's. The latter group is one of the new liberal organizations that sprang up in the wake of the 1980 presidential election. Founded by Pamela Harriman (the wife of Averell Harriman), the PAC raised over $1 million in 1981–1982 and spent over $375,000 for Democratic congressional contenders in 1982.

PAC Strategy and Targeting

Until the 1980 presidential election, most corporate and trade PACs had practiced "incumbent politics," contributing money to key congressional incumbents on both sides of the aisle without regard to party affiliation or ideology. But in 1980, many business PACs began to give significant sums to Republican challengers in House and particularly Senate races, especially in the campaign's closing weeks. Although many of these successful GOP challengers did not spend as much as Democratic incumbents, the PACs helped the challengers to accumulate a war chest of sufficient size to produce victory. At the time, Republicans hoped, and Democrats feared, that the change in strategy for business PACs would be a permanent one, the beginning of a more ideologically aggressive phase of PAC development.

To the displeasure of Republicans, however, PACs once again embraced an incumbent strategy that regarded challengers as dubious "risk capital ventures." Overall, PACs favored incumbents by a margin of better than 3 to 1 (compared with a spread of slightly more than 2 to 1 during the two previous election cycles), and corporate and trade PACs preferred incumbents to challengers in 1982 by more than 5½ to 1. Every 1982 Senate incumbent in both parties save two (Democrats William Proxmire of Wisconsin and Lawton Chiles of Florida, who will not accept any or many PAC gifts) raised more PAC money than their opponents. Of thirty-one widely targeted races in the House, including those where the incumbent was clearly endangered and did in fact lose, in twenty-seven the incumbent still received more PAC money.[56] Corporate and trade PACs lost their zest for Republican challengers for three primary reasons. First of all, business PACs had a major stake in the freshman Republican House class, which had first been elected in 1980 in part thanks to "challenger" PAC targeting and financing. Quite naturally, PACs sought to shelter and augment their earlier prize investment. Second, the election handicappers among PACs and in the press saw 1982 as being at least a mildly Democratic year, which encouraged corporate PACs even more to protect vulnerable GOP incumbents and also, where possible, to swim with the Democratic tide rather than make enemies unnecessarily.

Third, the Democrats made adjustments in their own campaign and legislative strategy to attract corporate and trade PAC money, though their efforts met with only limited success. As will be discussed later, the Democratic party sought to open new channels of communication with business, hoping to secure more money for Democratic candidates or at least slow the flow to the GOP. Earlier, many Democrats in the House had tried to approach business by offering special tax breaks to PAC-connected interest groups during the 1981 Ways and Means Committee debate on President Reagan's proposed three-year tax cut.[57] (The result was a virtual bidding war between the White House and congressional Democrats, to the delight of business.) While they may have succeeded with some selected industries, the Democrats' work may have been for naught overall. A comparison of corporate and trade PAC gift totals in 1981–1982 with those of 1979–1980, for example, reveals that Democrats received 39.8 percent of the 1980 money ($14.8 million of the $37.2

million total) but just 38.0 percent of the corporate and trade bounty in 1982 ($19.8 million of the $52.1 million total).

Not all PACs practiced incumbent politics in 1982. The independent committees on the right and left were somewhat kinder to challengers. So was labor, in a shift in direction from its often passive behavior in past years when it frequently gave away much of its resources in "thank-you" grants to incumbents who were sure to win. On the conservative side, Sunbelt interests, particularly independent oil, continued to pursue a challenger strategy, though with much less success than in 1980.[58] The Dallas Energy PAC (or DALENPAC), for example, one of about a dozen independent oil PACs, had channeled $244,000 into fourteen Senate and sixty-three House races by November 1982. Much of it was donated relatively early in the election cycle as seed money. But although DALENPAC won 77 percent of its Senate races and 60 percent of its House races in 1980 using the same tactics, in 1982 it won only 29 percent of its Senate contests and 22 percent of its House battles. DALENPAC's 1982 debacle illustrates an important principle: PACs, even powerful ones such as independent oil, working in concert with many other monied interests, cannot buck a significant trend in candidate preferences among the electorate; at most, they can hope, as they did in 1980, that other significant issues will also help elect the candidates they favor.

In its 1982 targeting, DALENPAC was clearly the exception among PACs. Most of them gave more heavily to incumbents, even occasionally incumbents unfriendly to their cause or industry, in order to ensure "access." If access is the goal, then unopposed representatives are obviously the ones to benefit most from contributions. In fact, in 1982, twenty-four representatives who were actually or virtually unopposed in both primary and general elections received at least $50,000 from PACs; eight of them were the recipients of over $100,000.[59] Democrat Kent Hance of Texas, for instance, a member of the House Ways and Means Committee, received well over $400,000 overall, with $141,825 from PACs, and Ways and Means Chairman Dan Rostenkowski of Chicago collected almost a half-million dollars, nearly $300,000 from PACs—"for a rainy day," as he explained it.[60] On the same principle of access, it was not uncommon in 1982 to find two incumbents, pitted against each other because of redistricting, receiving money from the same PACs, as the committees sought to hedge their bets. Similarly, some PACs followed Bank-PAC's practice of giving $10,000 each to the RNC, the DNC, and both parties' Senate and House campaign committees.[61]

Although ideological independent committees and groups like labor on the left and oil producers on the right gave special emphasis to party affiliation and philosophy, practical and strategic questions were crucial indicators in 1982 for almost all PACs. In deciding *which* incumbents to support, for instance, the typical trade or corporate PAC in 1982 appears to have asked a set of questions somewhat like these: (1) Is the congressman on a key committee affecting our industry? (2) Do we have a plant in the district? (3) Has the incumbent voted "right" on issues affecting us? (4) Has the incumbent been accessible to us? (5) Has he attempted to get to know our problems and helped us to cut government red tape? Under this set of criteria, of course, committee chairmen and members of both houses' money committees (Ways and Means, House Appropriations, Senate Finance, and Senate Appropriations) and the business regulatory committees (House Energy and Commerce, and Senate Commerce, Science, and Transportation) were especially popular and worthy of PAC gifts in 1982. The expectations are borne out by Federal Electoral Commission records.[62]

PAC Selection of Candidate-Recipients

Political action committees no longer rely on mere guesswork in deciding which candidates fulfill their selection criteria. They are demanding—and getting—more information from the candidates, their staffs, and the political parties. Many PACs have chosen the questionnaire method of selection, whereby potential recipients of money submit to questioning orally or in writing on issues of concern to the PAC. PeacePAC, for instance, required its 1982 candidates to complete and sign the following statement:

> As a candidate for Congress in 1982, I will support efforts to develop national security and arms control policies for the United States that avoid nuclear confrontation and waste of resources.
>
> Specifically, I will support:
>
> ———An immediate, verified, mutual freeze on the testing, construction and deployment of new nuclear weapons by both the United States and the Soviet Union.
>
> ———Continuous negotiations by the Reagan Administration with the Soviet Union to reduce existing nuclear weapons and to prevent nuclear war.
>
> ———The stated policy of the Reagan Administration to abide by the SALT II limits as long as the Soviet Union does.
>
> ———The termination of the MX missile program.
>
> ———The termination of the B-1 program.
>
> ———A continuation in force of the 1972 anti–ballistic missile (ABM) treaty between the U.S. and the U.S.S.R. that limits the deployment of new ABM systems.

————A negotiated end to *all* nuclear testing by the United States, the Soviet Union and other nuclear powers.

————Efforts to limit the huge increase in military spending planned over the next five years.

The R-PAC of the National Association of Realtors insisted that each candidate seeking its funds fill out a six-page questionnaire. The number of "correct" answers—and the right responses were not always obvious—were crucial to a candidate's chances. "Sometimes candidates call me and plead with me to give them the correct answers," reported R-PAC's political director.[63]

R-PAC and other PACs supplemented information from questionnaires with the voting records of incumbents on issues important to them. They also used field reports from paid staffers on the election odds in each district and state. The voting records often served a dual purpose: they provided decision-making information for candidate selection and also served as campaign fodder as a "report card" released to the press, the general public, and PAC constituency groups. Many of the report cards are based on just a few votes or issues, but they can be devastatingly effective in raising money from an "offended" constituency group or in damaging a candidate's chances with a segment of the population. The Christian Voice Moral Government Fund, for example, distributed 3 million "moral report cards" in thirty congressional districts to evangelical churchgoers on the Sunday before the 1982 election. Some candidates who flunked the group's test were dismissed with this sentence: "He deserves our prayers but not our votes."

Communication and Coordination among PACs

Report cards are sometimes used to communicate with the public, but other, more sophisticated means are used to keep PACs in touch with one another. In 1982 there was a greater degree of coordination than ever before among PACs with similar interests. Moreover, the PACs have developed a set of leadership organizations whose cues became increasingly significant in targeting races in the midterm elections. Leading PACs have begun to issue periodic lists of targeted races, to assist other PACs in making decisions, and to inform and alert political activists about their judgments. Both liberal groups, such as COPE and the National Committee for an Effective Congress, and conservative organizations, including the Committee for the Survival of a Free Congress and the National Association of Realtors, employ this technique.[64]

Two business groups, the U.S. Chamber of Commerce and the

Business-Industry Political Action Committee (BIPAC), have perhaps the best-known and most widely disseminated lists of targeted races on the Republican side. A place on either register is highly coveted by a candidate, since it can mean tens of thousands of dollars in PAC gifts. The Chamber of Commerce publishes and frequently updates its overwhelmingly Republican "opportunity race" slate throughout the election season. It lists only those candidates who "support the business viewpoint," whose opponents do not, and whose races are close and winnable with adequate financial support. In 1982 the Chamber of Commerce produced an innovative show-and-tell version of its list in a four-hour, closed-circuit television presentation called "See How They Run," broadcast to 200 regional, state, and local PAC managers in seven cities.

If anything, BIPAC's list is read even more widely, particularly since BIPAC tends to focus its attention on open-seat races and challengers. Formed by several officials of the National Association of Manufacturers in 1963 as business's answer to COPE, BIPAC holds monthly briefings in Washington and occasionally in other cities, and over 100 PAC staffers can normally be found in attendance. BIPAC contributes to candidates itself and tries to do so early in the election year, since other business PACs look to it for leadership. It donated more than $200,000 to 145 congressional candidates in 1982, and its targeted list was updated in print about every three weeks.

New Activities of PACs

The more useful a PAC is to a candidate in his election campaign, the more it will be remembered and the more "access" the PAC is likely to have if the candidate wins. A trend toward substantive and visible campaign activities, at least among the larger PACs, appears to be developing.

In 1982, for example, the American Medical Association's PAC commissioned extensive benchmark polls for thirty-five incumbents and one challenger[65] and was able to give the surveys to the campaigns at a fraction of their cost under the Federal Election Commission's so-called sixty-one-day rule. According to this provision, the value of a poll is considered to have depreciated by 50 percent if sixteen days have elapsed since its completion, and by 95 percent if it is sixty-one days old. In this fashion, by delaying release of the results of the polls, AMPAC could donate polls costing $10,000 or more for less than the $5,000 contribution limit per candidate per election. The PAC could be sure its generosity would come prominently to the attention of the candidate, since polls, as vital political intelligence, are eagerly sought and carefully guarded by a campaign's top echelon. The practice also permitted AMPAC to exercise control over the manner in which its money was spent and to obtain yet another organizational bonus: about a half-dozen questions on most polls were devoted to medical issues, the results of which were added to AMPAC's bank of data on various congressional districts for use in future elections and lobbying battles. Besides the polling operation, for which it spent $381,000 in undepreciated cost, AMPAC contributed some $1.7 million directly to selected candidates and spent another quarter of a million dollars on independent positive advertising, an area in which it has been a pioneer.[66]

The R-PAC of the National Association of Realtors also had a diverse and effective program of activity in the midterm elections. As the richest of the trade association PACs, with about a $3 million kitty, R-PAC could afford to donate more than $2.1 million in direct contributions to candidates as well as to mount a number of independent campaign activities on behalf of favored politicians. In Montana, for instance, R-PAC decided to conduct an independent get-out-the-vote program for hard-pressed Democratic U.S. Senator John Melcher.[67] Contracting with National Management Associates of Washington, D.C., a firm that specializes in telephone banks, R-PAC concentrated preelection phone canvassing in western Montana, where Melcher's organization was considered weak. On election day, voters previously identified as pro-Melcher were called and urged to vote. (In an R-PAC postelection poll, about a third of the sample reportedly credited R-PAC calls with making them more likely to cast a ballot.)

In other areas, R-PAC sent out thousands of independent direct mail letters marked "URGENT: 1982 Voter Information Enclosed," which lavished praise on favored incumbents. Just to make sure that a representative was properly appreciative, R-PAC attached a postcard, addressed to the candidate, for the voter to send in, which read in part: "I have just received a letter from the REALTORS® Political Action Committee in support of your reelection for U.S. House of Representatives, and I wanted you to know that I will cast my vote for you on November 2." Finally, to maximize its personal touch, R-PAC established a program to get 50,000 realtors to devote at least twenty-four hours to the fall campaigns of endorsed candidates.

Solicitation of PACs by Candidates and Parties

The candidates and the parties do not wait passively for an AMPAC or R-PAC to make its selections. Rather, the contenders and their party sponsors energetically seek to reach and impress the PAC decision makers, and this effort became far more intense and elaborate than ever before in 1982. Most serious candidates had a prefabricated "PAC-kit" sent to all major PACs, containing information about the candidate, his or her voting record or stand on issues, and optimistic projections of victory. Favorable polls and mention of contracts with big-name political consultants were usually included. The PAC-kit was intended to get the candidate's name on the table for discussion and was often followed by a personal visit from the candidate himself. It is not uncommon now for candidates to spend more time in the PAC suites than on the campaign trail in the pre–Labor Day period, and a trip to see the PAC managers in Washington (and also in satellite centers such as Dallas and Houston) is almost obligatory. Sometimes the PACs make it a bit easier on the candidates. The National Association for (Trade) Association PACs hosted a June reception on Capitol Hill; eighty congressmen responded to a form invitation and outnumbered the PAC managers in attendance by better than 2 to 1.

The political parties are just as attentive to PACs as their candidates are. This is a bit ironic, since PACs in many ways rival parties for the affection and loyalty of candidates, but the parties recognize that PAC money—usually lots of it—is necessary for the success of their team. Both sets of party committees regularly contact and court PACs, sometimes even unfriendly ones, and they attempt to help allied PACs identify close races where party incumbents are endangered or party challengers are on the brink of an upset. The parties also act as congenial intermediaries for their candidates, making introductions and arranging appointments, when they visit the Washington PAC community. The GOP uses its early money contributed to promising contenders as a substantive signal to PACs as well.

As with most campaign tasks, the Republicans have gone about their PAC work very thoroughly and systematically. A PAC relations unit operating within the RNC held numerous briefing sessions for PACs in Washington and other cities, passing along the GOP list of targeted districts. The RNC was assisted by two influential Republicans, Washington lobbyist and former Nixon-Ford aide William Timmons and Clark MacGregor, once chairman of Nixon's 1972 reelection committee and now senior vice president of United Technologies.[68] Timmons and MacGregor organized sessions with important individuals and PACs in various segments of American industry and coordinated gift giving to the GOP in cooperation with RNC operatives. Other former Republican officeholders and party staffers in strategic positions were also of value. The executive director of R-PAC and the political director for the U.S. Chamber of Commerce, for instance, are former RNC employees.

For the first time, the Democrats sought in 1982 to communicate with business PACs. Chairman Tony Coelho of the Democratic Congressional Campaign Committee was especially active in sending a new message to business PACs. His realistic goal was as much to stop the hemorrhage of PAC funds to Republicans as to secure large sums from business for Democratic candidates. Coelho frankly told business: "Don't let your ideology get in the way of your business judgment."[69] Although in specific instances Coelho's advice may have been heeded, the overall PAC contribution figures mentioned earlier suggest that the Democrats' message was not persuasive—at least in 1982.

PACs as a Campaign Issue

Because of the intense press focus on PAC activity and the correlations between votes cast in Congress and PAC campaign contributions, PACs became not only a means to election but also a possible obstacle to victory in 1982. Candidates were forced to begin to weigh the benefits of PAC money against the costs of appearing "bought" to the electorate. Although the term "PAC" is not yet a household word (unless confused with the video grame), it is fast becoming one. The voters are clearly receptive to the issue: as early as January 1980, an ABC News/Louis Harris survey found that 71 percent of those questioned believed PACs "are pouring too much money into the whole political process."[70]

For some 1982 candidates, PACs proved to be an effective campaign weapon. Democratic House challenger Robert G. Torricelli of New Jersey gained considerable political mileage from his demand that district candidates limit PAC gifts to a third of their treasuries. His opponent, incumbent Republican Harold C. Hollenbeck, had received 58 percent of his 1980 receipts from PACs. Democrat Joseph Kolter of Pennsylvania repeatedly pointed out that his incumbent opponent, Democrat-turned-Republican U.S. Representative Eugene Atkinson, had secured $40,000 from business PACs since his party conversion. Republican candidate Jake Held of Ohio hammered hard at his target, Democratic Representative Thomas Luken, using a *Wall Street Journal* story that showed Luken receiving $275,000 from PACs in 1980 and 1982 to work in behalf of legislation favorable to some of his benefactors. Republican Richard C. Freeman heavily criticized incumbent Representative James R. Jones of Oklahoma for securing a majority of his campaign contributions from out-of-state PACs (a charge Jones disputed). Challengers Torricelli and Kolter won, but Held and Freeman did not—although in all four cases the charges in connection with PACs seem to have stung the incumbent.

Some congressional candidates have resolved the PAC money dilemma by refusing to take PAC funds. Among incumbents, four U.S. senators (Republican Warren Rudman of New Hampshire and Democrats David Boren of Oklahoma, Lawton Chiles of Florida, and William Proxmire of Wisconsin) and at least a dozen House members take either no PAC money at all or only very small amounts. As the campaign issue of PAC gifts becomes more prominent in the future, other candidates may follow suit even at the risk of increasing their chances of defeat through inadequate funding. That risk, however, with probably keep the number of naysayers low.

Independent Groups in 1982: Financial Success and Electoral Failure

One vital category of PAC activity in 1982 has yet to be examined: the independent groups. Ever since the U.S. Supreme Court's decision in *Buckley* v. *Valeo*[71] in 1976, it has been possible for PACs (and also individuals) to spend *without limit* in advocating one candidate's election or another's defeat.[72] The only major condition placed on such an independent expenditure is that it be made without the consent or cooperation of any candidate or campaign. Only about $700,000 was spent independently on congressional races in the elections of 1976 and 1978 combined. But in 1980, independent congressional expenditures amounted to $2.3 million, about $1 million of that directed against liberal Democratic U.S. senators by the National Conservative Political Action Committee. In 1982 a new high-water mark was reached, and independent congressional spending more than doubled from 1980 to a total of $5.3 million.

The vast majority of independent expenditures are made by a handful of PACs. Until 1982 these PACs were heavily weighted in number and financial power toward the right; some diversification took place in the 1981–1982 election cycle, and the left is now better represented. Whether right or left, the organization of independent PACs in 1982 followed the still developing precepts of independent political groups. First, very little of the money raised was contributed directly to political candidates. Instead, most of their treasury was expended for fund raising (mainly by direct mail) and other administrative overhead, as well as for those campaign activities (especially television and radio advertising) under their control.[73] For this reason, though eight independent PACs were ranked among the top ten money raisers in the 1981–1982 election cycle, none could be found on the list of top contributors.

Second, once business and trade PACs returned to an incumbent strategy, the independent PACs became the only groups regularly devoting a large share of their funds to challengers. Third, the vast majority of the independent money was once again spent on negative efforts—attempts to defeat certain disfavored candidates—rather than on positive campaigns. NCPAC, for example, made positive contributions of just $257,000, while spending almost $3 million to defeat Democratic candidates and $200,000 against certain GOP contenders.

The Conservative PACs

In the midterm elections the conservative independents found themselves spending more and enjoying it less. Whereas in 1980 NCPAC had assisted in the defeat of four liberal incumbent U.S. senators (George McGovern of South Dakota, Frank Church of Idaho, Birch Bayh of Indiana, and John Culver of Iowa), only one of twenty senators targeted by NCPAC in 1982 (Democrat Howard Cannon of Nevada) lost.[74] All three of NCPAC's top House targets won reelection as well. NCPAC's Chairman John T. "Terry" Dolan claimed that his committee's campaign efforts were sabotaged in some areas by television and radio stations which refused to carry his negative ads; moreover, in states where NCPAC was especially active, the incumbents did less well on election night than in their previous contests and were more unpopular (as measured by private NCPAC polls) than before. Nevertheless, it would be difficult to characterize the 1982 elections as an NCPAC victory.

In part, NCPAC was a victim of the same Democratic tide that had given business PACs lower win-loss ratios in 1982 than in 1980. The fact that NCPAC maintained its preference for challengers in a strong incumbent year only worsened its position. But candidates have also learned how to deal effectively with negative charges, adapting to changed conditions by using NCPAC—which has become an antichrist for the left—to great advantage. It used to be a cardinal rule of politics that incumbents stayed, statesmanlike, above the fray, refusing to answer charges or to return them in kind. Thanks to NCPAC and other independent groups, incumbents have learned to assume a combative, not a passive, posture in the face of attack.

So when NCPAC struck in Montana against Democratic Senator John Melcher, Melcher retaliated with anti-NCPAC television spots. One showed actors furtively carrying NCPAC briefcases as an announcer related: "For more than a year now a pack of East Coast politicos have been scurrying into Montana with briefcases full of money, trying to convince us that our John Melcher is out of step with Montana. Montana isn't buying it, especially those who know bull when they hear it." Another ad used "talking cows" to point out, none too gingerly, that a cow pasture was full of material much like NCPAC's.

Democratic Senator Paul Sarbanes of Maryland also came out swinging once NCPAC chose him as its top target for defeat and aired negative advertisements against him beginning in 1981. Ironically, NCPAC actually improved Sarbanes's chances of reelection. A reluctant campaigner, Sarbanes was forced out on the campaign trail early, and he became a cause célèbre for discouraged Democrats nationally. Campaign contributions and volunteer help flowed as a result.[75] NCPAC's advertising also received a less than rousing evaluation from the electorate. A *Washington Post* poll found that, of the 33 percent of the sample who reported seeing the ads, 73 percent disapproved of them.[76] Sarbanes's frustrated GOP opponent, Lawrence J. Hogan, threw up his hands in exasperation in one televised debate and exclaimed, "I hereby denounce NCPAC!"

NCPAC was of even greater value to Democratic Senator Daniel P. Moynihan of New York.[77] In 1981, NCPAC launched what it hoped would be a $750,000 radio and television campaign labeling Moynihan a "big spender." A Moynihan ally in the legal profession wrote an ominous-sounding letter to New York stations, pointing out that the stations were not immune from libel action for misrepresentations in any NCPAC ads they aired. As a consequence, not a single television spot from NCPAC was ever broadcast in the state.[78] As icing on the cake, Moynihan skillfully used NCPAC's threats to raise a considerable sum by direct mail, as well as to defuse lingering opposition to him within the Democratic party and to secure the endorsement of the Liberal party (whose leaders had once forsworn just such a course of action).

Conservative independent groups besides NCPAC had a disastrous year. Jesse Helms's Congressional Club, the PAC that raises more money than any other in the nation,[79] was trounced in its own backyard, losing all five targeted House races in North Carolina (including two incumbent Republican representatives). The Committee for the Survival of a Free Congress not only fared poorly in the general election but lost eight of eleven important party primary contests.[80]

In light of the record, the *Washington Post* not surprisingly judged the independent PACs' 1982 expenditures "the most futile since John Connally spent $11 million for one presidential delegate in

1980."[81] The conservative independent PACs certainly did not have a banner year, but to conclude from this that they are on the wane or even that their tactics are always ineffective is wrong. There is considerable evidence that negative advertising works,[82] and also that independent groups using negative tactics *can* be effective if the voters' mood and electoral circumstances permit.[83] New Right leaders, in fact, insist that the Republican failure to do better in 1982 can be traced to the White House's adoption of a defensive, stand-pat, stay-the-course theme rather than a negative, confrontational attack stance that tied Democrats to liberal positions on emotional issues (such as school prayer, busing, and racial quotas).[84]

A fair evaluation of the conservative PACs' future must take into account their phenomenal fund-raising abilities, the ideological fervor that motivates their leaders, the power of negative advertising, and the populist appeal of certain right-wing issues (from "welfare abuse" and school desegregation to crime and judicial leniency). A modification in tactics (perhaps toward more subtle negative advertising) and pioneering in other campaign technologies (from telephone banks to cable television) are both likely to occur, and those changes will keep the PACs politically influential. The independent conservatives were probably given too much credit for the 1980 election results and too much blame for the 1982 conservative defeats. They are but one element in a complex electoral stew, but they will remain part of the American election recipe so long as *Buckley* v. *Valeo* stands and their fund-raising efforts succeed. As one of their opponents, a liberal independent PAC leader, commented after the 1982 results were in: "It's foolish to dismiss any organization that can raise $7 million to $10 million in a political cycle. NCPAC and the Congressional Club are going to be around for a long time."[85]

New Liberal Independent Groups

Just as the Democratic party began the long climb to parity with its Republican rival in 1982, so too did liberal independent PACs organize to combat NCPAC and its kind.[86] The Progressive Political Action Committee (ProPAC), Independent Action (started by Democratic U.S. Representative Morris Udall and liberal direct mailer Roger Craver), and the Harrimans' Democrats for the '80s joined a short list of established liberal PACs headed by the thirty-four-year-old National Committee for an Effective Congress. But while the NCEC concentrated on direct and in-kind contributions to endorsed candidates, some of the new liberal PACs adopted the negative tactics of NCPAC.

Although their fund-raising proceeds were small compared with those of conservative groups,[87] the liberal PACs' first efforts secured press notice and met with some success. Democrats for the '80s rushed to Senator Paul Sarbanes's defense in Maryland after NCPAC's televised attacks, independently placing $20,000 of pro-Sarbanes radio spots. ProPAC introduced its own brand of negative advertising in New Mexico's Senate race, where Republican strategists later conceded that ProPAC had "softened up" incumbent Senator Harrison Schmitt for Jeff Bingaman, his eventually successful Democratic challenger. ProPAC also launched a two-year effort to defeat Senator Jesse Helms of North Carolina, who was not up for reelection until 1984. Full-page newspaper advertisements on the abortion issue appeared in North Carolina, captioned, "If you think Jesse Helms is against Big Government, think again! To keep government and Jesse Helms out of your bedroom, you must first get Jesse Helms out of the Senate."

If the limited-purse liberal groups played David to the conservative Goliath in 1982, the relationship is not necessarily a permanent one. As their donor lists expand and their coffers grow with time, they may be able to compete on a more equal footing. New Right activist Richard Viguerie, the most successful of all direct mailers, sized up the new liberal PACs well before the midterm elections: "Their effectiveness . . . is going to be limited this year and, though somewhat less so, in '84. But by '86, they should be up and around."[88]

Concluding Remarks

Even though they were the focus of much press coverage, then, political action committees in general and independent groups in particular had less of an effect in several ways on the congressional elections of 1982 than they had in 1980. The return of mainstream PACs to an incumbent strategy, the growing diversification and balance among PACs, the increased levels of contributions and services given by the political parties, and the evolution of PACs into a double-edged sword in election campaigns—all had a limiting effect. PACs are obviously still a very significant political force. Their war chests ensure as much, and predictions—such as the ones uttered about the independent groups—of PACs' declining in influence or even disappearing are wishful thinking. Greater sophistication of PAC targeting, coordination, technology, and campaign activity in 1982 suggests the more likely direction of political action committees' influence.

The PAC evolution in the midterm elections was a fascinating

phenomenon, but of greater long-term consequence were developments in the realm of the political parties. A major change in the
way parties influence, and are perceived by, candidates, officeholders,
and the voters themselves may be in the making.

Martin P. Wattenberg has recently shown that American voters
have *not* grown more alienated from the parties, but rather have
become more *neutral* in their evaluations of the parties. Why has this
happened? As Wattenberg explains it:

> The reason for party decline has not been that people no
> longer see any important differences between the parties. . . .
> Rather the problem which the parties must face is that they
> are considered less relevant in solving the most important
> domestic and foreign policy issues of the day. *In the voters'
> minds, the parties are losing their association with the can-
> didates and the issues which the candidates claim to stand
> for.* [Emphasis added.] [89]

The association between parties and candidates weakened partly
because the parties ceased to be very important in the process of
electing their candidates. Since candidates were not beholden to the
party for their elections, they were not responsive to the party's
needs or platform once in office.

The new directions in which both major parties are moving
appear to be changing the relationship between party and candidate
in a fundamental way. The coordinated expenditures, institutional
advertising, media services, tracking polls, candidate schools, and all
the rest are having the effect of drawing candidates closer to the
parties. Particularly on the Republican side, where party renewal is in
full bloom, the candidates voice similar policy themes, take much the
same approach on at least some basic issues, and have a stake in the
party's present well-being and future development. They are beholden
to the party, too; sizable contributions and significant campaign
services are not easily forgotten, and there is always the implied threat
of their withdrawal in reelection campaigns should the officeholder
prove too much of a maverick. The best illustration to date can be
seen in 1981, when House and Senate Republicans were unusually and
exceedingly unified on the Reagan budget and tax votes.[90] It may well
be that congressional party cohesion on basic issues will increase, that
voters will begin to perceive more strongly the connection between
the party and its issues and candidates, and that a more party-
responsible system will gradually emerge in the future. If so, the
national party committees, thanks to their institutional adaptation of
the new campaign technologies, will be able to take much of the credit.

Notes

1. Personal interview, New York, July 24, 1979.
2. "Running with the PACs," *Time*, October 25, 1982, p. 20.
3. As quoted in the *Washington Post*, November 5, 1982.
4. 1971 FECA: 86 Stat. 3 (1971); 1974 amendments: 88 Stat. 1263 (1974); 1976 amendments: 90 Stat. 475 (1976); 1979 amendments: Public Law 96-187.
5. See Larry Sabato, *The Rise of Political Consultants: New Ways of Winning Elections* (New York: Basic Books, 1981), pp. 267–301.
6. The primary, the runoff, and the general election are each considered separate elections; thus, one House candidate could receive as much as $15,000 from the national party (*and* $15,000 from the national congressional campaign committee *and* $15,000 from the state party) if he takes part in all three elections. Since most states do not provide for runoffs, the most a House candidate could hope to collect from his party committees would be $30,000 in direct contributions.
7. 2 U.S.C. § 441 a(d); 11 CFR 110.7.
8. Coordinated expenditures differ from direct contributions in that the party, as well as the candidate, must exercise some control over the spending of coordinated funds, whereas direct money can be spent at the sole discretion of the candidate.
9. These figures combine the maximums for both direct contributions and coordinated expenditures.
10. The Democrats challenged this device, but the U.S. Supreme Court ruled against them in 1981.
11. See Richard E. Cohen, "Giving Till It Hurts: 1982 Campaign Prompts New Look at Financing Races," *National Journal*, December 18, 1982, pp. 2144–53. The GOP gave $7.5 million in aid to House candidates and $9.2 million to Senate contenders. The comparable figures for the Democrats were $753,000 and $2.5 million.
12. Gary C. Jacobson, *The Politics of Congressional Elections* (Boston: Little, Brown and Company, 1983), pp. 58–59.
13. Figures cited are official Federal Election Commission totals for the 1981–1982 election cycle. See also U.S. House of Representatives, Democratic Study Group, *Party Campaign Funds—A Widening Gap*, Special Report No. 98-1, Washington, D.C., January 5, 1983.
14. As quoted in the *Washington Post*, October 17, 1982.
15. Sabato, *The Rise of Political Consultants*, pp. 220–63.
16. See Federal Election Commission, *FEC Reports on Financial Activity: 1981–82 Interim Report No. 2, Party and Non-party Political Committees*, Washington, D.C., October 7, 1982. See also Rhodes Cook, "Democrats Develop Tactics: Laying Groundwork for 1984," *Congressional Quarterly Weekly*, July 3, 1982, p. 1595.
17. So-called soft money is any contribution to a party that cannot be legally spent in federal campaigns for federal candidates. As opposed to

hard money given by individuals and PACs to be spent on congressional or presidential campaigns, soft money is donated directly from corporate treasuries, union dues, or individuals (over and above the FECA contributory limits). Under the 1979 amendments to FECA, unlimited sums may be spent by political parties for getting out the vote, for purchasing articles such as bumper strips and buttons, and for other party-building activities. Also, soft money can be used for state candidates (for governor, etc.) in states without restrictions on direct corporate and union contributions. Often a party will allocate the cost of certain activities to both hard and soft money accounts, based on the proportion of assistance provided to federal versus state candidates by the activity. Obviously, this is a difficult determination to make in many cases, and so the parties have had considerable flexibility in such matters. In 1982 the Republicans spent soft money primarily on their various institutional advertising programs. Democrats devoted their soft money partly to advertising but mainly to voter registration and get-out-the-vote drives in key districts and states.

18. A sample size of 150 to 200 has a large margin of error; thus, a single night's sample would be insufficient to establish public opinion with accuracy. That is why it is necessary to accumulate several evenings' totals in a rolling or moving average.

19. It should be noted, however, that tracking polls with samples of 500 can offer only rough estimates of shifts in the electorate. The margin of error is still relatively high and by itself may account for the variations in sample results from day to day. Tracking polls should always be interpreted with caution.

20. See David S. Broder, "Tracking: Daily Polls Helped GOP Keep Senate Edge," *Washington Post*, November 7, 1982.

21. The national GOP committees and their contracted pollsters cannot actually give the individual campaigns precise polling figures without charging the considerable cost of the poll against the permissible level of party contributions to the campaign. But the strategists *are* allowed to describe general trends and to suggest remedial action—which is, of course, all any campaign really needs to know. (This is yet another illustration of the ability of inventive political professionals to circumvent the strictures of FECA.)

22. These savings are hardly insubstantial, given the size of most campaign advertising budgets. See Sabato, *The Rise of Political Consultants*, pp. 179–82.

23. Ibid., pp. 293–94.

24. The commercial was soon taken off the air after criticism about the appropriateness of the caricatures of Carter and O'Neill.

25. According to Wirthlin, though in June most of the elderly believed that Reagan had decreased their social security, by late July a majority of those willing to express an opinion thought Reagan had actually increased payments.

26. The AP/NBC poll was taken by telephone on October 18 and 19,

1982. A total of 1,595 adults were questioned, and the survey had a margin of error of ± 3 percent.

27. As quoted in Elizabeth Drew, "Politics and Money—I," *New Yorker*, December 6, 1982, p. 68.

28. Ibid., pp. 67–68.

29. Patrick Caddell, "Why the Democrats May Win Big," *Washington Post*, October 17, 1982.

30. In both 1980 and 1982, Democrats, as a congressional candidate group, were more successful than Republicans in raising funds from individuals *and* PACs. But the disproportionately large number of Democratic incumbents causes the figures to be skewed. In marginal and open seat races, GOP candidates have had a clear financial edge in the past two elections.

31. See Edward R. Tufte, "Determinants of the Outcomes of Midterm Congressional Elections," *American Political Science Review*, vol. 69 (1975), pp. 816–26; Tufte, *Political Control of the Economy* (Princeton, N.J.: Princeton University Press, 1978). See also Gerald H. Kramer, "Short-Term Fluctuations in U.S. Voting Behavior," *American Political Science Review*, vol. 65 (1971), pp. 131–43.

32. Gary C. Jacobson and Samuel Kernell, "Strategy and Choice in the 1982 Congressional Election," *PS*, vol. 15 (Summer 1982), pp. 423–30.

33. As quoted in *National Journal*, December 18, 1982, p. 2172.

34. For an explanation of the direct mail process, see Sabato, *The Rise of Political Consultants*, pp. 226–33.

35. The spot was conceived by DNC communications director Robert Newman and produced by First Tuesday, a Phoenix, Arizona, advertising firm.

36. These ads were produced by political consultant David Sawyer of New York.

37. Besides the radio ad on social security mentioned earlier, the party also produced a twenty-minute film for candidates to use before senior citizen groups and centered much of the direct mail effort on the social security issue.

38. Willders also made a second GOP ad in 1981, a radio commercial supporting the Reagan tax cut bill.

39. The NRCC had paid Willders $3,400 plus residuals for his 1980 ad. The DNC paid him nothing, but radio-television director Robert Hirschfeld, who produced the spot, arranged for Willders to meet Senator Edward M. Kennedy, the quid pro quo set by Willders.

40. See *Federalist* No. 10. See also Michael J. Malbin's discussion of PACs' influence in "The Problem of PAC-Journalism," *Public Opinion*, vol. 5 (December/January 1983), pp. 15–16, 59.

41. A review of the history and development of PACs is beyond the scope of this paper. See instead Joseph E. Cantor, *Political Action Committees: Their Evolution and Growth and Their Implications for the Political System* (Washington, D.C.: Congressional Research Service, Re-

port No. 82-92 GOV, November 6, 1981; updated May 7, 1982). See also Herbert E. Alexander, *Financing Politics: Money, Elections, and Political Reform* (Washington, D.C.: Congressional Quarterly Press, 1980); Congressional Quarterly, Inc., *Dollar Politics*, 3d ed. (Washington, D.C.: Congressional Quarterly, 1982), pp. 43–61; Edwin M. Epstein, "An Irony of Electoral Reform," *Regulation*, vol. 3 (May–June, 1979), pp. 35–41; Gary C. Jacobson, *Money in Congressional Elections* (New Haven, Conn.: Yale University Press, 1980); Michael J. Malbin, ed., *Parties, Interest Groups, and Campaign Finance Laws* (Washington, D.C.: American Enterprise Institute, 1979); and Sabato, *The Rise of Political Consultants*, pp. 267–84.

42. Total includes 103 corporations without stock.

43. Total includes general membership and health organizations.

44. Although 3,371 PACs were in existence as of the end of 1982, it should be noted that only 2,124 of them (1,181 corporate, 209 labor, 246 independent, 452 trade, and 36 cooperatives) actually made contributions to 1982 congressional candidates.

45. Actually, Reagan is now only "chairman emeritus" of CFR. Former Reagan White House aide Lyn Nofziger chairs the committee.

46. Another potential presidential candidate, Senator Jesse Helms of North Carolina, had the largest PAC of all, the Congressional Club, though its official purpose is not to promote Helms.

47. The $83.1 million donated to congressional candidates by PACs in 1981–1982 includes only direct contributions in congressional races; more than double that amount ($190.4 million) was spent on local and state contests, independent activities, and administrative costs.

48. See Norman J. Ornstein, Thomas E. Mann, Michael J. Malbin, and John F. Bibby, *Vital Statistics on Congress, 1982* (Washington, D.C.: American Enterprise Institute, 1982), table 3-5.

49. Cohen, "Giving Till It Hurts," pp. 2150–51.

50. Maxwell Glen, "Labor Trying to Bring Its Rebellious Members Back to the Democratic Fold," *National Journal*, October 30, 1982, pp. 1837–40.

51. *Washington Post*, November 9, 1982.

52. Dom Bonafede, "Women's Movement Broadens the Scope of Its Role in American Politics," *National Journal*, December 11, 1982, pp. 2108–11.

53. Dale Russakoff, "Getting Out 'Green Vote' for Friends of Nature," *Washington Post*, October 5, 1982; and *National Journal*, November 6, 1982, p. 1891.

54. *National Journal*, November 6, 1982, pp. 1875, 1910.

55. Whether the council and PeacePAC had any major part in the victories is debatable. In a good Democratic year, liberal groups will obviously have a high win ratio; in a good Republican year, conservative organizations will do well. But in either case, the groups may have had relatively little to do with the victories they claim credit for.

56. The thirty-one key races are listed in the *National Journal*, December 18, 1982, pp. 2150–51.

57. See Drew, "Politics and Money—I," pp. 78–88.

58. Thomas B. Edsall, "Business Tries Hand at Feeding GOP Early in Marginal Races," *Washington Post*, September 12, 1982; "PACs Bankrolling GOP Challengers," *Washington Post*, September 14, 1982; "Independent Oil's Political Prospectors Drill a Lot of Dry Wells," *Washington Post*, November 17, 1982.

59. Drew, "Politics and Money—I," p. 123.

60. Ibid.

61. Dom Bonafede, "Some Things Don't Change—Cost of 1982 Congressional Races Higher Than Ever," *National Journal*, October 30, 1982, p. 1834.

62. Drew, "Politics and Money—I," pp. 122–23. However, see final FEC figures on this point.

63. Mark Green, "Political Pac-Man," *New Republic*, December 13, 1982, p. 21.

64. See, for example, Drew, "Politics and Money—I."

65. Paul Taylor, "AMA Finds It Can Use Polling Data to Boost Election Donations Legally," *Washington Post*, October 6, 1982.

66. Sabato, *The Rise of Political Consultants*, pp. 282–83.

67. *The Political Report*, December 16, 1982, p. 5.

68. Drew, "Politics and Money—I," pp. 67–68.

69. Paul Taylor, "For Business PACs This Year, Suitable Targets Are in Short Supply," *Washington Post*, July 27, 1982.

70. About 19 percent disagreed, and 10 percent were unsure. From *Public Opinion*, vol. 5 (August/September 1982), p. 53.

71. 96 S.Ct. 612 (1976) or 424 U.S. 1 (1976).

72. See Sabato, *The Rise of Political Consultants*, pp. 281–84.

73. See, for example, the excellent series by Robert Timberg, "The PAC Business," *Baltimore Sun*, July 11–19, 1982.

74. NCPAC, however, claims an overall success rate of 70 percent, once NCPAC-endorsed incumbents are included in the total. See Terry Dolan, "NCPAC Didn't Lose—We Won," *Washington Post*, November 7, 1982. But as David Broder points out, NCPAC lost virtually all of the races where it spent most of its money. See David Broder, "NCPAC's New Math," *Washington Post*, November 10, 1982.

75. *Washington Post*, October 25, 1982.

76. The poll was a random-sample telephone survey of 609 registered Maryland adults taken October 7–10, 1982, by the Survey Research Center of the University of Maryland. The margin of error is ± 4 percent.

77. *New Republic*, October 11, 1982, p. 15.

78. Some radio spots, however, had already been aired. Interestingly, media stations throughout the country appeared to be much more reluctant in 1982 to air negative independent advertising of any stripe. Nuclear freeze spots, sponsored independently by a liberal group seeking to publicize certain congressmen's opposition to a nuclear weapons freeze, were also refused air time in a number of localities. See Philip M. Stern, "How TV Gagged Our Freeze Ads," *Washington Post*, November 21, 1982.

79. For background on the Congressional Club, see Paul Taylor, "Helms Modernizes GOP Political Machine for the Electronic Age," *Washington Post*, October 15, 1982. See also Irwin B. Arieff, Nadine Cohodas, and Richard Whittle, "Sen. Helms Builds a Machine of Interlinked Organizations to Shape Both Politics, Policy," *Congressional Quarterly Weekly*, March 6, 1982, pp. 499–505.

80. Richard E. Cohen, "Business, Conservative PACs—Bigger Yet, but Their Influence May Be Waning," *National Journal*, August 7, 1982, p. 1373.

81. "A Vote against the Aginners," *Washington Post*, November 5, 1982.

82. Sabato, *The Rise of Political Consultants*, pp. 165–74.

83. See, for instance, V. Lance Tarrance, Jr., *Negative Campaigns and Negative Votes: The 1980 Elections* (Washington, D.C.: Free Congress Research and Education Foundation, 1982).

84. Morton Kondracke, "Hard Times for the Hard Right," *New Republic*, December 20, 1982, p. 22.

85. Victor Kamber of the Progressive Political Action Committee (Pro-PAC), quoted in the *Washington Post*, November 15, 1982.

86. See Maxwell Glen and James K. Popkin, "Liberal PACs Learning It Won't Be Easy to Stem the Conservative Tide," *National Journal*, March 20, 1982, pp. 500–501.

87. Jeremy Gaunt, "Money Flows to the Right in 1982 Campaigns," *Congressional Quarterly Weekly*, February 27, 1982, p. 482.

88. Glen and Popkin, "Liberal PACs Learning," p. 501.

89. Martin P. Wattenberg, "The Decline of Political Partisanship in the United States: Negativity or Neutrality?" *American Political Science Review*, vol. 75 (1981), pp. 941–50.

90. See *National Journal*, May 8, 1982, pp. 800–810; and Drew, "Politics and Money—I," pp. 101–5.

4

State House Elections at Midterm

John F. Bibby

After each midterm election there is a consuming desire on the part of commentators and partisans to find in the election results an answer to the question of whether or not the electorate approves or disapproves of the president's policies. Interpreters of midterm elections, however, show a marked lack of consensus. In 1982, the Republican loss of twenty-six House seats was viewed by the Democratic Speaker of the House, Thomas P. O'Neill, as a "disastrous defeat" for the president's party; the same numbers were seen by the Republican White House as normal losses for a midterm election and, therefore, not as a reason to change course. Besides partisanship, one of the reasons for the difficulty in interpreting the midterm congressional elections is that the net change of party seats is normally such a small percentage of the total chamber membership. The 1982 elections were no exception to this pattern: a net switch of twenty-six (6.0 percent) seats in the House and no change in the partisan composition of the Senate. Like most recent midterm elections, the 1982 House and Senate elections convey more of an impression of stability than they do of change in spite of the controversial nature of administration policies.

Ironically, it was not at the national level that the effect of the 1982 midterm elections was greatest. Rather, it was in the states that partisan change was most apparent. There was a change in party control in eleven of the thirty-six states in which governorships were at stake, resulting in a net Democratic gain of seven (see table 4–1). Change was no less visible in the state legislative races. Democrats captured eleven legislative chambers from the GOP while surrendering two chambers and in four states gained control of both houses of the legislature. As a result, in January 1983 the Democrats

An earlier version of this paper was presented at the Public Policy Week conference sponsored by the American Enterprise Institute, Washington, D.C., December 6–9, 1982, and published in *Public Opinion* (February/March 1983).

TABLE 4–1
Extent of Change in Partisan Control of State Governments, 1982

Governorships[a]	Republicans	Democrats
Pre-1982 election lineup	23	27
Post-1982 election lineup	16	34
Governorships gained	2	9
Governorships lost	9	2
Net gain/loss	−7	+7
Incumbents reelected	6	13
Incumbents defeated	4	1
Open seats won	2	10

State Legislatures[b]	Republicans	Democrats
Pre-1982 election lineup		
Chambers controlled	35	63
States in which party controlled		
both houses	15	29
Number of state legislators	2,941	4,478
Post-1982 election lineup		
Chambers controlled	26	72
States in which party controls		
both houses	11	34
Number of state legislators[c]	2,718	4,655
Chambers gained	+2	+11
Chambers lost	−11	−2
Net chambers gained/lost	−9	+9
State legislatures where party gained		
control of both houses	−4	+4
Chambers in which party gained seats[d]		
(no change: 14 chambers)	24	51

a. Elections held in 36 states. Republicans were defending 16 seats; Democrats were defending 20 seats.
b. Elections held in 45 states; Nebraska's nonpartisan legislature not included.
c. Pre- and post-election numbers do not match because Illinois elected to eliminate fifty-nine seats in its State House of Representatives, and four states, North Dakota, Nevada, New York, and Wyoming, decided to increase membership in six legislative chambers by a total of fifteen seats. Sixteen seats nationwide are vacant or held by independents.
d. Both parties lost seats in New Hampshire because of the election of two independents and a tie in one district.
Sources: *Congressional Quarterly Weekly Report* (November 13, 1982), pp. 2848–49; *1981 Republican Almanac* (Washington, D.C.: Republican National Committee, 1981), pp. 695, 699; state legislative election data provided by the National Conference of State Legislatures. William Pound, "The Election's Over, but the Party's Just Beginning," *State Legislatures*, vol. 9, no. 1 (January 1983), pp. 10–12.

controlled both houses of the legislature in thirty-four states while the Republicans controlled eleven legislatures; in four states control was split between the two parties.

The Outcome of Midterm Gubernatorial Elections

Shifts in Party Control. The significant losses suffered by the president's party in the 1982 midterm elections were consistent with the pattern of gubernatorial elections since 1950.[1] In every midterm election between 1950 and 1982 the president's party has lost governorships, except in 1962 when there was no net change in the number of state houses held by each party (see table 4–2). During this period, the average loss of governorships for the president's party has been six. Republican governors have been particularly vulnerable at midterm. The party has never lost fewer than five governorships at midterm and has averaged a loss of seven. Democratic losses at midterm have been less severe, with an average loss of five governorships.

These data demonstrate that midterm gubernatorial elections are highly susceptible to national trends. Indeed, change in partisan control of governorships is likely to be greater than the extent of switched party control of seats in Congress. A further irony concerning gubernatorial elections is their marked independence from national trends in presidential years. In four of the eight presidential elections since 1950, the party of the winning presidential candidate has actually lost governorships (1956, 1960, 1964, and 1972). Even in landslide years such as 1964 and 1972, the party of the successful presidential candidate suffered a loss of governorships. These data clearly evidence the increased incidence of ticket splitting between presidential and gubernatorial elections since the turn of the century.

In the period 1896–1908, however, presidential and gubernatorial results coincided in 89.5 percent of elections. The 1920 election illustrates this tendency for the same party to win simultaneous presidential and gubernatorial elections. In that year, the Republicans won the governorship in each of the twenty-eight nonsouthern states carried by their party's presidential nominee, Warren G. Harding. The same pattern was also present in the Franklin D. Roosevelt and Dwight D. Eisenhower landslides of 1936 and 1952, when the same party won the electoral college votes and the governorship in 90 percent of the states holding simultaneous elections.[2] By contrast, only 63 percent of the presidential and gubernatorial results coincided in the 1976 and 1980 elections (see table 4–3). Recently, the Democrats have been least effective in capturing state houses while winning the

113

TABLE 4–2

RESULTS OF GUBERNATORIAL ELECTIONS, 1950–1982

Year	Party Winning Presidential Election	Governorships at Stake Total	Rep.	Dem.	Ind.	Republican Percentage of Major-Party Vote	Election Result Rep.	Dem.	Ind.	Gains/Losses Rep.	Dem.
1950		33	15	18	0	53.1	25	23	0	+6	−6
1952	Rep.	31	15	16	0	47.0	30	18	0	+5	−5
1954		33	23	10	0	47.2	21	27	0	−9	+9
1956	Rep.	30	15	15	0	46.8	19	29	0	−2	+2
1958		33	13	20	0	44.1	14	35	0	−5	+6
1960	Dem.	27	12	15	0	46.5	16	34	0	+2	−1
1962		35	14	21	0	50.0	16	34	0	No change	
1964	Dem.	25	7	18	0	45.2	17	33	0	+1	−1
1966		35	14	21	0	53.1	25	25	0	+8	−8
1968	Rep.	21	8	13	0	47.3	31	19	0	+6	−6
1970		35	24	11	0	48.6	21	29	0	−10	+10
1972	Rep.	18	8	10	0	49.7	19	31	0	−2	+2
1974		35	11	24	0	43.6	13	36	1	−6	+5

1976	Dem.	14	6	8	0	50.8	12	37	1	−1	+1
1978		36	9	26	1	47.8	18	32	0	+6	−5
1980	Rep.	13	3	10	0	50.0	23	27	0	+5	−5
1982		36	16	20	0	45.6	16	34	0	−7	+7

Summary

Midterm elections
Average number of governorships lost by:

President's party	6.2
Republicans	7.4
Democrats	4.8

Presidential election years

Average gain/loss for party of winning presidential candidate	+1.4
Average gain/loss when winning presidential party is Republican	+2.4
Average gain/loss when winning presidential party is Democratic	−0.33

SOURCES: *1981 Republican Almanac* (Washington, D.C.: Republican National Committee, 1981), p. 695; *Congressional Quarterly Weekly Report* (February 19, 1983), p. 387; *Statistical Abstract of the United States, 1953–1981*.

TABLE 4–3

TICKET SPLITTING IN PRESIDENTIAL AND
GUBERNATORIAL ELECTIONS, 1880–1980
(percent)

Period	States with Gubernatorial and Presidential Candidates of Same Party Carrying the State	States with Split Outcomes for Governor and President
1880–1892	93.1	6.9
1896–1908	89.5	10.5
1912–1924	81.2	18.8
1928–1940	77.8	22.2
1944–1956	75.5	24.5
1960–1972	56.0	44.0
1976–1980	63.0	37.0

SOURCE: Data for the years 1880 to 1972 are taken from Larry Sabato, *Goodbye to Good-Time Charlie* (Lexington, Mass.: Lexington Books, 1978), p. 147. His data have been supplemented with 1976–1980 election returns.

presidency. Between 1950 and 1980, the party netted a governorship only once during a successful presidential campaign (1976). The GOP, by contrast, has more frequently registered gubernatorial gains when winning the presidency (their average gain has been two governorships).

One of the reasons for the modest shifts in partisan control of governorships in presidential years is the declining number of state executives elected with the president. Whereas in 1932–1934, thirty-four states chose governors in presidential election years, that number was reduced to thirteen by 1980. Thirty-six of the states now elect their governors at midterm. Part of the rationale for moving gubernatorial elections to the midterm time slot was to insulate state elections from national trends. It is apparent from the data presented here, however, that this objective has not been achieved. Indeed, national trends appear to have a greater impact on midterm gubernatorial elections than on those occurring simultaneously with presidential elections.

In presidential years, the gubernatorial candidates are not the most prominent persons on the ballot. But at midterm, they are the most visible candidates seeking public office. Governors are widely perceived to be powerful officials, and they are usually involved in their state's major policy controversies. With this policy involvement comes inevitable discontent with past actions; and with perceived power and visibility comes a strong likelihood of being held accountable for the condition of the state. As the candidate at the head of the ticket, a governor stands exposed as the most readily available target of voter discontent, since the president is not on the ballot.

The extent of negative voting (a tendency of voters disapproving of the president and his policies to turn out and vote against his party) in state elections has never been systematically measured. Yet this pattern has been identified in congressional midterm elections.[3] It is, therefore, quite likely that the phenomenon of negative voting is even more pronounced in gubernatorial elections than in congressional ones because of the governor's higher visibility. Negative voting may also be encouraged when conditions make it possible to launch harsh attacks on virtually all candidates of the president's party.

The 1982 elections certainly found the Republican gubernatorial aspirants in an exposed and defensive posture because of the depressed state of the economy nationally. Democratic nominees sought to exploit this Republican vulnerability by nationalizing their campaigns to focus on the adversity created in their states by the recession. The specific issues used by Democratic nominees varied from state to state, but the theme of Republican responsibility for the recession and Democratic concern for the disadvantaged was pervasive; for George Wallace in Alabama it was a campaign against "rich Republicans" and unemployment; Bob Kerrey in Nebraska stressed the effect of high interest rates on farmers and recession-induced state deficits; Michigan's James Blanchard emphasized jobs and economic development; Mark White in Texas sought to capitalize on Governor William Clements's support for Reagan's policies while railing in a neopopulist manner against high interest and utility rates; William Clinton in Arkansas campaigned against cuts in Medicaid services to the poor; and Wisconsin's Anthony Earl talked of meeting the challenges of mounting state deficits and economic revitalization while preserving the state's progressive heritage. Nationwide, Democrats used the economic hard times to advantage and fought their elections on state variations of a national campaign theme. A significant Republican loss of governorships was, therefore, to be expected. The actual GOP loss of seven was consistent with the average loss (6.2) suffered by the president's party at midterm.

Most of the successful Republicans and those that ran better than expected were able to deflect attention away from the national issue of the economy. Winner George Deukmejian (California), for example, and narrow loser Lewis Lehrman (New York) linked their campaigns to anticrime themes and ballot initiatives (anti–gun control and recall of judges). In Iowa, Terry Branstad capitalized on his opponent's failure to pay state income taxes, while New Hampshire's John Sununu pledged opposition to new income and sales taxes—a pledge that Democratic incumbent Hugh Gallen did not take. Others like William Janklow (South Dakota), Richard Thornburgh (Pennsylvania), and Victor Atiyeh (Oregon) built personal followings and stressed their stewardship in office. These successful Republicans managed to divorce their campaigns from the national campaign and focus voter attention on state matters. But in most states, the 1982 midterm gubernatorial elections were also national elections, and as a result the GOP suffered.

Incumbency

The governorships of thirty-six states were at stake in 1982. In twenty-five of those states the incumbent governor sought renomination, and twenty-four (96 percent) were successful. Only Edward King failed to gain renomination when he lost the Democratic primary. Most incumbents, however, had a relatively easy time securing renomination. Twelve were renominated without primary opposition (six Democrats in Colorado, Connecticut, Idaho, New Hampshire, Rhode Island, and South Carolina; and six Republicans in Arkansas, Illinois, Pennsylvania, South Dakota, Tennessee, and Vermont). In addition, nine incumbents were renominated with only minor opposition (Republicans in Oregon and Texas; Democrats in Arizona, Florida, Kansas, Maine, Maryland, Oklahoma, and Wyoming). Only the Republican incumbents in Nebraska and Nevada, each of whom was defeated in the general election, and the Democrat in Hawaii faced significant primary opponents.[4] The normal pattern of incumbent governors' securing their parties' nomination without serious difficulty in the vast preponderance of instances was, therefore, maintained again in 1982.[5]

Eleven of the incumbent governors in 1982 did not seek reelection. Four (Republicans in Alaska and Ohio and Democrats in Georgia and New Mexico) were constitutionally banned from running for an additional consecutive term. Seven of the incumbent governors chose not to stand for reelection, and of that number at least three—Albert Quie (Minnesota), Hugh Carey (New York), and Forrest James (Alabama)—faced serious challenges either in the primary or in the general election. Only one governor, Jerry Brown of California, decided to forgo another term as governor in order to seek election to the U.S. Senate. Those retirees who sought to select their successors were notably unsuccessful: Quie's handpicked successor, Lieutenant Governor Lou Wangberg, won the Minnesota Republican Convention's endorsement but failed to win the primary; in Michigan outgoing Governor William Milliken supported the bid of Lieutenant Governor James H. Brickley, who also lost the primary; and Mayor Edward Koch of New York City lost the Democratic primary even though he was endorsed by Governor Hugh Carey.[6]

The greater vulnerability of governors compared with that of representatives and senators in general elections is well documented. House incumbents have averaged over 90 percent reelection rates since 1960, and senators have had a reelection average of almost 80 percent. By contrast, gubernatorial incumbents have won on the average 71 percent of the time (see table 4–4). The fate of incumbent governors in 1982 was similar to this longer-term pattern. Five incumbents (21 percent) of the twenty-four nominated for reelection in 1982 were defeated (see table 4–1). The effect of the national Democratic trend was strongly in evidence as thirteen of fourteen (93 percent) incumbent Democrats and six of ten GOP governors renewed their state house franchises. Not only did all but one of the Democratic incumbents win reelection, but nine of the thirteen winners also increased their percentage of the vote over that which they had received in 1978. The exceptions were John V. Evans (Idaho), George Ariyoshi (Hawaii), and Harry R. Hughes (Maryland).[7] Only three of the successful Republican incumbents were able to increase their vote percentage: Lamar Alexander (Tennessee), Victor G. Atiyeh (Oregon), and William J. Janklow (South Dakota).

The national Democratic trend in gubernatorial elections also had an effect in states where no incumbent was on the ballot. In ten (83 percent) of the twelve open seat races, the Democrats emerged victorious. They seized control of four midwestern states with retiring GOP governors (Minnesota, Michigan, Ohio, and Wisconsin) and in Alaska. Only in California did the Republicans capture a governorship occupied by a retiring Democratic incumbent. In a sea of Democratic state house victories about the only Republican island was the nation's largest state—California.

Interparty Competition. A pattern of increased interparty competition in gubernatorial elections was maintained in 1982. In seventeen states the winner received less than 55 percent of the vote (twelve Democrats and five Republicans). In only four states did the successful candidate receive more than 65 percent of the vote (see table 4–5). There is no distinct regional pattern in the extent of interparty competition that was present. States from all regions, including the old Confederacy, are found in the most competitive category, while the least competitive races also took place in various regions (for

TABLE 4-4

INCUMBENCY AND PARTISAN TURNOVER IN GUBERNATORIAL ELECTIONS, 1957–1982

Year	Number of Elections	Elections with Incumbents			Elections with No Incumbents		Percentage of Incumbents Who Lost	Percentage of All Elections with Incumbents
		Total	Incumbent won	Incumbent lost	Total	Party turnover		
1957–58	36	22	13	9	14	4	41	61
1959–60	30	14	8	6	16	7	43	47
1961–62	37	26	16	10	11	3	38	70
1963–64	28	14	12	2	14	3	14	50
1965–66	37	22	15	7	15	6	32	59
1967–68	24	14	10	4	10	6	29	58
1969–70	37	24	17	7	13	10	29	65
1971–72	21	9	7	2	12	4	22	43
1973–74	37	22	17	5	15	9	23	59
1975–76	17	9	7	2	8	5	22	53
1977–78	38	22	17	5	16	8	23	58
1979–80	16	10	7	3	6	2	30	63
1981–82	38	24	19	5	14	9	21	63
Total	396	232	165	67	164	76	29	59

SOURCE: The data compiled by Malcolm Jewell and David Olson, *American State Political Parties and Elections*, rev. ed. (Homewood, Ill.: Dorsey Press, 1982), p. 213, have been updated to reflect the 1981–1982 elections.

TABLE 4–5

INTERPARTY COMPETITION: WINNING GUBERNATORIAL
CANDIDATES' PERCENTAGE OF THE TOTAL VOTE, 1982

	Winners' Percentage of Vote				
	Under 55	55.0–59.9	60–64.9	65–70	70.1+
Republicans	5	2	1	0	1
Democrats	12	5	7	2	1
Total					
Number	17	7	8	2	2
Percentage	47.2	19.4	22.2	5.6	5.6

SOURCE: *Congressional Quarterly Weekly Report* (February 19, 1983), pp. 386–94.

example, in the Mountain, Southern, New England, and West North
Central regions). With the decline in the influence of party identification on voter choice, it is possible for both parties to compete
effectively in every part of the nation.

Regional Patterns. The most significant GOP losses occurred in the
North Central (midwestern) regions, where the party lost control of
five states, including the large industrial states of Ohio and Michigan,
along with Minnesota, Nebraska, and Wisconsin (see table 4–6).
The Democrats also reasserted their dominance in the South by
winning back the states of Arkansas and Texas and leaving the GOP
with only one southern governor, David Treen of Louisiana.

A review of the regional distribution of partisan control of
governorships reveals that control of governorships has little relationship to patterns of presidential voting in 1980. Ronald Reagan's
strongest area in 1980 was the Mountain states, yet Democratic
governors reside in the executive residences of all eight Mountain
states. A similar pattern emerges for the southern and Border states.
These areas of Reagan strength in 1980 find the GOP in control of
only two of fifteen state houses. Ironically, the Republicans picked
up a governorship (New Hampshire) in New England, Reagan's
weakest region. The state electorates of 1982 were obviously highly
volatile and susceptible to mobilization by either party in a given year.

The Outcome of Midterm State Legislative Elections

Shifts in Party Control. Shifts in partisan control of state legislatures,
like shifts in party dominance of governorships, have frequently been

TABLE 4–6
REGIONAL DISTRIBUTION OF GUBERNATORIAL
SEATS BY PARTY, 1982

Region	Republican	Democratic	Change
Northeast			
New England	2	4	+1 Rep.
Middle Atlantic	3	1	No change
North Central			
East North Central	2	3	+3 Dem.
West North Central	4	3	+2 Dem.
South and Border			
South	1	9	+2 Dem.
Border	1	4	No change
West			
Mountain	0	8	+1 Dem.
Pacific	3	2	No change

NOTE: The states within each region are as follows: *New England:* Connecticut, Maine, Massachusetts, New Hampshire, Rhode Island, Vermont; *Middle Atlantic:* Delaware, New Jersey, New York, Pennsylvania; *East North Central:* Illinois, Indiana, Michigan, Ohio, Wisconsin; *West North Central:* Iowa, Kansas, Minnesota, Missouri, Nebraska, North Dakota, South Dakota; *South:* Alabama, Arkansas, Florida, Georgia, Louisiana, Mississippi, North Carolina, South Carolina, Texas, Virginia; *Border:* Kentucky, Maryland, Oklahoma, Tennessee, West Virginia; *Mountain:* Arizona, Colorado, Idaho, Montana, Nevada, New Mexico, Utah, Wyoming; *Pacific:* Alaska, California, Hawaii, Oregon, Washington.

SOURCES: *Congressional Quarterly Weekly Report* (February 19, 1983), pp. 386–94; *1981 Republican Almanac* (Washington, D.C.: Republican National Committee, 1981), p. 693.

a more sensitive barometer of political change at midterm than congressional elections. In each midterm election since 1950 the president's party has lost control of legislative chambers. The net average number of chambers lost in this period has been thirteen. The 1982 GOP loss of nine chambers is, therefore, slightly below average (see table 4–7).

The consistent pattern of midterm losses of legislative chambers by the president's party is reflected, of course, in the number of states where party control of *both* houses of the legislature changed (table 4–8). In some midterm years, these shifts in party control can be of substantial magnitude, as in 1966 when the Democrats lost control of twelve state legislatures. The average loss of legislative control at

TABLE 4–7
RESULTS OF LEGISLATIVE ELECTIONS, 1950–1982

Year	Republicans Control Both Houses	Split Control	Nonpartisan Legislature	Democrats Control Both Houses	Net Number of Chambers Gained/Lost Republicans	Net Number of Chambers Gained/Lost Democrats
1982	11	4	1	34	− 9	+ 9
1980	15	5	1	29	+ 5	− 5
1978	11	8	1	30	+12	−12
1976	4	10	1	35	+ 2	− 2
1974	4	8	1	37	−24	+24
1972	16	8	2	24	No change	
1970	16	8	2	24	− 8	+ 8
1968	20	8	2	20	+ 7	− 7
1966	17	7	2	24	+18	−18
1964	7	9	2	32	−19	+19
1962	18	6	2	24	+ 9	− 9
1960	14	5	2	29	+ 9	− 9
1958	7	8	2	32	−18	+18
1956	17	6	2	23	− 6	+ 6
1954	20	6	2	20	− 8	+ 8
1952	26	2	2	18	+ 2	− 2
1950	22	4	2	20	+ 9	− 9

Summary

Midterm elections[a]
  Average number of chambers lost by:

President's party	12.7
Republicans	13.4
Democrats	12.0

Presidential election years[b]
  Average gain of chambers for:

Party of winning presidential candidate	2.0
Republicans	1.6
Democrats	2.7

a. In each midterm election since 1950 the president's party lost control of legislative chambers.
b. In four of eight presidential election years the winning presidential candidate's party did *not* have a net gain in legislative chambers.
SOURCES: *1973 Republican Almanac* (Washington, D.C.: Republican National Committee, 1973), p. 86B; *1981 Republican Almanac* (Washington, D.C.: Republican National Committee, 1981), p. 702; 1982 election data provided by the National Conference of State Legislatures.

TABLE 4–8

MIDTERM LOSSES OF STATE LEGISLATURES BY THE PRESIDENT'S PARTY, 1950–1982

Year	State Legislatures in Which President's Party Lost Both Houses	President's Party
1982	4	Republican
1978	5	Democratic
1974	12	Republican
1970	4	Republican
1966	12	Democratic
1962	5	Democratic
1958	10	Republican
1954	6	Republican
1950	2	Democratic

SOURCES: *1981 Republican Almanac* (Washington, D.C.: Republican National Committee, 1981), p. 702; *Congressional Quarterly Weekly Report* (November 13, 1982), pp. 2847–49; 1982 election data provided by the National Conference of State Legislatures.

midterm for the president's party between 1950 and 1982 has been seven legislatures. The GOP loss of four legislatures is, therefore, quite close to the average.

Although state legislative elections are strongly influenced by the anti–presidential party trends at midterm, these elections show less susceptibility to national trends during presidential election years. In four of the eight presidential elections since 1950, the winning presidential candidate's party has failed to gain control of an additional state legislative chamber. Between 1950 and 1980, the party of the successful presidential candidate has averaged a net gain of only two legislative chambers.

These data on the effect of national trends on state legislative contests are similar to those for gubernatorial elections. Both types of state elections are more dramatically affected by national trends during midterm elections than they are in presidential election years. Significant political change in state elections—for both the governorship and the legislature—is, therefore, more likely to occur in off-year elections than in presidential elections.

Despite the significant 1982 changes in party control of legislative chambers in favor of the Democrats, the shift to the Democrats was not consistently observable in each state. In twenty-four legislative chambers, the Republicans actually gained seats (table 4–1). Republicans increased their representation in seventeen chambers in spite of Democratic governors' being elected simultaneously. Further evidence of state electorates' tendency to split their tickets can be seen in Iowa and Illinois, where the GOP retained its control of the governorship while Democrats achieved control of both houses of the legislature.

Democratic ascendancy in state legislatures is now almost as great as it was in the post-Watergate era (1975–1976) when the party controlled both houses in thirty-seven states (table 4–7). The significant Republican gains of 1978 and 1980 have been partially removed.

Divided Control of State Government. The 1982 elections have left almost half of the states with divided partisan control of state government. In twenty-nine states the same party controls both the legislature and the governorship, but in twenty others one party holds the governorship while the opposition has a majority in at least one house of the legislature (Nebraska has a nonpartisan legislature). This pattern of divided control of state government is consistent with the trends that have been prevalent since the 1960s. It reflects the individualized nature of campaigns and the increasing incidence of split-ticket voting.

Divided control of state government does not necessarily mean that nearly half of the states are doomed to at least two years of partisan deadlocks in the conduct of state business. Governors and legislators intent on maintaining state services will be able, as in the past, to compromise their differences. But this normally occurs only after partisan maneuvering, publicity seeking, and protracted delays in enacting such critical legislation as the state budget. Divided government also falls short of the model of party responsibility and accountability to the electorate for the conduct of state affairs. In divided government, it is always more difficult for the voter to assess blame and credit for the state of the state.

Minority Parties and Traditional One-Party State Legislatures. Although much has been made of the ability of minority-party Republicans to turn the South into a competitive two-party area, competition is still largely restricted to statewide and congressional races. At the sub–congressional district level, competing with the traditional majority party has proved much more difficult. In spite of their demonstrated capacity to contest and win federal and gubernatorial offices, the Republicans control no legislative chambers in the South or in Border states. In Louisiana they hold no seats in the upper chamber, and in ten of eleven states of the old Confederacy there are fewer than ten Republicans in the state senates. In much of the South, therefore, one finds a two-tiered electoral system in which there is competition for the governorship and for federal office, but one-partyism prevails at the substate or legislative election level. The 1982 election revealed that true two-party politics is not yet a reality in the South.

The minority party's difficulty in mobilizing votes at the state legislative level, while competing effectively for federal and state-wide office, is not just a southern phenomenon. In the Democratic bastions of Hawaii, Massachusetts, Rhode Island, and West Virginia, the GOP holds fewer than ten seats in any of these states' legislative chambers. Similarly, in such traditionally Republican states as South Dakota, the Democrats are not an important force in legislative politics.

Conclusions and Implications

State-Level Elections and National Trends at Midterm. Since the 1950s, gubernatorial and state legislative elections have been particularly sensitive to national trends working against the president's party at midterm. Indeed, the extent of loss for the president's party is greater at the state level than it is at the congressional level in spite of the fact that state elections are supposedly fought over state issues. The 1982 state midterm elections were typical in that the president's party (in this case, the GOP) suffered significant losses. Adverse economic conditions combined with the high visibility of governors made GOP candidates convenient targets for unhappy voters.

The shift to the Democrats was most pronounced in the North Central region and in southern states, where voter turnout was up most significantly since 1978. Low-income and minority voters turned out in unusually large numbers, and they voted Democratic in these regions. In Illinois, for example, 240,000 new names were added to the voter rolls—140,000 in Chicago. The Chicago registration drive was funded by the campaign organization of the Democratic gubernatorial nominee, Adlai E. Stevenson, and run by a group called POWER, representing twenty-one community organizations. Among the minority and low-income white population toward whom this drive was directed, turnout on election day was up from 58 percent in 1978 to 77 percent in 1982. Similarly, in Texas, turnout increased substantially from approximately 2.4 million in 1978 to almost 3.2 million in 1982, and it was particularly high in minority and blue-collar precincts. In some black wards of Houston, the balloting was so intense that voting had to be suspended temporarily because the demand for ballots exceeded the supply. The benefits for the Democrats of increased turnout can be seen by the fact that in seven of the nine states where Democrats replaced GOP governors there was an increase in voter turnout over 1978. The only exceptions were Wisconsin and Nevada. In the two states (California and New Hampshire) lost by the Democrats to the Republicans, turnout among registered voters declined between 1978 and 1982.

The responsiveness of American gubernatorial and state legislative elections to adverse economic conditions and to a national trend against the chief executive's party is consistent with Seymour Martin Lipset's findings in a study of elections in seventeen Western-style democracies. He notes that when implementing their programs, governments outside the United States "have three to five years before parliamentary elections, but they typically face the prospect of earlier repudiation in local or regional elections and in the ever present opinion polls." Losses in local elections and evidence of diminished public support in the polls, Lipset believes, create conditions for governmental paralysis. The opposition, with evidence of the public's declining support for the government's policies, is likely to use all available means to resist the partisans in power, while the latter become demoralized and divided among themselves as to the correctness of their policies.[8] Because House and Senate elections in the United States occur simultaneously with state elections at midterm, the likelihood of political stalemate is potentially even greater here after an off-year election than it is in other Western democracies.

GOP Realignment Deferred. Speculation was rampant about the imminence of a Republican realignment of the electorate after its sweeping 1980 victory, and it was thought that a strong GOP showing in 1982 would confirm the trend toward Republican ascendancy. Obviously, 1982 was not a realigning year. Instead, GOP party-building initiatives at the state level have suffered a setback, and the Republicans are in approximately the position they were in after the 1976 elections.

Party growth over the long term requires more than presidential victories. Control of governorships and state legislatures is needed. Governors can provide state parties with the resources and leadership to build effective organizations. Legislatures are the recruiting ground for future representatives, senators, and governors. Without a strong contingent of state legislators, a party's talent pool is severely restricted.

State legislatures also control congressional and legislative redistricting, which can affect a party's fate for a decade. It was with these hard realities in mind that the Republican National Committee (RNC) under the leadership of Ray Bliss in the 1960s and Bill Brock in the 1970s sought to strengthen its state organizations and give significant aid to state parties and candidates. The RNC's Local Elections Division, under Brock's leadership, gave direct financial and technical support to legislative candidates at an unprecedented level during the 1978 and 1980 campaigns.[9] These national party investments in state legislative races paid handsome dividends. Between 1976 and 1981, the Republicans picked up 321 legislative seats, enabling them to control both houses of the legislature in fifteen states—eleven more than they had controlled after the 1976 elections. Control of the White House and Senate, of course, altered the party's organizational priorities for the 1982 campaign. The national Republican party focused its resources on protecting the House and Senate gains it had made in 1980. The RNC did not provide direct funding for state legislative candidates and relied upon a program of providing technical assistance to legislative candidates and state parties through its extensive field staff. It is clear from the 1982 results, however, that party building still occurs from the bottom up and that true majority status will elude the GOP unless the election of governors and state legislators is a continuing priority.

The Democratic National Committee (DNC), which had virtually ignored state legislative races in 1978 and 1980, started to provide modest assistance to state and local parties in 1982. The Political Affairs Division of the DNC worked with state and local party organizations to develop campaign organizations capable of mobilizing Democratic voters through the use of phone and mail lists, data bases, and political consulting services.[10] The Democrats' halting steps into state legislative campaigns, however, leave them far behind the RNC in the level of support provided state candidates and parties.

National Policy Directions. Decisions of the national government dramatically affect state budgets and policy. Governors can, therefore, be expected to seek to influence the direction of national policy through their respective state congressional delegations, direct liaison with the White House, and public relations channels. At their November 1982 meeting, the members of the National Governors Association showed an inclination to become involved in federal budgetary issues. An increased contingent of activist and liberal Democratic governors can make it more difficult for a Republican White House to achieve its policy objectives. This will be most evident in the New Federalism initiatives where the cooperation of the governors is required for successful implementation.

By December 1982, the chairman of the National Governors Association, Scott Matheson (Democrat, Utah), had already advised the Reagan administration that its New Federalism proposals should be postponed until the states' economic problems were resolved. He also opposed a revised New Federalism plan being considered by the White House that would have lumped Medicaid, food stamps, and welfare into one large block grant program.[11] When Richard Snelling (Republican, Vermont), the past chairman of the National Governors Association and its principal negotiator with the administration, also pronounced the original New Federalism proposal dead,[12] it was apparent that the likelihood of cooperation between the governors and the administration during 1983–1984 would be remote.

All Is Not Rosy for the Democrats. Even though the Republicans can hardly take pleasure in the results of state elections in 1982, they can perhaps be permitted to smile at the prospect of Democratic governors and state legislatures confronted with enormous budgetary deficits with no hope that the federal government will step in to help. The choice these Democrats face is not a happy one. They may cut services, raise taxes, or do both. Whatever choice they make, few voters are likely to be pleased.

Adding to the Democrats' difficulty is the fact that their constituency expects existing services to be at least maintained if not increased. The armies of public employees, teachers, union members, and minorities who worked for Democratic candidates across the country will not be easily satisfied by gubernatorial policies of service cutbacks and higher taxes. Therefore, one of the tests of Democratic governors in the 1980s will be their ability to convince their left-of-center cadre of supporters of what the governors themselves probably have already learned: the money to finance new social welfare programs or even provide full funding for existing programs just is not there.

How the new Democratic governors handle the dilemma of an electoral coalition that wants increased government services in an era of scarce resources will go a long way toward shaping the policy orientation of the Democratic party in the 1980s. Given the need of the states for additional financial resources, it is likely that they will opt for the politics of economic growth and production rather than the politics of income redistribution, which was the party's orientation in the 1970s.

Implications for the 1984 Presidential Election. Just as there was a rush to interpret the 1982 midterm elections as a referendum on the Reagan administration's policies, there was also an attempt to determine the implications of the election for the 1984 presidential contest. A prominent line of reasoning concerning the Republicans was that the moderate wing of the party would have significantly reduced influence, should Reagan not run for reelection, because GOP moderates no longer sit in the governors' chairs in the key midwestern states of Ohio, Michigan, Wisconsin, Minnesota, and Iowa. What this type of analysis ignores is the singular ineffectiveness of moderate Republican governors in presidential nominating politics since 1964. They have not been successful either as presidential candidates themselves or in forming a bloc of delegates at national conventions. The reduced number of GOP governors is likely, therefore, to have only a minimal effect on 1984 nominating politics, even if Ronald Reagan decides to forgo running for a second term.

Nor is the enlarged contingent of Democratic governors likely to change the nature of Democratic nominating contests in a significant way. Democratic governors, like their Republican counterparts, have not played an effective role in selecting Democratic nominees since the McGovern-Fraser rules were implemented for the 1972 convention. The minor changes in delegate selection procedures (making governors, representatives, and senators national convention delegates) that were instituted as a result of the Hunt Commission are not likely to change the fact that Democratic presidential nominations, like Republican nominations, are decided by forces over which governors have little control. It would, therefore, be a mistake to assume that a candidate such as former Vice President Walter Mondale, who has close ties to organized labor and minority groups, would gain a significant advantage, because most of these new Democratic governors are dependent upon these same groups for their electoral survival.

The 1982 midterm elections fueled speculation not only concerning 1984 presidential nominations but also concerning the general election contest. There is a widely held belief that failure to control the governorship in key states risks the loss of those states' electoral votes in the presidential elections. It is for this reason that commentators have given special attention to the Republican gubernatorial losses in the big states of Texas, Michigan, Ohio, Wisconsin, and Minnesota (with ninety-three total electoral votes). Some pundits also point to other ominous signs for the GOP, especially its lack of success in western and southern states—key blocs of electoral votes

TABLE 4–9

PARTY CONTROL OF GOVERNORSHIPS AND THE OUTCOME OF
PRESIDENTIAL VOTING IN THE STATES, 1968–1980

	1980	1976	1972	1968
Number of states in which party that controlled governorship *carried* the state for its presidential candidate	23 (46%)	25 (50%)	19 (38%)	23 (46%)
Number of states in which party that controlled governorship did *not* carry the state for its presidential candidate	27 (54%)	25 (50%)	31 (62%)	27 (54%)

SOURCE: *Statistical Abstract of the United States, 1969–1981.*

in Reagan's 1980 winning coalition. Analysis of recent presidential elections, however, reveals that there is virtually no relationship between control of a state's governorship and the outcome of presidential voting in the state. In 1980, for example, the party holding the governorship in twenty-seven states did not carry the state for president. The same pattern was present in the 1968, 1972, and 1976 presidential elections (see table 4–9). Thus, whatever the substantial benefits of holding a governorship, they do not extend to winning electoral votes for the party's presidential candidate. The 1982 midterm elections, therefore, offer no real clues concerning the outcome of the 1984 presidential contest.

What does stand out from this analysis of elections for governor and the state legislature is that at midterm these contests take on the character of national elections. Attempts to insulate state politics from national issues and trends by scheduling state elections in nonpresidential years has, therefore, been unsuccessful.

Notes

1. For the most complete consideration of gubernatorial elections and the relationship between national and state elections, see Malcolm E. Jewell and David M. Olson, *American State Political Parties and Elections*, rev. ed. (Homewood, Ill.: Dorsey Press, 1982), pp. 199–238; Sarah McCally Morehouse, *State Politics, Parties and Policy* (New York: Holt, Rinehart and Winston, 1981), pp. 45–84.

2. V. O. Key, Jr., *American State Elections* (New York: Knopf, 1956), p. 29.

3. Samuel Kernell, "Presidential Popularity and Negative Voting: An Alternative Explanation of Midterm Congressional Decline of the President's Party," *American Political Science Review*, vol. 71 (March 1977), pp. 44–66.

4. "State Gubernatorial Primaries," *Comparative State Politics Newsletter*, vol. 3 (October 1982), p. 2.

5. Between 1946 and 1980, incumbent governors received on average 64.6 percent of the vote in primary elections. See Jewell and Olson, *American State Elections*, p. 122.

6. "State Gubernatorial Primaries," p. 2.

7. Lt. Gov. William O'Neill succeeded Connecticut Gov. Ella Grasso in 1981 after she resigned, suffering from cancer.

8. Seymour Martin Lipset, "No Room for the Ins: Elections around the World," *Public Opinion*, vol. 5 (October–November 1982), p. 43.

9. John F. Bibby, "Political Parties and Federalism: The Republican National Committee Involvement in Gubernatorial and Legislative Elections," *Publius*, vol. 9 (Winter 1979), pp. 229–36.

10. "Democrats Recoup State Legislative Losses," *Congressional Quarterly Weekly Report* (November 13, 1982), p. 2849.

11. Howard Kurtz, "White House Studies Scaled-down Version of New Federalism," *Washington Post*, December 16, 1982.

12. "Reagan's Idea of Federalism Called 'Dead,'" *New York Times*, December 12, 1982.

5

Sending a Message:
Voters and Congress in 1982

Thomas E. Mann and Norman J. Ornstein

Congressional elections are devilishly difficult to generalize about. They are a crazy-quilt combination of local and national forces, of personalities and parties. Each of nearly five hundred separate contests has its own idiosyncrasies and dynamics. Aggregating them into some coherent set of principles is no easy task.

Still, we always do aggregate and generalize. Congressional elections generate results, and every observer of the political scene, whether journalist, academic, politician, or campaign professional, feels the need to draw lessons from an election. The process is not merely intellectual; lessons learned or messages received can and do lead to different behavior on the part of these political elites. The message of 1980 was that we were quite likely in the midst of a sea change in American politics, a realignment;[1] that message deeply affected the legislative behavior of congressional Democrats and Republicans alike in 1981 and 1982.

In this chapter, we shall examine in some detail the messages that have been drawn—or might be drawn—from the 1982 election. We shall first look into the vagaries of constructing broad interpretations of elections, with particular reference to 1980 and 1982. Second, we shall examine the tea leaves of 1982 more closely, contrasting different areas of results for explanation. Third, we shall dissect the many levels of interpretation to which elites look for cues in the next Congress, noting that, for particular groups of members of Congress, specific election results may be more important than the overall pattern in shaping their own political behavior.

Earlier versions of this essay were presented at Public Policy Week, sponsored by the American Enterprise Institute, December 6-9, 1982, Washington, D.C., and published in *Public Opinion* (December/January 1983).

Interpreting Election Results

Congressional elections matter, because they affect policy results. First, they replace departing members of Congress with a set of new members who may have entirely different policy preferences and voting patterns. In 1982, the departure of eighty-one members of the House of Representatives and their replacement by eighty-one newcomers meant a clear shift in votes, perhaps twenty-five or more on any given issue, away from the more "conservative" policies favored by President Reagan—enough to change many vote outcomes. Elections matter too because they often result in the departure of powerful committee and subcommittee chairmen and their replacement by new individuals. Senator Harrison "Jack" Schmitt of New Mexico, for example, who served in the Ninety-seventh Congress as chairman of the appropriations Subcommittee on Labor, Health, and Human Services, was defeated in 1982 and was replaced as chairman in the Ninety-eighth Congress by Senator Lowell Weicker (Republican, Connecticut), whose policy preferences on these key issues are distinctly different. The departure of a key individual like Rules Committee Chairman Richard Bolling (Democrat, Missouri), after thirty-four years in the House, meant a major difference in legislative strategy for Democrats in the Ninety-eighth Congress. One result has been a lesser ability for Democrats to gain substantive victories through parliamentary maneuvering. For example, the 1983 House resolution calling for a nuclear freeze was brought up in April under a pure open rule; the result was a conservative Republican "filibuster by amendment" that tied up the House for weeks. It is doubtful that the Rules Committee under Bolling would have allowed this type of rule to make it through.

Congressional elections also matter because they can result in the removal of prime spokesmen for particular policy positions, or the appearance of such individuals on the political scene. In 1982, the departure of Representatives Paul N. "Pete" McCloskey, Jr. (Republican, California) and Paul Findley (Republican, Illinois), who were the two major congressional proponents of a close American association with the Palestine Liberation Organization, meant a considerably different dialogue on the Middle East in the Ninety-eighth Congress from that in the Ninety-seventh Congress, since no other individuals in Congress appeared to be on the scene to replace the viewpoint expressed by McCloskey and Findley. Whatever congressional pressure there was on Israel to deal with the PLO was exerted by these two; in the next Congress, this limited movement virtually disappeared.

Congressional elections also may affect considerably the ideological and partisan makeup of particular committees. Even though the 1982 election did not dramatically affect the United States Senate —the turnover of only five members was the lowest in at least seventy years—the effect on the Senate Armed Services Committee was considerable. Two senior Democrats on that committee, Howard W. Cannon of Nevada and Harry F. Byrd of Virginia, left the Congress and the committee. They were replaced by two Democrats—Edward M. Kennedy (Massachusetts) and Jeff Bingaman (New Mexico)—with different points of view on defense. The hand of advocates of military reform is likely to be strengthened, and the role of such Armed Services powers as Senators John Tower (Republican, Texas), John Stennis (Democrat, Mississippi), and Henry Jackson (Democrat, Washington) will be altered. The results may be a different focus on the debate on American national defense.

Congressional elections thus can matter a great deal. But these particular elements of change, with one exception,[2] are rarely focused on in the immediate aftermath of an election, by either media analysts or political observers. Rather, our focus on the effect of congressional elections tends to move away from individuals and votes and toward a broader interpretation. We look to congressional elections first and foremost as a broad message from the electorate that can be read as a referendum on the presidency, a harbinger of political trends, and a predictor of future presidential politics.

All of these elements are important—indeed, the broader message of an election can have just as powerful an effect on attitudes, and therefore on policy behavior, as the election results themselves. But coming up with a "message" for an election that is the collective expression of individual judgments made by more than 60 million people voting for over 460 separate officeholders is a tricky and uncertain business. The sum of individual judgments may belie the collective result. Different ways of weighing a collective message may lead to widely varying interpretations of what that message is. The change in votes may be quite different from the change in seats. Margins of victory may tell us more than the victories themselves.

Difficulty aside, a public consensus commonly develops on the message of an election result. Usually, it is based on two elements: the combination of election *outcomes* (measuring wins and losses or changes in seat totals), and the extent to which these outcomes conform to or depart from preelection expectations.

Both of these factors had an enormous effect on the consensus interpretation of the 1980 election—one that worked greatly to the benefit of Republicans. The interpretation of the 1980 election, shared widely by press, public, and politicians, was of earthshaking change, with every potential of being the beginning of a realignment. Common perceptions of the 1980 election in the weeks following the election suggested that this one might have broken the mold; that we were quite possibly in the middle of a historic realignment that would make the Republican party the majority party in the United States for a decade or more; that the public had rejected not just President Jimmy Carter but also the New Deal, the Fair Deal, the Great Society, and all that the Democratic party stood for.

What made the difference in 1980 was not the solid victory of Ronald Reagan but the stunning election result in the Senate. For the first time in twenty-six years, Republicans took control of a house of Congress, in striking fashion, and against the preelection prognostication of nearly every political pundit. Republicans picked up twelve Senate seats in 1980, only the third party shift in double digits since World War II. This stunning election result, unusual and unexpected, greatly colored the interpretation given to the broader 1980 election results, moving it beyond the electorate's rejection of Carter and his presidency to the rejection of the Democrats.

Beyond doubt, the Senate results in 1980 *were* stunning and impressive and worthy of special emphasis. Had the Senate gone the other way, with the Democrats retaining control of the institution even while losing seats, the interpretation would have been far less sweeping. Most likely, the policy outcomes of 1981 and the Ninety-seventh Congress would also have been quite different.

Unnoticed in the pandemonium that followed the 1980 election was that *this* alternative election outcome came very close to happening. Of thirty-four Senate seats in 1980, fourteen were decided by the narrowest of margins—the winner receiving 52.1 percent of the vote or less. Of these fourteen contests, Republicans won eleven. Senate election contests of 1980 were so close, in fact, that a shift of merely 50,000 votes distributed appropriately nationwide would have moved seven Senate seats back into the Democratic column, leaving the Senate with a 54–46 Democratic edge. The outcome of 1980 would then have been much like that of 1972, when Richard Nixon's presidential landslide victory (much greater than Reagan's) was interpreted in narrow terms because the Democrats retained comfortable control of Congress. A 1980 *Republican* victory would have become simply a Reagan victory, and Democrats, still in the saddle in Congress for the twenty-seventh straight year, would have put their own mandate up against Reagan's.

The GOP's success at narrowly winning the lion's share of many tossup Senate elections gave us firm clues at the time that the Republican win in 1980 was not nearly so sweeping as it appeared to be—

and thus that Republicans were not in the middle of a realignment that would lead to unprecedented GOP gains in the off-year 1982 elections. But the margins of victory were overshadowed by the victories themselves—and by the fact that no political professionals really thought before November 1980 that the Senate would switch its membership so dramatically. The result was an overinterpretation of the meaning of 1980.

Interestingly, the 1982 Senate elections had a comparable importance for the election interpretation and were in many ways a replay of their 1980 counterparts. With substantial losses in the House and in state houses, the lone bright spot on election eve for Republicans was the Senate, where they managed to hold Democrats to a draw. In fact, if we use as a base the Senate of 1981, Republicans actually *gained* a seat. The combination of 1982 election results led to a prevailing interpretation that 1982 was "mixed." To postelection pundits, there was no message to "reverse the course," but rather, as *Time* magazine put it, to "trim the sails." Few observers, if any, saw the election as a widespread repudiation of President Reagan, the Republican party, and current policies.

Imagine, though, what the election interpretation would have been had the Republicans lost control of the Senate to the Democrats. A return of the Democrats to power in the Senate combined with their gain of twenty-six seats in the House and seven governorships would have led to widespread headlines that the 1982 elections showed a rejection of Reagan, Republicans, and Reaganomics. Although no one can project how *this* interpretation would have affected President Reagan's behavior and the likely policy directions pursued, it is undoubtedly true that the attitudes of Democrats and Republicans in Congress would have been different and policy outcomes would have reflected those new attitudes. Different too would have been the dynamics of 1984 presidential campaign politics.

The Democrats, of course, did not regain control of the Senate— but just as in 1980, the results were very close. Republicans won eight of ten "tossups" among Senate races. A switch of less than 35,000 votes would have given Democrats control of the Senate in 1983! Yet, would this small shift in votes have meant that the real wishes of tens of millions of American voters had changed from trim the sails to reverse the course? Of course not—but that is how the interpretations would have been read.

Republicans were fortunate to be able to take advantage of an overinterpretation of election results of 1980 and to avoid by a narrow margin being the victims of a negative interpretation of the 1982 results. They were also fortunate in 1982 that the prevailing interpretation of the 1980 election had been largely forgotten two years later and was not used as the base for interpreting the 1982 results.

Not surprisingly, Republicans were extremely optimistic in the first half of 1981. Excited by the prospect of a realignment, buoyed by the early Reagan policy victories in the House, and encouraged by the fact that, as in 1980, many more Senate Democrats than Republicans were up for reelection, Republicans confidently predicted a big GOP year in 1982. GOP National Chairman Richard Richards, for example, in a National Press Club speech in June 1981 flatly predicted both big Senate gains *and* a House takeover.

By these standards, Republicans fell flat on their faces in 1982. These, however, were not the prevailing standards. Instead, the 1982 standards of measuring election meaning were set by expectations or conventional wisdom in the days immediately preceding the election. By that time, any hopes for big GOP Senate gains—or for *any* GOP House gains—had vanished. Although it was still remote, many observers saw a real chance for Democrats to recapture the Senate. They did not gain a seat—thus, disappointment for the Democrats. Yet if we choose the 1981 standards, the Senate results were a disappointment for the Republicans.

It is no wonder, then, that members of both parties work so hard at setting the standards by which the media and politicians will judge the election outcomes. White House officials worked long hours in October 1982 to convince the political community that a big GOP defeat was forthcoming. If it then occurred, it would not be so surprising, and thus would be given less weight (this was one lesson of the 1980 Senate changes); if it did *not* occur, Republicans could proclaim victory. Democrats worked long hours to convince the same people that they would be lucky to gain ten seats in the House and to hold the Senate to a draw. Any larger gains, then, would be *their* big victory.

Admittedly, setting just the right level of expectations is a tricky business. Too much pessimism can turn off the money spigots (or divert them to the opponents) and can demoralize candidates. To avoid this, GOP congressional leaders countered the White House's preelection doom and gloom with their own rosy scenario. The point remains that attempts to mold expectations and set standards in advance of the election are now a key component of party strategy in congressional elections.

The 1982 Congressional Elections

Divining the message of a congressional election is neither illegitimate nor entirely arbitrary. Voters *do* make judgments, and those judgments *should* be understood and felt by policy makers. But discerning what the message (or messages) is can be difficult. Different measures may yield very different results, particularly given the nature of our electoral system. Nowhere is this more true than in efforts to explain the national political significance of the Republicans' loss of twenty-six seats in the House in 1982.

What is the appropriate measure of the normal midterm loss by the president's party—the average loss sustained in all midterm elections since 1900 (thirty-four), in midterms during the first term of a president (thirty-two), or only in midterms after a change in the White House party (twenty-five)? If we limit the universe to post–World War II elections, those three measures produce average losses of twenty-eight, twenty, and thirteen, respectively. Some analysts fixed on the latter standard, which led them to conclude that the Republican loss of House seats, double the "normal" midterm loss, constituted a sharp repudiation of President Reagan and his policies. Others were inclined to interpret the net shift as more or less typical of midterm elections.

A less arbitrary way of gauging the significance of the 1982 House results is provided by Edward Tufte's referendum model of congressional elections.[3] Tufte's scheme, which has had a remarkably good fit with midterm elections since the war, ties the drop in support for the president's party to the state of the economy (measured by the percentage change in real disposable income per capita over the year preceding the election) and the popular standing of the president (percentage approving the job the president is doing in the last pre-election Gallup poll). Tufte's equation, updated by Jacobson and Kernell[4] to cover the period 1946 to 1978, is

Standardized vote loss = − 10.56 + 0.663 change in income
+ 0.130 presidential popularity

With real income unchanged during 1982 and the president's approval rating in the Gallup poll at 42 percent, Tufte's model predicts a standardized Republican vote loss of 5.1 percent, which translates into a 7.7 percent drop in the national Republican House vote from 1980 to 1982.

Tufte offers no precise formula for converting votes into seats, but as a rule of thumb, he suggests that "an extra 2.5 percent of the vote . . . would typically translate into an extra 20 to 30 seats in the House of Representatives."[5] Hence, a gain of 7.7 percent of the vote by the Democrats should produce a gain of sixty to ninety seats. Using the equation estimated by Jacobson and Kernell,

Percentage of seats held by Democrats $= - 42.5$
$+ 1.90$ percentage of votes
won by Democrats

a model which fits very well the vote/seat relationship in postwar House elections, we see that a 7.7 percent drop in the vote should produce a loss of fifty-nine seats.

A referendum model of midterm elections predicts a Republican loss of 7.7 percent of the votes and fifty-nine seats, yet the Republicans actually lost 5.2 percent of the vote and twenty-six seats in the House. By these standards, the Republicans fared reasonably well in 1982. Given the dismal economic conditions and the relatively low level of presidential popularity, the Democrats could have made much more substantial gains had the public responded as it has in the past to these national forces. The 1982 losses for the president's party were greater than all recent first midterm elections because President Reagan presided over very bad economic conditions—in that sense, the election registered a Republican failure—but the losses would have been much deeper had these national conditions alone determined the net shift in House seats. Some combination of factors must have intervened to soften the blow to the president's party.

The discrepancy between prediction and outcome can most usefully be divided into two questions: Why didn't the Democrats attract a larger portion of the votes nationwide? Why did the votes they did gain translate into so few seats?

A part of the answer to the first question is suggested by what appears to have been on voters' minds on election day. Public opinion as measured in the network exit polls was divided in its evaluation of Reagan's economic program: 53 percent felt Reagan's economic program would eventually help the country, but 47 percent said it would hurt; 38 percent blamed Reagan for the country's economic ills, while 48 percent blamed the Democrats; 55 percent said the Democrats were better able to handle the nation's most important problem, and 45 percent said the Republicans were better able to do so.[6] Moreover, roughly equal numbers of voters mentioned a candidate's support or opposition to Reaganomics as a reason for their House vote (23 percent and 25 percent, respectively). On these and other questions posed to voters as they left the polls, there was a very strong partisan coloration to the responses. Yet even though self-identified Democrats greatly outnumber Republicans, there was no Democratic advantage apparent in the exit polls on matters of national economic policy.

Just what accounts for this ambivalence in the public at a time of great economic distress is uncertain. Memories of a troubled economy under a Democratic president only two years earlier may be partly responsible. So too might have been the Republican party's national television ads urging voters to "stay the course." Both may have been most effective in holding the support of rank-and-file Republicans for their party's candidates at the same high level as it was in 1980. In any case, the predicted referendum on President Reagan was clouded by the public's confusion and uncertainty over which party to blame for and how best to deal with the nation's economic problems.

Another key element in explaining the Democratic shortfall is to be found in the relationship between the change in votes from one election to the next and the change in seats. In 1982, the Democrats won just over five percentage points more of the votes cast for the House of Representatives than they had in 1980. Although a similar gain in *votes* had in previous elections produced a sizable gain in *seats*—forty-nine in 1958 and 1974, thirty-seven in 1964—the Democrats saw their majority increase by only twenty-six seats in 1982. This number is all the more striking in light of the apparent Democratic victory in the redistricting sweepstakes. As Alan Ehrenhalt reports in chapter 2, the Democrats actually gained five to ten seats from the reapportionment of seats from Frostbelt to Sunbelt states and from the redrawing of district boundaries, an advantage that should have magnified their seat gains on election night.

Why did so many votes translate into so few seats for the Democrats? The answer begins with a recognition that Ronald Reagan was not on the November 2 ballot, that voters across the country were faced most immediately with a choice of who should represent them in the House. The local character of U.S. congressional elections has always proved troublesome for national interpretations of midterm results—and 1982 was no exception. The national Democratic vote gain of five percentage points obscured some modest regional variation (+ 5 percent in the East, +4 percent in the South, +7 percent in the Midwest, and +3 percent in the West), substantial fluctuations among states (+12 percent in Illinois, 0 percent in Indiana and Florida, −3 percent in Oregon), and widely divergent patterns of change across congressional districts (+25 percent in Arkansas's second district, −25 percent in California's twenty-first district). In spite of the strong national Democratic tide, a number of Republicans managed to hold their own or increase their 1980 margins. Who ran and how they ran clearly made a difference in many districts across the country.

Herein lies a partial explanation of why the Republicans lost fewer seats than their drop in votes would appear to have warranted.[7]

As Larry Sabato describes in chapter 3, the national Republican party, with a massive campaign chest at its disposal, was able to alter the balance of resources in key districts—by attracting strong candidates in open seats and by contributing funds and technical assistance to their candidates in close races—that prevented deeper losses. Their success was particularly striking in the open seats where they lost a net of only two seats, a pittance compared with the open seat Republican losses of fourteen in 1958 and eleven in 1974.

Some analysts, noting that most of the successful Democratic challengers were outspent by their GOP incumbent opponents, concluded that money was not an important factor in 1982 and that the Democrats' concern about their financial disadvantage was overstated. It is certainly true that outspending one's opponent is no guarantee of victory, especially when national political forces are working against one's party. Nonetheless, there is little doubt that money was an important factor in the victories of Republican open seat candidates and shaky incumbents. The normal midterm pattern of out-party candidates outspending administration partisans in marginal seats was reversed in 1982. The success of these Republican candidates is a testament less to the staying power of the Reagan administration than to the impressive political machinery of the Republican party.

Another way of discerning the message or mandate of an election is to see whether the voters discriminate among types of candidates. Are there signs, for example, of public antipathy toward senior incumbents, as in 1980, or freshman Republicans, called "Reagan robots" by House Democratic leaders, or conservative Democrats who gave the president his margin of victory on the major votes in 1981?

House incumbents as a group did very well in the election, dashing any interpretation that the voters sought to "throw the rascals out." A total of thirty-nine House incumbents were defeated in their reelection bids (ten in primaries, twenty-nine in the general election), and fully twelve of these in contests where redistricting forced them to run against another incumbent. Setting aside the latter, 93 percent of all incumbents seeking reelection against nonincumbents were successful (86 percent for the Republicans, 99 percent for the Democrats), about average for House elections. Moreover, though several senior Republicans were defeated and Minority Leader Robert Michel was given a real scare, the returns reveal no evidence that a long-term association with the House was an electoral liability.

In fact, most observers were struck by the heavy concentration of freshmen among the Republican losers—thirteen of twenty-six GOP incumbents defeated in the general election were seeking their first reelection. Recent freshman classes, using all of the resources of incumbency at their disposal, have enjoyed a "sophomore surge,"[8] running on average six percentage points better than their more senior party colleagues. The Watergate class of 1974 rode that surge to an extraordinary victory in 1976, losing only two of seventy-four seats. The Republican class of 1980 proved to be much less durable in 1982—a fourth of the fifty-two freshmen running were defeated.

Yet in several other respects, the freshman Republicans performed quite well. They ran on average two percentage points ahead of their showing as challengers in 1980, while the entire Republican ticket fell five points off its 1980 pace (producing a 1982 Republican sophomore surge of 7 percent). Moreover, 71 percent of the GOP freshmen who unseated Democrats in the 1980 elections succeeded in keeping those seats in the Republican column. And what is most striking is that nine of the thirteen Republican freshmen who lost ran in districts heavily altered by redistricting.[9] Although GOP first-termers suffered from the adverse political climate in 1982, their efforts as individual candidates largely overcame this liability and blunted any clear message from the voters.

The "Gypsy Moths," the moderate northern Republicans who took steps to demonstrate some independence from President Reagan after their initial support of his budget proposals, fared slightly worse than their party colleagues. The group as a whole dropped about six percentage points from its margins two years earlier, and five of the twenty-two seeking reelection were defeated.

Yet one of the defeated Gypsy Moths (Heckler) was forced to run against a Democratic incumbent; two others (Dunn and Hollenbeck) were weakened significantly by redistricting; and the final two (DeNardis and Dougherty) represented traditionally strong Democratic districts. Anti-Reaganomics sentiment was successfully exploited by Democratic candidates in rallying the party faithful, making it even tougher than usual for a Republican to win in a Democratic district.

Yet being a conservative Democrat willing to support President Reagan on budget and tax votes was no problem whatsoever on election day. All of the "Boll Weevils" who sought reelection in November were successful, and most padded their already comfortable margins. There is not a shred of evidence that Democrats who deserted their party to support President Reagan were punished by the voters. At the same time, Democratic candidates did not need to advertise themselves as Boll Weevils to get elected from the South —the fourteen new Democratic seats are held by a largely moderate contingent not far from the party mainstream. Whatever national political forces were set in motion by the bad economic times, they worked to the advantage of all Democrats—liberals, moderates, and conservatives.

The Democratic party gained nationally in the House elections largely because some of the voters who called themselves Democrats but who voted for Republican candidates in 1980 came home in 1982.[10] The net shift was not large—about 4 to 5 percent of all Democrats changed their vote and 2 to 3 percent of all voters—nor was it ideologically motivated or policy laden. Very bad economic conditions appear to have set in motion forces that, mediated by local candidates and campaigns, differences in turnout, and the increasingly distinctive orientation of women, gave the Democrats a midterm lift. The message is that in times of economic adversity and policy uncertainty, more voters than usual are loyal to their own political party, particularly those who identify with the party out of power.

The message sent by the voters in the Senate elections was even less clear than in the House races. As we noted earlier, many observers saw the absence of any party change in the Senate, in contrast to the Democratic gains in the House and in the state capitols, as a sign that the voters had made a discerning judgment—that the most glaring excesses of Reaganomics had to be trimmed by an invigorated Democratic party in the House, but continued Republican control of the Senate was needed to prevent any return to the "tax and tax, spend and spend" programs long associated with the Democratic party. However well this subtle message fits the collective outcome of 1982 elections, it had little basis in public opinion or in voter behavior.

The stability of the Senate results is remarkable in light of the volatility and precariousness of recent Senate elections. Only two of thirty incumbents seeking reelection were defeated in November (none in the primaries), producing a 93 percent success rate that matches the House and far exceeds the 60 percent average over the preceding three Senate elections. In 1980, a strong Republican tide led to an average gain of almost ten percentage points over the 1974 division of the vote and a gain of twelve seats. Yet in 1982, with signs of a Democratic year all around, the Democrats gained not a single seat and barely improved their showing over 1976.

Why did Senate incumbents and Republicans in particular not suffer at the polls in 1982? Were there no signs of Democratic resurgence in the Senate comparable to that in the House? Is the now standard characterization of Senate elections as both more competitive (and thereby risky for incumbents) and more tied to national political forces flawed?

We think not. The Senate results obscured a showing by the Democrats as impressive as that in the House and portend a continuation, not an end, to the pattern of relatively low incumbent success in the years ahead. Overall, the Democrats won the same percentage of seats contested in the Senate as in the House (61 percent). For the Democrats to hold their own in seats in 1982 and even to increase, however slightly, their margins over 1976, a pretty good Democratic year, was a victory. With twenty seats on the line in 1982, including nine rated as highly vulnerable in early 1981, the Senate Democrats were poised to absorb their third consecutive beating at the hands of the Republicans. The national political tides carried the vulnerable Democrats to high ground—indirectly, by discouraging the ablest Republican challengers and giving the Democrats the rhetorical advantage, and directly, by prompting Democratic voters to go with their party—thereby averting a Democratic loss and raising the incumbent reelection rate. The same national conditions worked in reverse on presumably safe Republican incumbents, carrying five within a whisker of defeat. Their ultimate survival, attributable in part to the quality of their candidacies and the vigor of their campaigns, did not erase the powerful effect national politics had on their races.

Had the Republicans had the same number and type of seats up in 1982 as the Democrats had in 1980, there is little doubt that party control of the Senate would have changed once again. The message coming from the public in 1982, therefore, was not fundamentally different from that of 1980, but the opportunities for registering that message in the Senate elections were. In 1980, some fraction of the public felt it was time for a change and voted accordingly. In 1982, the comparable response to economic adversity was to go with the out-party, the Democrats. As in House elections, however, these generalized public responses were mediated by a host of factors specific to individual races.

Sending Messages to the Members

We have explored the intricacies of interpreting the message sent by voters in the 1982 congressional election and examined in some detail the often contradictory and puzzling results. But to this point we have focused largely on the election as seen by the broader public and by the political audience. Although the consensus election message as seen by these groups can be and usually is shared by the members of Congress who populate the Capitol in the following session, they receive many other election messages that condition their attitudes and legislative behavior. These additional cues may come from the campaign and its rhetoric, from particular contests and outcomes, and from sets of victory margins. It remains to explore some of these particular effects of 1982 on the members of the Ninety-eighth Congress.

The Campaign Is the Message. In every campaign, members of Congress use rhetoric, focus on issues, press their opponents, or see these things happening to them in ways that either have an effect or fall flat. These thrusts and counterthrusts in campaign rhetoric are shared in the cloakrooms when the next Congress convenes. A campaign may box in members of Congress to vote the next year for or against particular things because of grandiose statements or particular promises they made during a campaign, or a campaign may make a member of Congress wary of taking a step like one he took in the previous Congress that backfired and hurt him during the campaign.

The voters sent many such messages during the 1982 election campaign. Among the substantive messages: cut back on defense growth, do something—anything—about unemployment, treat social security as a ticking time bomb and not, certainly, as a budget issue. In virtually every campaign, candidates of both parties talked about the need to maintain some control over unchecked Pentagon spending. The phrase "we can't give the Pentagon a blank check" could have been used interchangeably by Democrats and Republicans in virtually every congressional campaign across the country. This rhetoric spilled over into the Ninety-eighth Congress and began immediately to affect the votes on defense bills in the House and Senate budget committees and on the two floors. It will not result in an actual cut in the defense budget, nor will it result in deep cuts in the projected growth. But these campaign themes led the House in 1983 to pass a budget cutting President Reagan's defense increase by nearly two-thirds and will almost certainly lead to $6–15 billion less in the 1984 defense budget than what President Reagan asked.

We immediately saw the results of campaign experiences with unemployment. Within days after the election, Republican Senate leader Howard Baker and Democratic House Speaker Tip O'Neill had embraced a bill to create public works jobs to repair highways and bridges—in advance of any program proposed by the president. The president soon signed on, and this bill passed even before the Ninety-eighth Congress convened. Soon thereafter, another, larger jobs bill made its way through Congress.

As for social security, Democratic candidates outdid one another in claiming their fealty to the social security system. Having scored their political points, they then worked with the president to pass a comprehensive plan to overhaul the social security system. The plan was signed into law in April 1983—before serious deliberation of the budget became intertwined with social security reform. Republicans, deeply stung by Democratic charges on social security, began immediately after the 1982 election to try to "depoliticize" the issue. In 1981 and 1982, Republicans talked about social security as a budget issue; in 1983, Republicans talked about social security as a *social security* issue and swallowed most of the changes propounded by Democrats to eliminate the social security issue from the 1984 political agenda.

Social security will continue to have a big effect on politics in Congress in 1983 and 1984—because of the *way* it was used in 1982 campaigns by Democrats against incumbent GOP members of Congress. Virtually every Republican legislator across the country was stung by Democratic charges that he or she had voted to cut social security in the 1982 budget. The charges stung because they were true; elimination of a minimum benefit and other changes were incorporated into the omnibus Reagan budget proposals that Republicans signed onto nearly unanimously. While twenty-six incumbent Republican congressmen lost their seats in November, a much larger number saw their margins considerably reduced or barely escaped defeat. All these returning members will be particularly cautious in the future about voting for any omnibus measure that contains the potential seeds of destruction. Thus, Republican hopes of near-perfect party unity on an omnibus, blockbuster vote in 1983 or 1984 are dim indeed.

Often just as important in a campaign is the message that could be sent—but is not. In 1982, few candidates called for restoring every budget cut made in 1981 and adding more federal dollars for good measure, for increasing taxes over and above what they were in 1980, or for cutting national defense in real terms. The overall agenda of the campaign virtually *assumed* acceptance of the notions that we should cut back and streamline the role of government, reduce the tax burden to relieve citizens and enhance economic growth, and keep our country strong enough to avert an outside threat. Thus, the stronger and self-confident House Democrats, implementing their own budget resolution in early 1983, increased social spending only marginally over the Reagan request, did not cut defense, but increased it less than Reagan, and did not propose a wholesale rollback of the package of tax cuts passed two years earlier.

The Life of the Party. In the 1980 campaign, the Republicans ran a party-based effort. National television commercials buttressed the notion that voters should vote Republican. These campaign themes underscored the notion that 1980 was a Republican party victory, not just a Reagan victory. They helped to lead to the unprecedented party unity on key votes in Congress in 1981 that resulted in Reagan policy victories.

The 1982 campaign moved rapidly away from party-based politics. National Republican television commercials that focused on a party message flopped (although they may have helped the Republicans by blunting the steady stream of bad economic news). While Republican candidates everywhere relied heavily on the national party organization and national party resources of the GOP, few Republican candidates ran as Republicans, saying "vote for me because I am a Republican." Most Republicans ran the more traditional, individualistic campaigns, emphasizing their own personalities, their own service to constituents, their own independence. The Republican party organization and money helped candidates a lot; the Republican party label did not. Until events prove otherwise, independence from party is likely to be a prevailing theme for Republicans in Congress as we approach 1984.

Most Democrats ran *against* Republicans and the Republican party more than they ran *as* Democrats. (Of course, they benefited simply by *being* Democrats. On the whole, it helps to be a member of the party with more identifiers.) Moreover, Democrats, despite major strides made in 1981 and 1982, lacked the impressive organization and resources of their GOP counterparts. The use of party in campaigns in 1982 strongly underscores the notion that dealignment, rather than realignment, is the prevailing trend in American politics.

Carolina on My Mind. Specific elections often send specific messages to particular groups of legislators. Nowhere was this more true—or more important in 1982—than in North Carolina. President Reagan made a ballyhooed campaign appearance there, even though there were no statewide contests. Why? Republicans saw a chance to pick up as many as five House seats from moderate Democrats who had failed to support the president on the key economic issues of 1981— Representatives Bill Hefner, Steve Neal, and Charles Whitley, who voted against Reagan on all three key votes, Representative Ike Andrews, who supported Reagan on only one of the three, and the open seat vacated by Representative L. H. Fountain, who voted with the president two times out of three.

The White House anticipated sending a message, through several defeats or close calls, to all southern Democrats: support the president on the key issues or else the full resources of the Oval Office will be arrayed against you—and that means trouble. The results, however, sent the opposite message. All the Democrats won, and all except Andrews won comfortably (receiving between 58 and 64 percent of the vote). Although Ike Andrews received only 51 percent of the votes cast, his victory was the most significant; few observers expected it, since his early vulnerability had been compounded by a widely publicized arrest for drunk driving during the campaign. Underscoring these Democratic victories were two additional victories in North Carolina districts, where staunch Reagan Republican loyalists Eugene Johnston and Bill Hendon were unseated by moderate Democrats.

Every southern Democrat noted the numbers in North Carolina. All were reinforced in their judgment that they—not the White House—are the best judges of what works in their own districts. Few will be moved by fear of retribution or awe of President Reagan's political standing to support presidential initiatives in the Ninety-eighth Congress. Since, in addition, the new southern members elected in 1982 were almost all moderate, the chances of finding in the House a consistent majority coalition of the right—as opposed to the center—became virtually nonexistent.

Moths Too Close to the Flame. The Reagan conservative coalition of 1981 was composed of southern Democratic Boll Weevils—and a nearly totally united Republican party. Before 1981 was over, perfect Republican unity had disappeared, changing the coalition long before the 1982 election. Still, chances for presidential success in Congress remained—and remain—dependent on keeping Republican ranks as unbroken as possible.

Fissures in Republican unity were, however, widened by two sets of election results. First, the moderate Republican House members who were most reluctant to support Reaganomics—the so-called Gypsy Moths—generally saw their electoral margins drop significantly on November 2.

The clear message to moderate Republicans: get your distance from the president. This message was reinforced by the narrow escapes made by prominent GOP Senate moderates Lowell Weicker (Connecticut), John Chafee (Rhode Island), David Durenberger (Minnesota), Robert Stafford (Vermont), and John Danforth (Missouri); each was hurt by charges that he was too close to Reagan. Moderate Republicans up for reelection in 1984 will be sure to pay their reelection insurance premiums early, reinforcing their own independent stances and voting records.

The same message went to all Republicans with the narrow

escape of their House leader, Robert Michel. Running against an underfinanced, late-starting political novice in a bedrock Republican district, Michel won by a bare 3,000 votes. The terrible economic conditions in Peoria, worsened by the president's pipeline embargo, hurt Michel—but hurt far worse because of his near-total identification with the president and his policies. Afterward, Michel said that he had heard the message sent by his constituents. So too did his colleagues.

Liberalism Lives. Not all specific election messages went to Republicans. Liberal Democrats also received a message—the reverse of that sent to them in 1978 and 1980. In 1982, every liberal Democratic senator up for reelection won; nearly all increased their margin over their last election contest. Sarbanes (Maryland), Metzenbaum (Ohio), Riegle (Michigan), Matsunaga (Hawaii), and Mitchell (Maine) all were considered vulnerable a year before the election; all won handily. None shrank in the campaign from his voting record, philosophy, or feisty opposition to President Reagan's conservative policies. Democratic feistiness is likely to increase, as a result, in 1983 and 1984.

But feistiness does not mean returning to the Great Society. As we note above, the campaign demonstrated that the political agenda has shifted. There *is* a new liberalism, and it differs from that espoused in the 1960s, both in rhetoric and, as the House 1983 budget resolution shows, in action.

Conclusion

The 1982 elections will matter in policy terms. But the message sent by the voters in the elections was a message that had been sent in other ways long before the election. The dramatic changes in the president's coalition, which mass media analysts described on election night as a result of the twenty-six-seat shift in the House, in fact had occurred well before the November election. A message to trim the sails first went out in August 1981 after the foundation had been laid for the Reagan economic program and continued through much of 1982. The election most importantly reinforced and confirmed the validity of that message, among Republicans and Democrats alike.

All of this meant a tougher time for President Reagan in building a majority coalition on Capitol Hill. It meant too that it certainly would not be the majority coalition that Reagan constructed in 1981. But it does not mean that Reagan will be defeated in every battle he chooses to fight on Capitol Hill, only that the formula for a winning coalition will be that of 1982, not of 1981. The message is to compromise, to acknowledge the sources of public and congressional concern, to seek coalitions of the center as well as of the right. The president's actions on social security, jobs bills, and the budget in early 1983 show at least a partial acceptance of that message.

There is another message in this election, namely, that we should all be careful about interpreting what motivates the voters on election day. Public opinion and elite opinion can and often do diverge. Messages can be deceptive and easily misinterpreted. Sensitivity to how preelection expectations are drawn and to the margins of victory and shifts in support, not just to who wins and loses, can often lead to very different interpretations from those of the past—and usually to more correct ones.

Notes

1. This seems to be true in spite of contrary arguments by most academic observers. See, for example, Everett C. Ladd, "The Brittle Mandate," *Political Science Quarterly,* vol. 96 (Spring 1981), pp. 1–25; and Austin Ranney, ed., *The American Elections of 1980* (Washington, D.C.: American Enterprise Institute, 1981).

2. That one exception is the overall shift in seats and ideology, which got much attention on election night and in the days following, albeit in a rather overstated and simplistic fashion that ignored the major changes that had already taken place in voting behavior and coalition politics in Congress in the year that followed Reagan's "conservative coalition" victories in 1981 and preceded the 1982 election.

3. Edward R. Tufte, *Political Control of the Economy* (Princeton, N.J.: Princeton University Press, 1978), chap. 5.

4. Gary C. Jacobson and Samuel Kernell, "Strategy and Choice in the 1982 Congressional Elections," *PS,* vol. 15, no. 3 (Summer 1982), pp. 423–30.

5. Tufte, *Political Control of the Economy,* p. 112.

6. William Schneider, "Reaganomics Was on the Voters' Minds, but Their Verdict Was Far from Clear," *National Journal,* vol. 14, no. 45 (November 6, 1982), pp. 1892–93. See also "Opinion Roundup," *Public Opinion,* vol. 5, no. 6 (December/January 1983), pp. 21–38.

7. The explanation that follows was offered together with a prediction of modest Republican losses *before* the election by a number of analysts, most notably Jacobson and Kernell in "Strategy and Choice."

8. The term and the empirical phenomenon it describes were reported by Albert D. Cover and David R. Mayhew in "Congressional Dynamics and the Decline of Competitive Congressional Elections," in L. Dodd and B. Oppenheimer, eds., *Congress Reconsidered* (New York: Praeger, 1977), pp. 54–72.

9. Carolyn Smith, *The 1982 Vote: What Happened* (New York: ABC News, 1983), p. 14.

10. We note in passing that a simple presidential coattails surge-and-decline model, which explains midterm losses by the events of the preceding presidential election (the stronger the showing by the president in the previous election, the greater the loss by the president's party at midterm), predicts a Republican loss of thirty-one seats in 1982. See James E. Campbell, "Explaining Presidential Losses in Midterm Congressional Elections: A Test of Competing Theories," unpublished paper, Department of Political Science, University of Georgia, 1983.

Appendixes

Appendix A

	Party Holding Presidency	President's Party Gain/Loss of Seats in House	President's Party Gain/Loss of Seats in Senate
Year			
1862	R	− 3	8
1866	R	− 2	0
1870	R	− 31	− 4
1874	R	− 96	− 8
1878	R	− 9	− 6
1882	R	− 33	3
1886	D	− 12	3
1890	R	− 85	0
1894	D	− 116	− 5
1898	R	− 21	7
1902	R	9 [a]	2
1906	R	− 28	3
1910	R	− 57	− 10
1914	D	− 59	5
1918	D	− 19	− 6
1922	R	− 75	− 8
1926	R	− 10	− 6
1930	R	− 49	− 8
1934	D	9	10
1938	D	− 71	− 6
1942	D	− 55	− 9

Losses by President's Party in Midterm Elections, 1862–1982

APPENDIX A (continued)

Year	Party Holding Presidency	President's Party Gain/Loss of Seats in House	President's Party Gain/Loss of Seats in Senate
1946	D	−55	−12
1950	D	−29	−6
1954	R	−18	−1
1958	R	−48	−13
1962	D	−4	3
1966	D	−47	−4
1970	R	−12	2
1974	R	−48	−5
1978	D	−15	−3
1982	R	−26	+1

NOTE: Each entry is the difference between the number of seats won by the president's party in that midterm election and the number of seats won by that party in the preceding general election. Because of changes in the overall number of seats in the Senate and House, in the number of seats won by third parties, and in the number of vacancies, a Republican loss is not always matched precisely by a Democratic gain, or vice versa. D = Democratic; R = Republican.
a. Although the Republicans gained nine seats in the 1902 elections, they actually lost ground to the Democrats, who gained twenty-five seats after the increase in the overall number of representatives after the 1900 census.
SOURCES: For 1862–1978: Norman J. Ornstein, Thomas E. Mann, Michael J. Malbin, and John F. Bibby, *Vital Statistics on Congress, 1982* (Washington, D.C.: American Enterprise Institute, 1983), p. 41. For 1982: *Congressional Quarterly Weekly Report*, November 6, 1982, pp. 2779–81.

Appendix B

State	Candidates	Party	Vote	%	Expenditures ($)
	SENATE ELECTION RESULTS AND CAMPAIGN EXPENDITURES, 1982				
Arizona	Dennis DeConcini[a]	D	411,970	56.9	1,907,358
	Pete Dunn	R	291,749	40.3	884,517
	Randall Clamons	L	20,100	2.8	0[b]
California	Edmund G. Brown	D	3,494,968	44.8	5,367,931
	Pete Wilson	R	4,022,565	51.5	7,082,651
Connecticut	Toby Moffett	D	499,146	46.1	1,368,147
	Lowell Weicker, Jr.[a]	R	545,987	50.4	2,306,119
	Lucien Difazio	C	30,212	2.8	60,806
Delaware	David N. Levinson	D	84,413	44.2	1,247,054
	William V. Roth[a]	R	105,357	55.2	794,210
Florida	Lawton Chiles[a]	D	1,636,857	61.7	806,629
	Van Poole	R	1,014,551	38.3	472,505
Hawaii	Spark M. Matsunaga[a]	D	245,386	80.1	561,388
	Clarence J. Brown	R	52,071	17.0	0[b]
	E. F. Bernier-Nachtwey	I-D	8,953	2.9	0[b]
Indiana	Floyd Fithian	D	828,400	45.6	870,023
	Richard G. Lugar[a]	R	978,301	53.8	2,973,791
Maine	George J. Mitchell[a]	D	279,819	60.9	1,208,026
	David F. Emory	R	179,882	39.1	1,081,122
Maryland	Paul S. Sarbanes[a]	D	707,356	63.5	1,612,746
	Lawrence J. Hogan	R	407,334	36.5	580,953

Massachusetts	Edward M. Kennedy[a]	D	1,247,084	60.8	2,470,473
	Raymond Shamie	R	784,602	38.3	2,305,996
Michigan	Donald W. Riegle[a]	D	1,728,793	57.7	1,542,147
	Philip E. Ruppe	R	1,223,288	40.9	1,045,545
Minnesota	Mark Dayton	DFL	840,401	46.6	7,172,312
	David Durenberger[a]	I-R	949,207	52.6	3,969,408
Mississippi	John C. Stennis[a]	D	414,099	64.2	944,054
	Haley Barbour	R	230,927	35.8	1,133,384
Missouri	Harriet Woods	D	758,629	49.1	1,193,966
	John C. Danforth[a]	R	784,876	50.8	1,806,350
Montana	John Melcher[a]	D	174,861	54.4	823,924
	Larry Williams	R	133,789	41.7	708,286
	Larry Dodge	L	12,412	3.9	18,936
Nebraska	Edward Zorinsky[a]	D	363,350	66.6	522,616
	Jim Keck	R	155,760	28.5	489,186
	Virginia Walsh	I	26,443	4.9	99,330
Nevada	Howard W. Cannon[a]	D	114,720	47.7	1,625,042
	Chic Hecht	R	120,377	50.1	981,197
	"None of the Above"		5,297	2.2	—
New Jersey	Frank R. Lautenberg	D	1,117,549	50.9	6,435,743
	Millicent Fenwick	R	1,047,626	47.8	2,606,633
New Mexico	Jeff Bingaman	D	217,682	53.8	1,586,245
	Harrison Schmitt[a]	R	187,128	46.2	1,692,204
New York	Daniel Patrick Moynihan[a]	D	3,232,146	65.1	2,708,660
	Florence Sullivan	R	1,696,766	34.2	117,875
North Dakota	Quentin N. Burdick[a]	D	164,873	62.8	779,859
	Gene Knorr	R	89,304	34.0	406,601
	Anna Bougois	I	8,288	3.2	166
Ohio	Howard M. Metzenbaum[a]	D	1,923,767	56.7	2,815,967
	Paul E. Pfeifer	R	1,396,790	41.1	1,025,595
	Philip Herzing	L	36,103	1.1	0[b]
	Alicia Merel	I	38,803	1.1	0[b]

(Table continues)

APPENDIX B (continued)

State	Candidates	Party	Vote	%	Expenditures ($)
Pennsylvania	Cyril H. Wecht	D	1,412,965	39.2	424,507
	John Heinz[a]	R	2,136,418	59.3	2,607,983
Rhode Island	Julius C. Michaelson	D	167,283	48.8	438,630
	John H. Chafee[a]	R	175,495	51.2	1,019,020
Tennessee	Jim Sasser[a]	D	780,113	61.9	2,090,517
	Robin L. Beard	R	479,642	38.1	1,639,858
Texas	Lloyd Bentsen[a]	D	1,818,223	58.6	4,996,104
	James M. Collins	R	1,256,759	40.5	4,285,377
Utah	Ted Wilson	D	219,482	41.3	1,703,170
	Orrin G. Hatch[a]	R	309,332	58.3	4,685,836
Vermont	James A. Guest	D	79,340	47.2	282,600
	Robert T. Stafford[a]	R	84,450	50.3	397,015
Virginia	Richard J. Davis	D	690,839	48.8	1,192,203
	Paul S. Trible	R	724,571	51.2	2,170,961
Washington	Henry M. Jackson[a]	D	943,655	69.0	1,353,408
	Doug Jewett	R	332,273	24.3	241,695
	Jesse Chiang	I	20,251	1.5	14,079
	King Lysen	I	72,297	5.3	41,557
West Virginia	Robert C. Byrd[a]	D	387,170	68.5	1,763,156
	Cleve Benedict	R	173,910	30.8	1,098,218
Wisconsin	William Proxmire[a]	D	983,311	63.6	0[b]
	Scott McCallum	R	527,355	34.1	119,924
	William Osborne Hart	I	21,807	1.4	2,471
Wyoming	Rodger McDaniel	D	72,466	43.3	389,511
	Malcolm Wallop[a]	R	94,725	56.7	1,102,046

NOTE: C = Conservative; D= Democratic; DFL = Democratic Farm Labor; I = Independent; I-D = Independent-Democratic; I-R = Independent-Republican; L = Libertarian; R = Republican. Does not include candidates who received less than 1 percent of the vote.
a. Incumbent.
b. Did not file with the Federal Election Commission.
SOURCE: Elections Research Center, Washington, D.C.

Appendix C

SENATE INCUMBENTS REELECTED, DEFEATED, OR RETIRED AND
SEATS THAT CHANGED PARTY, 1954–1982

Year	Retired[a]	Total Seeking Reelection	Incumbents Defeated in Primaries	Incumbents Defeated in General Elections	Reelected as Percentage of Those Seeking Reelection	Incumbent Defeated in General Election		Open Seat	
						D→R	R→D	D→R	R→D
1954	6	32	2	6	75.0	2	4	1	1
1956	6	29	0	4	86.2	1	3	3	1
1958	6	28	0	11	60.7	0	11	0	2
1960	5	29	0	1	96.6	1	0	1	0

(Table continues)

159

APPENDIX C (continued)

Year	Retired[a]	Total Seeking Reelection	Incumbents Defeated in Primaries	Incumbents Defeated in General Elections	Reelected as Percentage of Those Seeking Reelection	Incumbent Defeated in General Election		Open Seat	
						D→R	R→D	D→R	R→D
1962	4	35	1	5	82.9	2	3	0	3
1964	2	33	1	4	84.8	1	3	0	0
1966	3	32	3	1	87.5	1	0	2	0
1968	6	28	4	4	71.4	4	0	3	2
1970	4	31	1	6	77.4	3	2	1	0
1972	6	27	2	5	74.1	1	4	3	2
1974	7	27	2	2	85.2	0	2	1	3
1976	8	25	0	9	64.0	5	4	2	3
1978	10	25	3	7	60.0	5	2	3	3
1980	5	29	4	9	55.2	9	0	3	0
1982	3	30	0	2	93.3	1	1	1	1

NOTE: This table reflects shift in party control of seats from immediately before to immediately after the November election. D = Democrat; R = Republican.

a. Does not include persons who died or resigned from office before the election.

SOURCES: For 1954–1980: *Vital Statistics on Congress, 1982,* pp. 44, 48. For 1982: *Congressional Quarterly Weekly Report,* November 6, 1982, pp. 2789–91.

Appendix D

	97th Congress			98th Congress			
	Seats	Dem.	Rep.	Seats	Dem.	Rep.	Gain/Loss
Alabama	7	4	3	7	5	2	+1D/−1R
Alaska	1	0	1	1	0	1	
Arizona	4	2	2	5	2	3	+1R
Arkansas	4	2	2	4	2	2	
California	43	22	21	45	28	17	+6D/−4R
Colorado	5	3	2	6	3	3	+1R
Connecticut	6	4	2	6	4	2	
Delaware	1	0	1	1	1	0	+1D/−1R
Florida	15	11	4	19	13	6	+2D/+2R
Georgia	10	9	1	10	9	1	
Hawaii	2	2	0	2	2	0	
Idaho	2	0	2	2	0	2	
Illinois	24	10	14	22	12	10	+2D/−4R
Indiana	11	6	5	10	5	5	−1D
Iowa	6	3	3	6	3	3	
Kansas	5	1	4	5	2	3	+1D/−1R
Kentucky	7	4	3	7	4	3	
Louisiana	8	6	2	8	6	2	
Maine	2	0	2	2	0	2	
Maryland	8	7	1	8	7	1	
Massachusetts	12	10	2	11	10	1	−1R
Michigan	19	12	7	18	12	6	−1R
Minnesota	8	3	5	8	5	3	+2D/−2R
Mississippi	5	4	1	5	3	2	+1R/−1D
Missouri	10	6	4	9	6	3	−1R

HOUSE MAKEUP, PARTY GAINS AND LOSSES, 1983

(Table continues)

APPENDIX D   (continued)

	97th Congress			98th Congress			
	Seats	Dem.	Rep.	Seats	Dem.	Rep.	Gain/Loss
Montana	2	1	1	2	1	1	
Nebraska	3	0	3	3	0	3	
Nevada	1	1	0	2	1	1	+1R
New Hampshire	2	1	1	2	1	1	
New Jersey	15	8	7	14	9	5	+1D/−2R
New Mexico	2	0	2	3	1	2	+1D
New York	39	22	17	34	20	14	−2D/−3R
North Carolina	11	7	4	11	9	2	+2D/−2R
North Dakota	1	1	0	1	1	0	
Ohio	23	10	13	21	10	11	−2R
Oklahoma	6	5	1	6	5	1	
Oregon	4	3	1	5	3	2	+1R
Pennsylvania	25	12	13	23	13	10	+1D/−3R
Rhode Island	2	1	1	2	1	1	
South Carolina	6	2	4	6	3	3	+1D/−1R
South Dakota	2	1	1	1	1	0	−1R
Tennessee	8	5	3	9	6	3	+1D
Texas	24	19	5	27	22	5	+3D
Utah	2	0	2	3	0	3	+1R
Vermont	1	0	1	1	0	1	
Virginia	10	1	9	10	4	6	+3D/−3R
Washington	7	5	2	8	5	3	+1R
West Virginia	4	2	2	4	4	0	+2D/−2R
Wisconsin	9	5	4	9	5	4	
Wyoming	1	0	1	1	0	1	
Total	435	243	192	435	269	166	+26D/−26R

SOURCE: *Congressional Quarterly Weekly Report*, November 6, 1982, p. 2788.

Appendix E

NATIONAL POPULAR VOTE AND SEATS WON BY PARTY IN
HOUSE ELECTIONS, 1954–1982

	Democratic Candidates		Republican Candidates		Change from Last Election[a]		Difference between Democratic Percentage of Seats and Votes Won
Year	Percentage of all votes	Percentage of seats won	Percentage of all votes	Percentage of seats won	Percentage of major-party votes	Percentage of seats won	
1954	52.1	53.3	47.0	46.7	2.6D	4.2D	+1.2
1956	50.7	53.8	48.7	46.2	1.5R	0.5D	+3.1
1958	55.5	64.9	43.6	35.1	5.0D	11.1D	+9.4
1960	54.4	60.0	44.8	40.0	1.2R	4.9R	+5.6
1962	52.1	59.4	47.1	40.6	2.3R	0.6R	+7.3
1964	56.9	67.8	42.4	32.2	4.8D	8.4D	+10.9
1966	50.5	57.0	48.0	43.0	6.0R	10.8R	+6.5
1968	50.0	55.9	48.2	44.1	0.3R	1.1R	+5.9
1970	53.0	58.6	44.5	41.4	3.4D	2.7D	+5.6
1972	51.7	55.8	46.4	44.2	1.7R	2.8R	+4.1
1974	57.1	66.9	40.5	33.1	5.8D	11.1D	+9.8
1976	56.2	67.1	42.1	32.9	1.3R	0.2D	+10.9
1978	53.4	63.7	44.7	36.3	2.8R	3.4R	+10.3
1980	50.4	55.9	48.0	44.1	3.2R	7.8R	+5.5
1982	55.6	61.8	42.9	38.2	5.2D	5.9D	+6.2

a. Data show percentage-point increase over previous election in votes or seats won by Republicans (R) or Democrats (D).

SOURCES: *Vital Statistics on Congress 1982*, pp. 38–39; *Congressional Quarterly Weekly Report*, February 19, 1983, p. 387.

Appendix F

				Incumbents Defeated	Reelected as Percentage of Those	Incumbent Defeated in General Election		Open Seat	
Year	Retired[a]	Total Seeking Reelection	Incumbents Defeated in Primaries	Defeated in General Elections	Seeking Reelection	D→R	R→D	D→R	R→D
1954	24	407	6	22	93.1	3	18	2	3
1956	21	411	6	16	94.6	7	7	2	4
1958	33	396	3	37	89.9	1	35	0	14
1960	26	405	5	25	92.6	23	2	6	6

HOUSE INCUMBENTS REELECTED, DEFEATED, OR RETIRED AND SEATS THAT CHANGED PARTY, 1954–1982

Year								
1962	24	12	22	91.5	9	5	2	3
1964	33	8	45	86.6	5	39	5	8
1966	22	8	41	88.1	39	1	4	3
1968	23	4	9	96.8	5	0	2	4
1970	29	10	12	94.5	2	9	6	8
1972	40	12	13	93.6	6	3	9	5
1974	43	8	40	87.7	4	36	2	13
1976	47	3	13	95.8	7	5	3	7
1978	49	5	19	93.7	14	5	8	6
1980	34	6	31	90.7	27	3	10	1
1982	40	10	29	90.1	1	22	3	5

NOTE: This table reflects shift in party control of seats from immediately before to immediately after the November elections. It does not include party gains resulting from the creation of new districts and does not account for situations in which two districts were reduced to one, thus forcing incumbents to run against each other. D = Democrat; R = Republican.

a. Does not include persons who died or resigned from office before the election.

SOURCES: For 1954–1980: *Vital Statistics on Congress, 1982*, pp. 42, 46–47. For 1982: *National Journal*, November 6, 1982, p. 1881.

Appendix G

					Percentage of Total Vote[b]	
District and Candidates[a]		Party	Expenditures ($)	1982	1980

HOUSE ELECTION RESULTS AND CAMPAIGN EXPENDITURES IN CLOSE RACES, 1982

District and Candidates[a]	Party	Expenditures ($)	1982	1980
Alabama				
2 William Dickinson[c]	R	287,346	50	61
Billy Joe Camp	D	141,373	50	
6 Ben Erdreich	D	214,886	53	
Albert Lee Smith, Jr.[c]	R	537,985	46	51
Arizona				
5 Jim McNulty	D	343,318	50	
Jim Kolbe	R	532,588	49	
Arkansas				
2 Ed Bethune[c]	R	229,050	54	79
Charles George	D	60,706	46	
California				
1 Douglas Bosco	D	271,990	50	
Don H. Clausen[c]	R	539,448	47	54
6 Barbara Boxer	D	531,401	52	
Dennis McQuaid	R	603,952	47	
17 Charles Pashayan, Jr.[c]	R	433,229	54	71
Gene Tackett	D	151,530	46	
30 Matthew G. "Marty" Martinez[c]	D	300,744	54	
John H. Rousselot[c]	R	990,236	46	71
36 George Brown, Jr.[c]	D	447,111	54	53
John Paul Stark	R	183,661	46	
38 Jerry Patterson[c]	D	278,994	52	56
William F. Dohr	R	248,435	43	

43	Ron Packard (write-in)	R	366,711	37	
	Johnie R. Crean	R	1,140,863	31	
	Roy "Pat" Archer	D	36,072	32	

Colorado

3	Ray Kogovsek[c]	D	334,206	53	55
	Tom Weins	R	142,463	45	

Connecticut

3	Bruce Morrison	D	313,517	50	
	Lawrence J. DeNardis[c]	R	330,644	49	52
6	Nancy Johnson	R	420,578	52	
	William E. Curry, Jr.	D	233,284	48	

Delaware

AL	Thomas Carper	D	146,451	52	
	Thomas B. Evans, Jr.[c]	R	605,413	46	62

Florida

9	Michael Bilirakis	R	299,558	51	
	George H. Sheldon	D	379,692	49	
12	Tom Lewis	R	346,124	53	
	Brad Culverhouse	D	289,570	47	

Idaho

1	Larry E. Craig[c]	R	372,393	54	54
	Larry LaRocco	D	211,149	46	

Illinois

4	George M. O'Brien[c]	R	309,393	55	66
	Michael A. Murer	D	81,840	45	
17	Lane Evans	D	238,155	53	
	Kenneth G. McMillan	R	295,044	47	
18	Robert H. Michel[c]	R	687,875	52	62
	G. Douglas Stephens	D	166,928	48	
19	Daniel B. Crane[c]	R	305,850	52	69
	John Gwinn	D	164,470	48	
20	Richard J. Durbin	D	777,043	50	
	Paul Findley[c]	R	780,105	50	56

Indiana

3	John Hiler[c]	R	356,239	51	55
	Richard C. Bodine	D	113,831	49	
8	Francis X. McCloskey	D	157,223	51	
	Joel Deckard[c]	R	286,682	48	55

Kentucky

4	Gene Snyder[c]	R	303,653	54	67
	Terry L. Mann	D	201,217	45	

(Table continues)

APPENDIX G (continued)

District and Candidates[a]	Party	Expenditures ($)	Percentage of Total Vote[b] 1982	1980
Maine				
1 John R. McKenan, Jr.	R	384,594	50	
John M. Kerry	D	288,924	48	
Maryland				
2 Clarence D. Long[c]	D	162,439	53	57
Helen Delich Bentley	R	209,059	47	
Michigan				
5 Harold S. Sawyer[c]	R	422,129	53	53
Stephen V. Monsma	D	269,339	47	
6 Bob Carr	D	388,057	51	49
Jim Dunn[c]	R	358,114	48	51
Minnesota				
1 Timothy J. Penny	DFL	182,226	51	
Tom Hagedorn[c]	I-R	390,795	48	61
2 Vin Weber[c]	I-R	565,465	54	53
James W. Nichols	DFL	151,635	46	
6 Gerry Sikorski	DFL	245,136	51	
Arlen Erdahl[c]	I-R	432,497	49	72
7 Arlan Stangeland[c]	I-R	441,649	50	52
Gene Wenstrom	DFL	329,298	50	48
Mississippi				
2 Webb Franklin	R	318,376	50	
Robert G. Clark	D	208,136	48	
4 Wayne Dowdy[c]	D	357,159	53	50
Liles Williams	R	608,202	46	50
Missouri				
4 Ike Skelton[c]	D	459,566	55	68
Wendell Bailey[c]	R	464,385	45	57
7 Gene Taylor[c]	R	251,305	51	68
David A. Geisler	D	103,881	49	
8 Bill Emerson[c]	R	452,291	53	55
Jerry Ford	D	113,127	47	
Montana				
2 Ron Marlenee[c]	R	367,269	54	59
Howard Lyman	D	189,084	44	

New Hampshire

1	Norman E. D'Amours[c]	D	202,605	55	61
	Robert C. Smith	R	123,793	45	

New Jersey

4	Christopher H. Smith[c]	R	319,212	53	57
	Joseph P. Merlino	D	365,435	47	
9	Robert G. Torricelli	D	266,401	53	
	Harold C. Hollenbeck[c]	R	194,346	46	59

New Mexico

1	Manuel Lujan, Jr.[c]	R	788,844	52	51
	Jan Alan Hartke	D	187,488	48	

New York

3	Robert J. Mrazek	D	319,999	52	
	John LeBoutillier[c]	R,C	549,431	46	53
15	Bill Green[c]	R	241,019	54	57
	Betty G. Lall	D,L	184,808	45	
22	Benjamin A. Gilman[c]	R	432,571	53	74
	Peter A. Peyser[c]	R	218,605	42	56
27	George C. Wortley[c]	R	325,100	53	60
	Elaine Lytel	D,L	65,234	44	

North Carolina

2	I. T. "Tim" Valentine, Jr.	D	368,732	54	
	John W. Marin	R	169,610	31	
	H. M. Michaux, Jr. (write-in)	D	298,652	14	
4	Ike Andrews[c]	D	205,982	51	53
	William Cobey, Jr.	R	690,889	47	
6	Charles Robin Britt	D	184,365	54	
	Eugene Johnston[c]	R	380,732	46	51
11	James McClure Clarke	D	277,890	50	
	Bill Hendon[c]	R	507,213	49	54

Ohio

12	John R. Kasich	R	373,093	51	
	Bob Shamansky[c]	D	527,700	47	53
17	Lyle Williams[c]	R	306,537	55	58
	George D. Tablack	D	90,325	45	

Oklahoma

1	James R. Jones[c]	D	635,844	54	58
	Richard C. Freeman	R	200,138	46	

Oregon

1	Les AuCoin[c]	D	482,176	54	66
	Bill Moshofsky	R	585,624	46	

(Table continues)

APPENDIX G (continued)

District and Candidates[a]	Party	Expenditures ($)	Percentage of Total Vote[b] 1982	1980
5 Denny Smith[c]	R	491,122	51	49
J. Ruth McFarland	D	205,062	49	
Pennsylvania				
3 Robert A. Borski	D	235,326	50	
Charles F. Dougherty[c]	R	316,992	49	63
8 Peter H. Kostmayer	D	553,459	50	49
Jim Coyne[c]	R	488,208	49	51
11 Frank Harrison	D	191,306	53	
James L. Nelligan[c]	R	284,240	47	52
18 Doug Walgren[c]	D	267,527	54	69
Ted Jacob	R	240,169	45	
21 Thomas J. Ridge	R	228,140	50	
Anthony "Buzz" Andrezeski	D	158,321	50	
South Carolina				
1 Thomas F. Hartnett[c]	R	323,373	54	52
W. Mullins McLeod	D	204,637	45	
6 Robert Tallon, Jr.	D	412,669	52	
John L. Napier[c]	R	489,456	48	52
South Dakota				
AL Thomas A. Daschle[c]	D	716,436	52	66
Clint Roberts[c]	R	549,799	48	58
Tennessee				
7 Don Sundquist	R	508,451	51	
Bob Clement	D	373,530	49	
Texas				
16 Ronald Coleman	D	374,821	54	
Pat B. Haggerty	R	318,180	44	
26 Tom Vandergriff	D	948,024	50	
Jim Bradshaw	R	516,701	50	
Utah				
2 Dan Marriot[c]	R	414,300	54	67
Frances Farley	D	234,319	46	
Virginia				
1 Herbert H. Bateman	R	257,335	54	

	John J. McGlennon	D	101,798	46	
4	Norman Sisiky	D	525,304	54	
	Robert W. Daniel, Jr.ᶜ	R	328,382	46	61
6	James R. Olin	D	245,708	50	
	Kevin G. Miller	R	260,976	49	
8	Stan Parrisᶜ	R	728,076	50	49
	Herbert E. Harris II	D	416,624	49	48
9	Frederick C. Boucher	D	238,373	50	
	William C. Wamplerᶜ	R	316,900	50	70
10	Frank R. Wolfᶜ	R	557,553	53	51
	Ira M. Lechner	D	418,044	46	
West Virginia					
1	Alan B. Mollohan	D	202,099	53	
	John F. McCuskey	R	213,159	47	

NOTE: Close races are those in which the winner received 55 percent of the vote or less. AL = At large; C = Conservative; D = Democratic; DFL = Democratic Farm Labor; I-R = Independent-Republican; L = Liberal; R = Republican.

a. First candidate listed for district indicates winner.

b. Total vote rounded to the nearest whole percent.

c. Incumbent.

SOURCES: Federal Election Commission; *Congressional Quarterly Weekly Report*, February 19, 1983, pp. 386–94.

Appendix H

House Vote by State, 1978, 1980, and 1982

State	Total House Vote, 1978 (thousands)	Percent Democratic	Turnout[a] (percent)	Total House Vote, 1980 (thousands)	Percent Democratic	Turnout[a] (percent)	Total House Vote, 1982 (thousands)	Percent Democratic	Turnout[a] (percent)
Alabama	642	68.4	24.1	1,012	62.1	36.8	961	70.4	34.2
Alaska	124	44.4	46.1	155	25.8	56.6	181	28.7	63.1
Arizona	519	50.4	29.4	854	46.1	43.7	711	42.3	34.5
Arkansas	293	33.4	21.3	202	21.1	18.0	759	52.4	46.0
California	6,526	51.1	39.4	8,180	44.8	46.7	7,586	50.3	41.5
Colorado	785	47.0	39.8	1,150	44.0	54.4	946	47.4	42.5
Connecticut	1,021	58.0	45.3	1,339	51.9	58.0	1,069	54.0	45.0
Delaware	158	41.1	37.1	217	37.3	50.2	188	52.4	42.5
Florida	1,620	58.5	23.6	3,094	58.6	40.8	2,212	59.3	27.1
Georgia	589	80.2	16.1	1,355	71.9	35.0	904	74.1	22.4
Hawaii	253	80.1	38.5	281	85.4	40.4	298	89.6	41.6

Idaho	285	41.4	46.6	415	43.9	64.5	321	47.0	48.6
Illinois	3,044	51.8	37.4	4,473	54.1	54.4	3,613	57.9	43.9
Indiana	1,449	51.9	38.0	2,189	49.7	56.4	1,796	49.1	46.0
Iowa	812	49.6	39.1	1,257	51.1	60.1	1,005	52.6	48.0
Kansas	676	34.5	40.2	933	43.4	54.1	756	45.7	43.0
Kentucky	477	55.5	18.9	1,056	57.8	40.8	700	59.0	26.7
Louisiana	770	61.3	27.9	730	59.9	25.0	517	65.0	16.9
Maine	370	38.1	46.8	513	26.9	63.3	452	41.4	54.4
Maryland	924	65.4	30.7	1,403	61.7	45.5	1,091	68.1	34.2
Massachusetts	1,809	69.0	42.9	2,256	65.3	52.7	1,457	70.5	33.2
Michigan	2,708	56.8	42.3	3,588	52.3	55.0	2,808	59.5	42.9
Minnesota	1,526	51.1	54.1	1,905	51.8	65.1	1,750	54.7	58.5
Mississippi	519	48.5	31.0	789	54.3	46.0	641	57.5	36.7
Missouri	1,546	56.7	44.2	2,051	54.1	57.3	1,528	57.0	42.0
Montana	283	50.6	51.6	339	52.1	60.6	317	52.4	55.6
Nebraska	495	37.2	44.7	625	26.7	55.4	519	22.4	45.4
Nevada	191	69.5	36.7	245	67.5	40.8	234	48.8	35.4
New Hampshire	258	47.3	40.4	364	48.6	54.3	269	42.5	38.6
New Jersey	1,934	54.0	36.3	2,741	48.0	50.6	2,146	56.2	38.7
New Mexico	285	58.5	33.9	409	43.0	45.7	395	51.4	42.1
New York	4,379	51.9	33.9	5,617	49.3	43.4	4,681	55.9	35.6
North Carolina	1,020	59.5	25.0	1,737	55.5	40.7	1,321	53.6	29.9
North Dakota	220	30.9	48.4	293	56.8	63.0	260	71.6	55.1
Ohio	2,780	46.0	36.4	3,952	45.2	51.1	3,326	54.3	42.7
Oklahoma	589	56.2	28.3	836	52.6	38.0	856	63.0	37.3
Oregon	874	67.2	48.3	1,106	59.4	57.6	1,015	56.9	51.9
Pennsylvania	3,542	51.0	40.8	4,321	47.6	49.2	3,629	52.7	40.9

(Table continues)

APPENDIX H (continued)

State	Total House Vote, 1978 (thousands)	Percent Democratic	Turnout[a] (percent)	Total House Vote, 1980 (thousands)	Percent Democratic	Turnout[a] (percent)	Total House Vote, 1982 (thousands)	Percent Democratic	Turnout[a] (percent)
Rhode Island	308	56.6	43.6	387	55.3	54.5	333	52.2	45.8
South Carolina	577	65.6	27.4	830	49.2	37.7	657	53.7	28.7
South Dakota	256	46.9	53.3	320	54.3	66.0	276	51.6	57.2
Tennessee	1,062	54.7	33.4	1,304	50.9	39.4	1,176	59.4	34.8
Texas	2,182	58.9	23.3	4,069	59.1	40.2	2,849	64.8	26.4
Utah	379	43.0	44.2	592	39.2	63.3	490	36.3	49.6
Vermont	121	19.0	34.3	195	0	52.9	165	23.2	43.5
Virginia	1,057	42.0	27.9	1,553	31.3	39.6	1,335	47.2	32.7
Washington	979	51.8	35.1	1,626	50.2	53.7	1,307	52.8	41.5
West Virginia	443	65.7	32.5	686	57.0	49.2	546	62.9	38.8
Wisconsin	1,450	53.0	44.4	2,134	50.2	63.1	1,450	53.0	41.9
Wyoming	129	41.9	43.6	170	31.2	51.2	159	28.9	45.0

NOTE: In some states, votes for unopposed candidates are not counted.

a. Turnout is the total vote as a percentage of voting-age population.

SOURCES: *Statistical Abstract of the United States*, tables 786 and 802; *Congressional Quarterly Weekly Report*, February 19, 1983, pp. 386–94.

Appendix I

	GUBERNATORIAL ELECTION RESULTS, 1982			
State	*Candidates*	*Party*	*Votes*	*Percent*
Alabama	George C. Wallace	D	650,538	57.6
	Emory Folmar	R	440,815	39.1
Alaska	Bill Sheffield	D	89,918	46.1
	Tom Fink	R	72,291	37.1
	Joseph Vogler	AKI	3,235	1.7
	Richard L. Randolph	LIBERT	29,067	14.9
Arizona	Bruce Babbitt[a]	D	453,795	62.5
	Leo Corbet	R	235,877	32.5
	Sam Steiger	LIBERT	36,649	5.0
Arkansas	Bill Clinton	D	431,855	54.7
	Frank D. White[a]	R	357,496	45.3
California	Tom Bradley	D	3,787,669	48.1
	George Deukmejian	R	3,881,014	49.3
	James C. Griffin	AMI	56,249	0.7
	Dan P. Dougherty	LIBERT	81,076	1.0
	Elizabeth Martinez	PFP	70,327	0.9
Colorado	Richard D. Lamm[a]	D	627,960	65.7
	John D. Fuhr	R	302,740	31.7
	Paul Grant	LIBERT	19,349	2.0
Connecticut	William A. O'Neill[a]	D	578,264	53.4
	Lewis B. Rome	R	497,773	45.9
Florida	Robert Graham[a]	D	1,739,553	64.7
	L. A. "Skip" Bafalis	R	949,023	35.3

(Table continues)

APPENDIX I (continued)

State	Candidates	Party	Votes	Percent
Georgia	Joe Frank Harris	D	734,090	62.8
	Bob Bell	R	434,496	37.2
Hawaii	George Ariyoshi[a]	D	141,043	45.2
	D. G. Anderson	R	81,507	26.1
	Frank F. Fasi	I-D	89,303	28.6
Idaho	John V. Evans[a]	D	165,365	50.6
	Philip E. Batt	R	161,157	49.4
Illinois	Adlai E. Stevenson III	D	1,811,027	49.3
	James R. Thompson[a]	R	1,816,101	49.4
	Bea Armstrong	LIBERT	24,417	0.7
	John E. Roche	TAX	22,001	0.6
Iowa	Roxanne Conlin	D	483,291	46.5
	Terry Branstad	R	548,313	52.8
Kansas	John Carlin[a]	D	405,772	53.2
	Sam Hardage	R	339,356	44.4
	James H. Ward	LIBERT	7,595	1.0
Maine	Joseph E. Brennan[a]	D	281,066	61.1
	Charles L. Cragin	R	172,949	37.6
Maryland	Harry R. Hughes[a]	D	705,910	62.0
	Robert A. Pascal	R	432,826	38.0
Massachusetts	Michael S. Dukakis	D	1,219,109	59.4
	John W. Sears	R	749,679	36.6
	Frank Rich	I	63,068	3.1
Michigan	James J. Blanchard	D	1,561,291	51.4
	Richard H. Headlee	R	1,369,582	45.1
	Robert Tisch	I	80,288	2.6
Minnesota	Rudy Perpich	DFL	1,049,104	58.8
	Wheelock Whitney	I-R	711,796	39.9
Nebraska	Bob Kerrey	D	277,436	50.7
	Charles Thone[a]	R	270,203	49.3
Nevada	Richard H. Bryan	D	128,132	53.4
	Robert F. List[a]	R	100,104	41.8
	Dan Becan	LIBERT	4,621	1.9
	None of the above		6,894	2.9
New Hampshire	Hugh Gallen[a]	D	132,287	46.4
	John H. Sununu	R	147,774	51.9
	Meldrim Thomson, Jr.	I	4,785	1.7

New Mexico	Toney Anaya	D	215,840	53.0
	John B. Irick	R	191,626	47.0
New York	Mario M. Cuomo	D, L	2,675,213	50.9
	Lew Lehrman	R, C, I[b]	2,494,827	47.5
	Robert J. Bohner	RTL	52,356	1.0
Ohio	Richard F. Celeste	D	1,981,882	59.0
	Clarence J. Brown	R	1,303,962	38.9
	Phyllis Goetz	LIBERT	39,114	1.2
Oklahoma	George Nigh[a]	D	548,159	62.1
	Tom Daxon	R	332,207	37.6
Oregon	Ted Kulongoski	D	374,316	35.9
	Victor G. Atiyeh[a]	R	639,841	61.4
	Paul J. Cleveland	LIBERT	27,394	2.6
Pennsylvania	Allen E. Ertel	D	1,772,353	48.1
	Richard L. Thornburgh[a]	R	1,872,784	50.8
Rhode Island	J. Joseph Garrahy[a]	D	247,208	73.2
	Vincent Marzullo	R	79,602	23.7
South Carolina	Richard Riley[a]	D	468,819	69.8
	William D. Workman, Jr.	R	202,806	30.2
South Dakota	Mike O'Connor	D	81,137	29.1
	William J. Janklow[a]	R	197,425	70.9
Tennessee	Randy Tyree	D	500,937	40.4
	Lamar Alexander[a]	R	737,963	59.6
Texas	Mark White	D	1,697,870	53.2
	William Clements[a]	R	1,465,937	45.9
Vermont	Madeleine M. Kunin	D	74,394	44.0
	Richard A. Snelling[a]	R	93,111	55.0
Wisconsin	Anthony S. Earl	D	896,812	56.8
	Terry J. Kohler	R	662,838	41.9
Wyoming	Ed Herschler[a]	D	106,427	63.1
	Warren A. Morton	R	62,128	36.9

NOTE: AKI = Alaskan Independence; AMI = American Independent; C = Conservative; D = Democratic; DFL = Democratic Farm Labor; I = Independent; I-D = Independent-Democratic; I-R = Independent-Republican; L = Liberal; LIBERT = Libertarian; PFP = Peace and Freedom; R = Republican; RTL = Right to Life; TAX = Taxpayers.
a. Incumbent.
b. The New York ballot listed Lehrman on three lines: R = Republican, C = Conservative, and I = Statewide Independent.
SOURCES: *Congressional Quarterly Weekly Report*, February 19, 1982, pp. 386–94; Elections Research Center, Washington, D.C.

Appendix J

Partisan Control of State Legislatures, 1968-1982

FIGURE J–1

NUMBER OF STATE LEGISLATORS BY PARTY

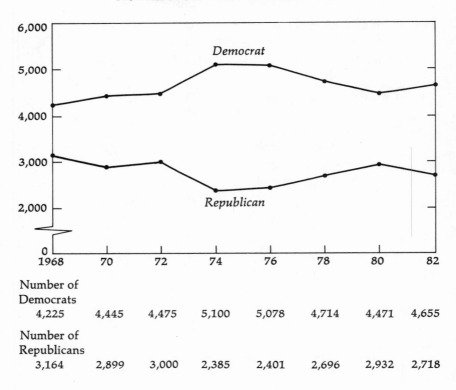

	1968	70	72	74	76	78	80	82
Number of Democrats	4,225	4,445	4,475	5,100	5,078	4,714	4,471	4,655
Number of Republicans	3,164	2,899	3,000	2,385	2,401	2,696	2,932	2,718

FIGURE J–2

NUMBER OF LEGISLATIVE CHAMBERS BY PARTY

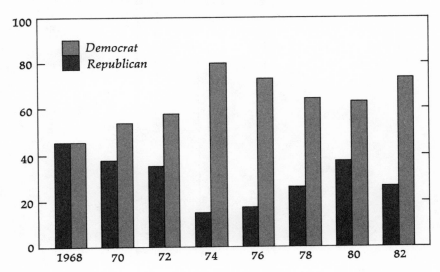

SOURCES: Figures for 1968, 1970, and 1972 are from *Statistical Abstract of the United States, 1973* (Washington, D.C.: Bureau of the Census, 1973), table 608, p. 377; figures for 1974, 1976, and 1978 are from *Statistical Abstract of the United States, 1979*, table 831, p. 511; figures for 1980 were compiled by Norman J. Ornstein; figures for 1982 are from *State Legislatures*, vol. 9, no. 1 (January 1983), pp. 10-12.

Appendix K

HOUSE CAMPAIGN EXPENDITURES, 1974–1982
(dollars)

	1974	1976	1978	1980	1982
All candidates					
Total expenditures	44,051,125	60,046,006	86,129,169	115,222,222	174,881,844
Mean expenditure	54,384	73,316	109,440	153,221	228,008
	(N=810)	(N=819)	(N=787)	(N=752)	(N=767)
Mean, Democrats	53,993	74,563	108,986	143,277	213,271
	(N=434)	(N=429)	(N=416)	(N=396)	(N=411)
Mean, Republicans	54,835	71,945	109,995	164,282	245,020
	(N=376)	(N=390)	(N=371)	(N=356)	(N=356)
Incumbents					
Mean, all incumbents	56,539	79,398	111,159	165,081	265,886
	(N=381)	(N=382)	(N=377)	(N=391)	(N=384)
Mean, Democrats	38,743	73,322	103,519	158,010	247,573

Mean, Republicans	80,339 (N=163)	91,456 (N=128)	126,022 (N=128)	177,345 (N=143)	289,430 (N=168)
	(N=218)	(N=254)	(N=249)	(N=248)	(N=216)
Challengers					
Mean, all challengers	40,015 (N=323)	50,795 (N=335)	74,802 (N=299)	121,751 (N=277)	152,075 (N=271)
Mean, Democrats	59,266 (N=162)	46,330 (N=122)	70,948 (N=109)	93,313 (N=105)	142,169 (N=138)
Mean, Republicans	20,644 (N=161)	53,352 (N=213)	77,012 (N=190)	139,111 (N=172)	162,354 (N=133)
Open seats					
Mean, all open seat candidates	90,426 (N=106)	124,506 (N=102)	201,049 (N=111)	201,790 (N=84)	281,870 (N=112)
Mean, Democrats	99,743 (N=54)	145,497 (N=53)	211,871 (N=58)	180,312 (N=43)	255,428 (N=57)
Mean, Republicans	80,751 (N=52)	101,802 (N=49)	189,205 (N=53)	224,316 (N=41)	309,273 (N=55)

NOTE: Includes primary and general election expenditures for general election candidates who filed reports with the Federal Election Commission. The 1979 amendments to the Federal Election Campaign Act exempted low-budget (under $5,000) campaigns from reporting requirements. A number of low-budget candidates who did file reports are included in the table. Because of these amendments, however, the data for 1980 and 1982 are not strictly comparable with those for previous years.

SOURCES: For 1974: Common Cause. For 1976–1982: Federal Election Commission.

Appendix L

SENATE CAMPAIGN EXPENDITURES, 1974–1982
(dollars)

	1974	1976	1978	1980	1982
All candidates					
Total expenditures	28,436,308	38,108,745[a]	64,695,510	74,163,669	114,035,370[b]
Mean expenditure	437,482 (N=65)	595,449[a] (N=64)	951,405 (N=68)	1,106,920 (N=67)	1,781,803 (N=64)
Mean, Democrats	487,775 (N=34)	569,902 (N=33)	762,831 (N=35)	1,170,580 (N=34)	1,761,694 (N=32)
Mean, Republicans	382,343 (N=31)	616,635 (N=30)	1,151,407 (N=33)	1,041,332 (N=33)	1,801,912 (N=32)
Incumbents					
Mean, all incumbents	555,714 (N=25)	623,809[a] (N=25)	1,341,942[c] (N=22)	1,301,692 (N=25)	1,858,112 (N=29)
Mean, Democrats	525,766 (N=15)	503,111 (N=17)	618,211[d] (N=11)	1,355,660[e] (N=19)	1,696,182 (N=18)
Mean, Republicans	600,636 (N=10)	891,342 (N=7)	2,065,674[c] (N=11)	1,130,792 (N=6)	2,123,089 (N=11)

Challengers					
Mean, all challengers	332,579 (N=22)	452,275 (N=23)	697,766 (N=21)	842,547 (N=24)	1,217,034 (N=29)
Mean, Democrats	390,297 (N=10)	645,441 (N=8)	830,282 (N=11)	557,006 (N=6)	1,516,015 (N=11)
Mean, Republicans	284,480 (N=12)	349,253 (N=15)	551,999 (N=10)	937,727 (N=18)	1,034,324 (N=18)
Open seats					
Mean, all open seat candidates	401,484 (N=18)	756,951 (N=16)	820,787 (N=25)	1,132,560 (N=18)	4,142,687 (N=6)
Mean, Democrats	532,691 (N=9)	636,295 (N=8)	828,127 (N=13)	1,188,903 (N=9)	3,055,589 (N=3)
Mean, Republicans	270,277 (N=9)	877,606 (N=8)	812,835 (N=12)	1,076,218 (N=9)	5,229,785 (N=3)

NOTE: Includes primary and general election expenditures for general election candidates only.

a. Includes one incumbent independent, Senator Harry F. Byrd of Virginia, $802,928.

b. Two candidates did not file reports with the FEC in 1982: incumbent William Proxmire (Democrat, Wisconsin) and challenger Clarence J. Brown (Republican, Hawaii).

c. These figures include the $7.5 million Helms reelection campaign in North Carolina. Without it the Republican mean would be $1,526,145, and the mean for all incumbents would be $1,050,560.

d. Includes incumbent J. Bennett Johnston (Democrat, Louisiana, $857,860), who was unopposed in the general election, but faced a primary challenger who spent $327,027.

e. Includes incumbent Russell B. Long (Democrat, Louisiana, $2,166,838), who was unopposed in the general election, but faced a primary challenger who spent $142,027.

SOURCES: For 1974: Common Cause. For 1976–1982: Federal Election Commission.

Appendix M

MEAN HOUSE CAMPAIGN EXPENDITURES, BY ELECTION OUTCOME, 1974–1982
(dollars)

	1974	1976	1978	1980	1982
Incumbent won with 60 percent or more[a]					
Democratic incumbent	35,146 (N=194)	56,937 (N=185)	85,424 (N=184)	117,773[b] (N=170)	206,670 (N=178)
Republican challenger	12,481 (N=137)	24,865 (N=144)	32,850 (N=125)	50,213 (N=95)	110,454 (N=101)
Republican incumbent	60,593 (N=57)	77,855 (N=87)	105,687 (N=103)	138,050 (N=114)	186,717 (N=86)
Democratic challenger	25,891 (N=56)	26,606 (N=81)	36,040 (N=84)	44,120 (N=75)	36,628 (N=62)
Difference between incumbents and challengers[c]	32,023 (N=192)	42,968 (N=226)	68,031 (N=209)	101,021 (N=170)	143,277 (N=163)
Incumbent won with less than 60 percent					
Democratic incumbent	68,513 (N=20)	119,440 (N=62)	145,065 (N=51)	223,345 (N=50)	446,542[d] (N=35)
Republican challenger	66,405 (N=20)	109,079 (N=62)	144,347 (N=51)	198,728 (N=50)	324,647[d] (N=31)

Republican incumbent	83,632 (N=70)	104,465 (N=36)	204,674 (N=20)	336,046 (N=26)	365,641[d] (N=56)
Democratic challenger	63,134 (N=70)	77,075 (N=36)	187,290 (N=20)	195,135 (N=26)	201,985[d] (N=54)
Difference between incumbents and challengers[c]	16,747 (N=90)	16,616 (N=98)	5,412 (N=71)	64,402 (N=76)	135,666 (N=85)
Incumbent was defeated					
Democratic incumbent	64,191 (N=4)	97,874 (N=7)	189,994 (N=14)	285,636 (N=28)	353,201[d] (N=3)
Republican challenger	71,404 (N=4)	144,883 (N=7)	226,028 (N=14)	341,499 (N=27)	373,093[d] (N=1)
Republican incumbent	105,203 (N=36)	234,435 (N=5)	230,323 (N=5)	295,170 (N=3)	465,027[d] (N=26)
Democratic challenger	103,661 (N=36)	144,491 (N=5)	192,037 (N=5)	353,855 (N=4)	292,781[d] (N=22)
Difference between incumbents and challengers[c]	1,185 (N=40)	10,055 (N=12)	-16,476 (N=19)	-56,537 (N=31)	123,361 (N=23)

a. Percentage of the vote received by two leading candidates.

b. For reasons explained in the note to appendix K, a number of nonfiling candidates with low-budget campaigns are not included.

c. Includes only races contested in the general election, both candidates filing.

d. The number of challengers does not equal that of incumbents because of the six races in 1982 in which an incumbent faced an incumbent because of redistricting. The mean expenditure for Democrats in these races was $585,205; for Republicans, $592,080. The mean expenditure for winners (four Democrats, two Republicans) was $600,337; for losers, $583,824.

SOURCES: For 1974: Common Cause. For 1976–1982: Federal Election Commission.

Appendix N

MEAN SENATE CAMPAIGN EXPENDITURES, BY ELECTION OUTCOME, 1974–1982
(dollars)

	1974	1976	1978	1980	1982
Incumbent won with 60 percent or more[a]					
Democratic incumbent	447,234	340,362	559,046[b]	1,220,616[c]	1,401,792
	(N=11)	(N=11)	(N=4)	(N=6)	(N=12)
Republican challenger	222,955	171,997	56,233	332,404	807,276
	(N=8)	(N=9)	(N=3)	(N=5)	(N=12)
Republican incumbent	—	—	318,749	1,075,038	—
			(N=3)	(N=4)	
Democratic challenger	—	—	38,458	265,822	—
			(N=3)	(N=4)	

Difference between incumbents and challengers[d]				
299,321 (N=8)	220,202 (N=9)	341,750 (N=6)	747,967 (N=9)	739,686 (N=12)
Incumbent won with less than 60 percent				
Democratic incumbent				
741,729 (N=4)	1,237,910 (N=1)	586,055 (N=2)	796,984 (N=4)	2,416,945 (N=5)
Republican challenger				
407,531 (N=4)	665,058 (N=1)	332,537 (N=2)	727,617 (N=4)	1,589,864 (N=5)
Republican incumbent				
497,945 (N=10)	320,239 (N=4)	3,133,293[e] (N=6)	1,242,300 (N=2)	2,117,088 (N=9)
Democratic challenger				
254,374 (N=10)	282,441 (N=4)	1,212,929 (N=6)	1,139,376 (N=2)	1,629,490 (N=9)
Difference between incumbents and challengers[d]				
314,376 (N=14)	241,346[f] (N=5)	1,503,653[g] (N=8)	80,553 (N=6)	608,842 (N=14)
Incumbent was defeated				
Democratic incumbent				
—	714,201 (N=5)	678,406 (N=5)	1,693,991 (N=9)	1,625,042 (N=1)
Republican challenger				
—	605,153 (N=5)	937,244 (N=5)	1,367,400 (N=9)	981,197 (N=1)

(Table continues)

187

APPENDIX N (continued)

	1974	1976	1978	1980	1982
Republican incumbent	513,456 (N=2)	1,319,440 (N=4)	1,483,203 (N=2)	—	1,692,204 (N=1)
Democratic challenger	679,614 (N=2)	1,008,440 (N=4)	870,079 (N=2)	—	1,586,245 (N=1)
Difference between incumbents and challengers[d]	−166,158 (N=2)	198,906 (N=9)	−9,706 (N=7)	326,591 (N=9)	374,902 (N=2)

NOTE: Dash indicates none.

a. Percentage of the vote received by two leading candidates.

b. Includes incumbent J. Bennett Johnston (Democrat, Louisiana, $857,860), who was unopposed in the general election, but faced a primary challenger who spent $327,027.

c. Includes incumbent Russell B. Long (Democrat, Louisiana, $2,166,838), who was unopposed in the general election, but faced a primary challenger who spent $142,027.

d. Includes only races contested in the general election, both candidates filing.

e. If one excludes the 1978 race between Republican Senator Jesse Helms of North Carolina and his challenger, John Ingram, this figure becomes $2,267,758.

f. Senate incumbents in 1976 who won with less than 60 percent included one independent, Senator Harry F. Byrd of Virginia, who spent $802,928.

g. If the Helms-Ingram race is excluded, this figure becomes $690,335.

SOURCES: For 1974: Common Cause. For 1976–1982: Federal Election Commission.

Appendix O

POLITICAL PARTY FINANCIAL ACTIVITY, 1976–1982
(dollars)

	Adjusted Receipts	Adjusted Disbursements	Contributions to Presidential, Senate, and House Candidates	Expenditures on Behalf of Presidential, Senate, and House Candidates
1976				
Democratic				
National committee	13,095,630	12,516,979	22,050	3,055,644
Senatorial	1,017,454	971,562	375,237	4,359
Congressional	937,717	1,011,157	423,200	500
Conventions, other national	3,164,573	3,062,675	0	0
State/local	n.a.	n.a.	n.a.	n.a.
Total Democratic	18,215,374	17,562,373	820,487	3,060,503
Republican				
National committee	29,118,930	26,679,143	1,871,726	1,442,773
Senatorial	1,774,815	2,010,629	445,902	113,976
Congressional	12,207,055	9,243,195	2,071,525	329,853
Conventions, other national	2,605,088	2,143,220	11,343	0
State/local	n.a.	n.a.	n.a.	n.a.
Total Republican	45,705,888	40,076,187	4,400,496	1,886,602
1978				
Democratic				
National committee	11,314,008	11,455,639	64,307	68,822

(Table continues)

189

APPENDIX O (continued)

	Adjusted Receipts	Adjusted Disbursements	Contributions to Presidential, Senate, and House Candidates	Expenditures on Behalf of Presidential, Senate, and House Candidates
Senatorial	269,981	893,773	427,000	0
Congressional	2,766,963	2,118,161	537,438	0
Conventions, other national	3,324,519	3,428,481	403,502	0
State/local	8,688,999	8,994,213	433,337	329,765
Total Democratic	26,364,470	26,890,267	1,865,584	398,587
Republican				
National committee	34,221,058	36,016,600	905,244	336,981
Senatorial	10,882,480	11,107,961	456,110	2,599,290
Congressional	14,062,070	15,695,690	1,817,424	839,421
Conventions, other national	4,400,216	2,330,882	598,382	0
State/local	20,960,029	20,728,829	745,191	579,974
Total Republican	84,525,853	85,879,962	4,522,351	4,355,666
1980				
Democratic				
National committee	15,418,300	15,150,984	41,051	3,942,526
Senatorial	1,653,849	1,618,162	481,500	589,316
Congressional	2,864,088	2,828,184	614,097	34,686
Conventions, other national	8,147,837	6,631,517	132,200	0
State/local	9,103,520	8,754,177	384,358	375,660
Total Democratic	37,187,594	34,983,024	1,653,206	4,942,188
Republican				
National committee	77,838,238	75,821,719	844,455	5,352,269
Senatorial	23,308,963	21,211,482	414,893	5,025,802
Congressional	20,287,961	34,790,731	2,005,663	1,229,110
Conventions, other national	6,031,367	6,080,735	482,159	0
State/local	33,781,069	32,545,199	781,207	837,292
Total Republican	161,247,598	170,449,866	4,528,377	12,444,473

APPENDIX O (continued)

	Adjusted Receipts	Adjusted Disbursements	Contributions to Presidential, Senate, and House Candidates	Expenditures on Behalf of Presidential, Senate, and House Candidates
		1982		
Democratic				
National committee	16,214,114	16,412,344	83,198	144,742
Senatorial	5,622,254	5,568,306	530,000	1,877,245
Congressional	6,525,419	6,481,665	560,605	197,936
Conventions, other national	3,107,038	3,887,834	0	0
State/local	7,558,084	7,667,280	546,660	1,071,950
Total Democratic	39,026,909	40,047,429	1,720,463	3,291,873
Republican				
National committee	83,531,947	84,309,088	1,648,667	229,127
Senatorial	48,879,354	47,680,853	548,626	8,707,537
Congressional	58,041,972	57,056,101	2,554,863	4,943,249
Conventions, other national	503,208	806,935	100	0
State/local	23,948,726	24,079,995	800,994	401,213
Total Republican	214,905,207	213,932,972	5,553,250	14,281,126

NOTE: n.a. = not available.

SOURCES: For 1976: Federal Election Commission, *Disclosure Series No. 4* (National Party Committee Receipts and Expenditures, Democratic and Republican, 1976 Campaign), November 1977. For 1978: Federal Election Commission, *Reports on Financial Activity, 1977-78* (Party and Non-Party Political Committees), vol. 1, summary tables, Final Report, April 1980. For 1980: Federal Election Commission, *Reports on Financial Activity, 1979-80* (Party and Non-Party Political Committees), vol. 1, summary tables, Final Report, January 1982. For 1982: Federal Election Commission, "FEC Reports Republicans Outspent Democrats by More Than 5-to-1 in '82 Elections," Press release, April 26, 1983.

Appendix P

Type of PAC	1972	1974[a]	1976	1978	1980	1982
Adjusted Expenditures of Political Action Committees by Category, 1972–1982 (millions of dollars)						
Labor	8.5	11.0	17.5	18.6	25.1	35.0
Business-related[b]	8.0	8.1	—	—	—	—
Corporate	c	c	5.8	15.2	31.4	43.2
Trade/membership/health	c	c	d	23.8	32.0	41.7
Nonconnected[e]	2.6	0.8	d	17.4	38.6	64.6
Other[f]	—	1.1	29.6	2.4	4.0	5.8
Total[g]	19.2	20.9	52.9	77.4	131.2	190.4

NOTE: Adjusted expenditures exclude transfers of funds between affiliated committees.

a. Data for 1974 do not correspond with those in table 3-8, which reflects an estimated amount, because the data in this table were thought to be low.

b. This category is based on a large assumption that the majority of PACs it encompasses do indeed have a basically probusiness orientation. It is included here for the purpose of listing the data for 1972 and 1974, before the specific breakdowns were devised by the FEC for the corporate and other categories, and it is only roughly comparable to the combined corporate and trade/membership/health data in 1978 through 1982. For 1972 it includes PACs listed by the Citizens Research Foundation as business/professional, dairy, education, health, and rural; for 1974 it includes those PACs grouped by Common Cause under the headings of business/professional, health, and agriculture/dairy. Most of these PACs would today fall into the corporate and trade/membership/health categories used by the FEC, although some would be scattered in the nonconnected, cooperative, and corporation without stock categories.

c. Included in business-related.

d. Included in other.

e. For 1972 and 1974 this represents spending by ideological PACs, as grouped by the Citizens Research Foundation (1972) or Common Cause (1974). After 1976 it corresponds directly to the FEC category by that name (which is dominated by the ideological groups).

APPENDIX P (continued)

f. This is a catchall category, for which only the 1978 through 1982 figures are comparable to each other. For 1974 this represents PACs grouped as "miscellaneous" by Common Cause and includes such groups as the NEA (and affiliates), environmentalists, and some cooperatives. For 1976 it includes all PACs now grouped by the FEC as trade/membership/health, nonconnected, cooperative, and corporation without stock. For 1978 through 1982, it combines the FEC categories of cooperatives and corporations without stock.

g. Figures may not add to totals because of rounding.

Sources: For 1972-1978: Cantor, *Political Action Committees*, pp. 83-84. For 1980: Federal Election Commission, *Reports on Financial Activity, 1979-80* (Party and Non-Party Political Committees), vol. 1, summary tables, Final Report. For 1982: Federal Election Commission,"1981–82 PAC Giving Up 51%," Press Release, April 29, 1983.

Contributors

JOHN F. BIBBY is a professor of political science at the University of Wisconsin–Milwaukee. He has been an adjunct scholar at the American Enterprise Institute and codirector of its Congress Project since 1979. He is coauthor of a number of books, including *On Capitol Hill* and the 1980 and 1982 editions of *Vital Statistics on Congress*.

ALAN EHRENHALT is political editor of *Congressional Quarterly* and contributes a regular column, "Congress and the Country," to the *Congressional Quarterly Weekly Report*. He is editor of *Politics in America: Members of Congress in Washington and at Home*.

ALBERT R. HUNT is congressional and national political correspondent for the *Wall Street Journal* and a regular participant in public television's "Washington Week in Review." He contributed to *The American Elections of 1980*.

THOMAS E. MANN is executive director of the American Political Science Association and an adjunct scholar at the American Enterprise Institute. He is the author of *Unsafe at Any Margin*, coauthor of the 1980 and 1982 editions of *Vital Statistics on Congress*, and coeditor of *The New Congress*.

NORMAN J. ORNSTEIN is professor of politics at Catholic University, visiting scholar at AEI, and political editor of "The Lawmakers" series on public television. He is the author of *Interest Groups, Lobbying and Policymaking*, coauthor of the 1980 and 1982 editions of *Vital Statistics on Congress*, and coeditor of *The New Congress*.

LARRY F. SABATO is associate professor of government at the University of Virginia. He is author of *The Democratic Party Primary*, *Goodbye to Good-Time Charlie: The American Governor Transformed*, and *The Rise of Political Consultants*.

Index

The New Congress

THOMAS E. MANN AND NORMAN J. ORNSTEIN, editors

Eleven scholars examine the changes that have taken place within Congress and its environment over the past several decades and the consequences of those changes for the policy process. The authors are R. Douglas Arnold, I. M. Destler, Roger H. Davidson, Charles O. Jones, Michael J. Malbin, Thomas E. Mann, Norman J. Ornstein, Nelson W. Polsby, Michael J. Robinson, Allen Schick, and Barbara Sinclair.

"The quality of anything written about the Congress depends heavily on whether the author has reflected on its complexity and respected the need for a reasonable level of precision. Here—overall, at least—the quality is high. . . . [deals] with contemporary changes in congressional politics, practices, and procedures. Its contributors are certifiably knowledgeable about both Congress in general and the particular subjects they cover. . . especially well organized."   *Congressional Staff Journal.*

"Eleven thoughtful essays. . . . This excellent book should contribute to a better understanding of congressional actions in the 1980s."   *Library Journal.*

"A more timely book cannot be imagined. This is really fascinating stuff about the very engine of popular government and how it works."   *Fayetteville Observer-Times.*

400 pp./1981/paper 3416-0 $9.25/cloth 3415-2 $17.25

After the People Vote
Steps in Choosing the President

EDITED BY WALTER BERNS

What if no presidential candidate gets an electoral college majority? What if a presidential candidate dies before the November election? after the November election but before the electoral votes are cast? after the electoral votes are cast but before they are counted? after they are counted but before the winning candidate assumes office?

Questions like these have puzzled even constitutional scholars. The authors of this guide address these matters and others as they explain the workings of the electoral college and the process of presidential selection.

39 pp./1983/paper 3540-X $3.95

How Capitalistic Is the Constitution?

ROBERT A. GOLDWIN
AND WILLIAM A. SCHAMBRA, editors

Is there a deep contradiction between the promises of democratic equality in the Constitution and the material inequalities generated by American capitalism? Or is capitalism not only compatible with but essential for democratic liberty? The controversy over how to understand and to reconcile our political and economic systems is presented in its full political, historical, economic, legal, and philosophic complexity in essays by Walter Dean Burnham, Edward S. Greenberg, Robert Lekachman, Forrest McDonald, Stephen Miller, Marc F. Plattner, and Bernard H. Siegan.
"Provocative."   *Reason.*

172 pp./1981/paper 3478-0 $6.25/cloth 3477-2 $14.25

How Democratic Is the Constitution?

ROBERT A. GOLDWIN
AND WILLIAM A. SCHAMBRA, editors

Some of the authors in this volume accept a version of Charles Beard's thesis, arguing that the Constitution was designed to protect the wealthy by frustrating popular rule, that it is an aristocratic document garbed in democratic rhetoric, or that it is a middle-of-the-road compromise between radical democrats and "accommodating conservatives." Other authors maintain that the Constitution is unqualifiedly democratic, that it was designed to establish a "deliberative democracy," or that its seemingly undemocratic institutions are intended to secure rights for all. The seven essays were written by Walter Berns, Joseph M. Bessette, Ann Stuart Diamond, Wilson Carey McWilliams, Michael Parenti, Gordon S. Wood, and Alfred F. Young.

"A splendid recent compendium of essays."
The Public Interest.

150 pp./1980/paper 3399-7 $5.25/cloth 3400-4 $12.25

The United States Senate:
A Bicameral Perspective

RICHARD F. FENNO, JR.

This study looks at the U.S. Senate in the context of its relationship to the House of Representatives. Comparisons are made of Senate and House campaigns on the basis of dependency on the media, remoteness from constituencies, and emphasis on personal trust and on public policy. The author explores the effect of the six-year term on senators.

Richard F. Fenno, Jr., a visiting scholar at the American Enterprise Institute in 1981–1982, is William J. Kenan Professor of Political Science at the University of Rochester.

"Deserves special note.... Fenno has few if any peers among his professional colleagues in his ability to confront the ordinary, the mundane, and even the banal about the Congress and to discover there the veins of meaning and understanding which should have been apparent to all, and to express his insights with a clarity and a straightforwardness so frequently lacking in others."

Congressional Staff Journal.

47 pp./1982/3499-3 $2.95

The Reagan Phenomenon— and Other Speeches on Foreign Policy

JEANE J. KIRKPATRICK

In these speech/essays, Ambassador Kirkpatrick describes, assesses, and articulates the foundations of what she calls "the Reagan phenomenon" as it relates to the liberal tradition, Western values, America's goals, and U.S. foreign policy.

"She is at once informed, incisive, and challenging.... in a fresh and vigorous fashion.... This is a stimulating and valuable book, the work of an activist and participant that nevertheless has about it the qualities of scholarship and objectivity."　　　　　*Contemporary Review* (London).

"Lucid, potent speeches.... Valuable reading on a number of levels—as a reflection of Kirkpatrick's work and views on foreign affairs; as an indication of the Reagan administration's policies and opinions; and as substantive material for further discussion of international politics."　　　*Booklist.*

"Ambassador Kirkpatrick... understands that truth is the main weapon of democracy."

Jean-François Revel, former editor, *L'Express.*

"The best thinking of the clearest mind in foreign policy today."　　　William Safire, columnist, *New York Times.*

230 pp./1983/cloth 1361-9 $14.95

• *Mail orders for publications to:* AMERICAN ENTERPRISE INSTITUTE, 1150 Seventeenth Street, N.W., Washington, D.C. 20036 • *For postage and handling, add 10 percent of total; minimum charge, $2* • *For information on orders, or to expedite service, call toll free* 800-424-2873 • *Prices subject to change without notice* • *Payable in U.S. currency only.*

A NOTE ON THE BOOK

This book was edited by Claire Theune,
Margaret Seawell, and Gertrude Kaplan of the
Publications Staff of the American Enterprise Institute.
The staff also designed the cover and format, with Pat Taylor.
The figures were drawn by Hördur Karlsson.
The text was set in Palatino, a typeface designed by Hermann Zapf.
Hendricks-Miller Typographic Company, of Washington, D.C.,
set the type, and R. R. Donnelley & Sons Company,
of Harrisonburg, Virginia, printed and bound the book,
using paper made by the S. D. Warren Company.

94400

JK
1968
1982

THE AMERICAN ELECTIONS OF 1982.

DATE DUE